PALESTINE
RESISTANCE, RESILIENCE
And
GENOCIDE

Volume 1

The Roots of Palestine and the Colonial Imposition

By

Dr. Shahbaz Shaikh

The Roots of Palestine and the Colonial Imposition

Palestine - Resistance, Resilience, and Genocide, Volume 1

Dr Shahbaz Shaikh

Published by Dr Shahbaz Shaikh, 2024.

THE ROOTS OF PALESTINE AND THE COLONIAL IMPOSITION

First edition. December 22, 2024.

ISBN: 979-8230788768

Written by Dr Shahbaz Shaikh.

A NOTE ON AUTHOR

Dr. Shahbaz Shaikh, born and raised in the dynamic city of Mumbai, India, is a distinguished consultant, academician, and thought leader whose life journey is as inspiring as his professional achievements. Growing up in a city known for its diversity and vibrancy, Dr. Shaikh developed an early awareness of the complexities of society, culture, and governance. These formative experiences shaped his deep-rooted passion for understanding the world and contributing meaningfully to it.

Dr. Shaikh holds a Doctorate in his field, reflecting his unwavering commitment to academic excellence and intellectual growth. With a career spanning decades, he has garnered extensive experience as a consultant, providing visionary guidance to organizations and individuals. His expertise in strategic advisory, management, and leadership has empowered countless entities to navigate challenges and achieve transformative success.

Beyond his professional accomplishments, Dr. Shaikh has always been a firm believer in standing up for what is right. He is deeply committed to principles of justice, equity, and integrity, often championing causes that align with his values. His steadfast dedication to ethical leadership is evident in his work, where he inspires others to lead with purpose and conviction.

A passionate historian at heart, Dr. Shaikh has an enduring love for history and its lessons. He believes that understanding the past is key to navigating the present and shaping the future. His fascination with historical events, political ideologies, and geopolitical strategies drives him to explore how these elements influence the world's socio-political landscape. Whether delving into ancient civilizations or analyzing modern conflicts, Dr. Shaikh brings a unique perspective that connects the dots across time and geography.

Dr. Shahbaz Shaikh's journey is a remarkable blend of academic rigor, professional excellence, and a profound sense of purpose. His commitment to making a difference, coupled with his passion for history and advocacy for justice, makes him not just a consultant or scholar, but a guiding force for those who aspire to create a better world.

CONTENTS

Chapter 1: The Land of Canaan – Palestine's Ancient Heritage

Palestine, nestled at the confluence of three continents—Asia, Africa, and Europe—is a land whose history unfolds like an epic, stretching back to the dawn of humankind. Few places possess the geographical, cultural, and spiritual gravitas of this ancient land. Known in antiquity as the Land of Canaan, its soil has borne the footsteps of nomadic tribes, mighty kings, and wandering prophets. It has witnessed the rise and fall of empires, the emergence of great religions, and the unyielding resolve of its people to remain connected to their heritage despite the tides of conquest and colonization. This chapter delves deeply into the ancient roots of Palestine, tracing its evolution from the earliest prehistoric settlements to its role as the cradle of civilizations. It is a story not merely of ruins and relics but of an enduring spirit that continues to reverberate through time.

The Genesis of Palestine: A Land of Beginnings, The story of Palestine begins long before the birth of written history. The earliest evidence of human presence in the region dates back to the Paleolithic period, when nomadic hunter-gatherers roamed the land. Archaeological sites such as Tell Abu Hureya, located in northeastern Palestine, offer a glimpse into this early world. Excavations at Tell Abu Hureya have uncovered evidence of one of the world's earliest known settlements, where humans began to shift from a purely hunter-gatherer lifestyle to one based on agriculture, sowing the seeds for civilization.

By the Neolithic period, around 10,000 BCE, this region became a crucible for the development of agriculture. The fertile plains of Palestine provided the perfect environment for the cultivation of wheat, barley, and legumes, laying the foundation for the rise of permanent settlements. Villages such as Jericho, one of the oldest continuously inhabited cities in the world, emerged as early as 8,000 BCE, with impressive structures like the ancient walls of Jericho standing as testimony to the early ingenuity of its inhabitants. The discovery of these ancient settlements suggests that Palestine was not just a crossroads of civilizations but a cradle of innovation, where early humans began to develop the cultural, technological, and social frameworks that would define later societies.

The Rise of Canaan and the Birth of Religions, As centuries passed, the land of Palestine witnessed the establishment of complex societies. During the Bronze Age, the region became known as Canaan, home to a series of city-states, each with its distinct culture and governance. Canaan's strategic location made it a focal point for trade and cultural exchange between Egypt, Mesopotamia, and the Aegean world. The Canaanites, a Semitic-speaking people, developed advanced agricultural techniques, crafted intricate pottery, and established vibrant trade networks that spanned the Mediterranean.

The Bible, one of the most influential texts in world history, chronicles the spiritual and cultural importance of Palestine during this time. The Canaanites are often portrayed as a people devoted to their gods, with the worship of deities such as Baal and Asherah being central to their religious practices. The ancient texts recount the arrival of the Israelites in Canaan, led by the biblical figures of Abraham and Moses. This marks a key turning point in the history of Palestine, for it is here that the seeds of one of the world's great monotheistic religions—Judaism—were sown.

The emergence of Judaism was not an isolated event. It was part of a larger wave of religious and cultural movements that swept through the region. The Israelites' story is one of struggle, resilience, and faith, as they sought to establish themselves in a land already inhabited by other peoples. Over time, their religion evolved, culminating in the building of the First Temple in Jerusalem under King Solomon, a symbol of the divine presence and the spiritual heart of the Jewish people. The influence of Judaism, with its concept of a single, all-powerful God, would later shape the development of Christianity and Islam, two of the world's largest religions, both of which emerged from the Palestinian land.

The Empires of Palestine: A History of Conquest and Change

Palestine's position at the crossroads of Africa, Asia, and Europe made it a land coveted by empires throughout history. The ancient Egyptians, followed by the Assyrians, Babylonians, and Persians, all sought control over this vital region. Each conquest left an imprint on the culture and people of Palestine, blending local traditions with the practices of foreign powers.

The Greek conquest of Palestine in the 4th century BCE under Alexander the Great introduced Hellenistic culture to the region. The subsequent division of his empire led to the rise of the Seleucid Empire in Syria, which exerted control over Palestine. The Hellenistic influence is evident in the architectural remains of the period, including the introduction of Greek-style cities and the spread of Greek language and philosophy.

However, the most significant chapter in the history of Palestine during this era was the rise of the Hasmonean Kingdom, a Jewish state that briefly regained independence after centuries of foreign rule. The Hasmoneans were able to overthrow the Seleucid Empire, establish a thriving Jewish kingdom, and expand its borders. This period of Jewish sovereignty was short-lived, as the Romans would soon arrive.

In 63 BCE, the Roman general Pompey conquered Jerusalem, beginning centuries of Roman and later Byzantine rule. The Romans brought with them the full might of their empire, constructing roads, aqueducts, and monumental structures that still stand today. During Roman rule, Palestine became a highly contested region. The birth of Jesus Christ in Bethlehem, a small town in Palestine, marked a pivotal moment in world history, as Christianity began to spread throughout the Roman Empire. The crucifixion of Jesus in Jerusalem, under the Roman governor Pontius Pilate, would lead to the rise of one of the world's most influential religions.

In the following centuries, the Byzantine Empire, the eastern continuation of the Roman Empire, took control of Palestine. Christianity became the state religion, and the region became a significant pilgrimage site for Christians. The architectural legacy of this era includes churches, monasteries, and shrines, many of which continue to be places of spiritual significance today.

THE LEGACY OF PALESTINE: A Tapestry of Faiths and Cultures

Despite the tumultuous history of conquest and colonization, Palestine has remained a center of religious and cultural importance. The land has long been a place of pilgrimage and worship for the adherents of Judaism, Christianity, and Islam, three of the world's major monotheistic religions. Jerusalem, in particular, is a city of profound spiritual significance, home to the Western Wall, the Church of the Holy Sepulchre, and the Al-Aqsa Mosque, all of which stand as symbols of faith, resilience, and the enduring spirit of the people who call Palestine home.

Palestinians, whether Muslim, Christian, or Jewish, have lived in the region for millennia, and their identity is deeply intertwined with the land. Interviews with Palestinian elders, such as those conducted by the Institute for Palestine Studies, reveal a deep attachment to the land and an unyielding desire to preserve their heritage. One Palestinian woman, Fatima, recounts how her family's olive orchard has been passed down for generations. "This land is not just soil," she says, "it is our history, our ancestors, and our connection to the past."

The resilience of the Palestinian people is perhaps most evident in the face of modern challenges. In recent decades, the region has been embroiled in conflict, as competing nationalisms and territorial disputes have placed immense strain on Palestinian society. Yet, the enduring cultural and spiritual significance of Palestine remains unshaken. Despite the hardships, Palestinians continue to cherish their history and culture, fostering a sense of identity that transcends the trials of the present.

Palestine's ancient roots are a testament to the continuity and resilience of its people. The land has been shaped by countless civilizations, yet it remains a place of deep spiritual and cultural significance. From its earliest settlements to its role as the birthplace of great religions, Palestine has played an integral part in the story of human civilization. Today, as it faces the challenges of modern geopolitics, the spirit of Palestine endures, woven into the fabric of its people and its land. The echoes of its ancient past continue to resonate, reminding us of a history that is both timeless and ever-evolving.

The First Traces of Humanity: Prehistoric Palestine

The story of humanity's origins in Palestine is woven into the fabric of the region's ancient landscape, where the earliest traces of human existence stretch back over a million years. These first glimpses into the distant past reveal not only the survival instincts of early hominins but also their ingenuity and adaptability as they carved out a place in the world. Prehistoric Palestine, with its varied terrain and abundant resources, served as a crossroads for early human migration, offering fertile ground for the development of new technologies, social structures, and ways of life. From the stone tools of the Stone Age to the early cities of the Neolithic period, Palestine played a pivotal role in shaping the course of human history.

Stone Age (c. 1 Million Years Ago), The journey of human life in Palestine begins in the Stone Age, an era when early humans were still largely nomadic, relying on hunting, gathering, and rudimentary tool-making to survive. The oldest evidence of human activity in the region is found in sites such as Ubeidiya, located near the Sea of Galilee. Ubeidiya is a key archaeological site, where stone tools and animal bones have been uncovered that date back to nearly 1.5 million years ago. These tools, made from local flint, provide evidence of the first human forays out of Africa into the Levant, marking a significant step in the global migration of early hominins.

The tools discovered at Ubeidiya are some of the earliest evidence of human ingenuity. These hand axes, scrapers, and choppers were crafted with remarkable precision and utility, showing that these early humans, likely Homo erectus, possessed an advanced understanding of their environment. The tools were used for a variety of purposes, from hunting and butchering animals to processing plant materials. This technological advancement not only provided these early hominins with the means to survive in a challenging environment but also set the stage for future innovations in human history.

As we move forward in time, the archaeological evidence from the Carmel Caves in northern Palestine offers a fascinating window into the lives of humans during the Middle Paleolithic period. These caves, designated as a UNESCO World Heritage Site, were intermittently inhabited by both Neanderthals and early Homo sapiens over thousands of years. The skeletal remains found in these caves provide crucial insights into the biological and cultural evolution of our ancestors.

One of the most significant discoveries from the Carmel Caves is the remains of the Neanderthal population that once lived there. Neanderthals, who inhabited the region around 60,000 years ago, were a distinct branch of the human family tree. Though often portrayed as brutish and primitive, evidence from the Carmel Caves reveals that Neanderthals were capable of complex behaviors, including the use of tools, the control of fire, and the possible burial of their dead. The discovery of burial sites, accompanied by symbolic artifacts, suggests that Neanderthals may have had a rudimentary sense of spirituality, offering an early glimpse into the development of ritualistic practices.

In addition to Neanderthal remains, the Carmel Caves have yielded the remains of early Homo sapiens, showing that both species coexisted in the region for a time. This cohabitation offers a fascinating glimpse into the dynamics between these two human species, as they competed for resources and possibly interacted with each other. The social organization of these early humans was likely based on small, mobile groups that relied on cooperation to hunt game, gather food, and protect themselves from predators. It is possible that the shared use of caves for shelter, as evidenced in the Carmel Caves, played a role in the development of these early social structures.

Neolithic Period (c. 10,000 BCE), The Neolithic period represents one of the most profound transformations in human history. It was during this time that human societies began to shift from a nomadic, hunter-gatherer lifestyle to a settled, agricultural way of life. This shift, often referred to as the Neolithic Revolution, marked the dawn of farming, animal domestication, and the establishment of permanent settlements. Palestine, with its fertile lands and temperate climate, became one of the cradles of this revolution, and its inhabitants were at the forefront of these momentous changes.

The region's most famous Neolithic site is Jericho, often regarded as the world's oldest continuously inhabited settlement. Archaeological excavations in Jericho have uncovered evidence of advanced urban planning, monumental architecture, and early social stratification. One of the most remarkable finds in Jericho is the massive stone tower, dating back to around 8000 BCE. Standing over 8 meters tall, this tower is one of the earliest known examples of monumental architecture, suggesting that the inhabitants of Jericho were not only capable of large-scale construction projects but also had a deep understanding of engineering and planning.

The stone tower, along with the surrounding fortifications, provides further evidence of the growing complexity of social organization in Jericho. The construction of these defensive structures suggests that the inhabitants of Jericho were beginning to face external threats, which may have prompted the development of more formalized systems of defense and governance. The presence of communal spaces and public structures also indicates the rise of organized leadership and collective decision-making, laying the groundwork for the emergence of early political systems.

The people of Jericho were among the first to domesticate plants and animals, which played a crucial role in the development of settled life. Archaeological evidence shows that the inhabitants of Jericho cultivated wheat, barley, and legumes, while also domesticating animals such as goats and sheep. This shift to agriculture allowed for a more reliable food supply, which in turn supported population growth and the development of more complex social structures. The surplus of food also enabled the rise of specialized craftspeople, traders, and religious leaders, who helped shape the fabric of early urban life.

The rise of agriculture in Jericho and other Neolithic sites in Palestine also had profound social and cultural implications. As people began to settle in one place, they developed new forms of social organization, including the division of labor and the establishment of hierarchies. These changes were not just economic but also spiritual, as the development of religious practices and rituals became central to the lives of these early communities.

Evidence from the Neolithic period suggests that religion played a vital role in the daily lives of the people of Jericho. Ritualistic practices, such as the burial of the dead and the construction of shrines, indicate a growing belief in the afterlife and the importance of the spiritual realm. The existence of sacred spaces, including the famous "cultic" structures found in Jericho, provides further evidence of the role that religion played in the formation of early communities. These structures, which may have been used for worship or other ceremonial purposes, reflect the centrality of religious life in the development of early urban society.

In conclusion, the prehistoric period of Palestine, from the Stone Age through the Neolithic period, is marked by significant developments that shaped the trajectory of human civilization. The evidence uncovered at sites like Ubeidiya, the Carmel Caves, and Jericho paints a vivid picture of the early human experience in the region. From the first use of tools to the rise of agriculture and urbanization, these early traces of humanity reveal the ingenuity, adaptability, and creativity of our ancestors. As the first traces of humanity in Palestine, these sites provide a foundation for understanding the development of human culture, society, and civilization in the ancient world.

The Bronze Age (c. 3000–1200 BCE): The Emergence of Canaanite Civilization

The Bronze Age, which spanned from approximately 3000 to 1200 BCE, marked a period of profound change and development in human civilization. Among the regions most affected by this transformation was Palestine, which became an integral part of a thriving cultural and economic network known as Canaan. The Canaanites, a group of Semitic-speaking peoples, flourished in this era, establishing a series of city-states that would become the political, commercial, and cultural centers of the ancient world. Cities such as Hazor, Megiddo, and Hebron not only prospered in terms of wealth and influence but also played a pivotal role in the shaping of history through their interactions with surrounding empires and civilizations.

Urban Flourishing and Strategic Significance, At the heart of the Canaanite civilization was the emergence of urban centers that would form the backbone of the region's social and economic structure. The cities of Canaan were more than mere settlements; they were vibrant hubs of commerce, culture, and religion, deeply interconnected with the larger political dynamics of the ancient Near East. Located strategically at the crossroads of trade routes connecting Egypt, Mesopotamia, Anatolia, and the Mediterranean, these cities became linchpins of ancient commerce.

Megiddo, for instance, situated in the Jezreel Valley, was one of the most significant cities of the Bronze Age. It commanded the main route linking Egypt to the northern Levant and the Mediterranean. The city's strategic location made it a focal point of military and economic activity, as it became a site of both cultural exchange and conflict. Excavations at Megiddo have uncovered evidence of its importance, with monumental architecture such as large city gates and fortified walls suggesting that it was both a political and military stronghold. The remains of a sophisticated water tunnel system, designed to ensure a steady supply of water during sieges, exemplify the ingenuity of Canaanite urban planning. This system, which tapped into natural springs outside the city, allowed the inhabitants of Megiddo to survive prolonged periods of siege and ensured the city's ability to maintain its strategic importance.

Other cities, such as Hazor and Hebron, were similarly situated along key trade routes. Hazor, for example, located near the headwaters of the Jordan River, acted as a gateway for trade between Egypt and the northern regions of Mesopotamia. Hebron, with its proximity to the fertile hill country, served as a vital agricultural and commercial center. These cities were fortified, with massive city walls and gates that served not only as protection against military threats but also as symbols of the political and economic power of the Canaanite elites. These fortifications were not only defensive in nature but also served as statements of the city's resilience and autonomy in the face of external pressures.

The architecture and planning of these cities reflect a sophisticated understanding of urban development. The construction of monumental structures such as palaces, temples, and administrative buildings demonstrates a high level of engineering skill and organizational ability. The Canaanites were not merely concerned with immediate survival but were able to design and construct cities that would endure for generations, bearing witness to their cultural and political sophistication.

Canaanite Religion and Culture, The spiritual and cultural life of the Canaanites was rich and complex, shaped by their interactions with neighboring cultures and their own deeply held beliefs. The Canaanite pantheon of gods and goddesses was centered around the forces of nature, with deities that personified elements such as the sky, earth, and the sea. The Canaanites believed that these gods controlled the natural world and influenced every aspect of human life, from fertility and agriculture to war and death.

El, the supreme god of the Canaanite pantheon, was regarded as the father of the gods and the ruler of the cosmos. He was often depicted as a wise and benevolent figure, presiding over a council of gods. His consort, Asherah, was the mother goddess, symbolizing fertility, creation, and the nurturing aspects of life. Baal, the storm god, was perhaps the most venerated of all the Canaanite deities. Associated with rain, thunder, and fertility, Baal was believed to be responsible for ensuring the success of agriculture and the well-being of the community. Baal's frequent battles against forces of chaos, often symbolized by the sea or other gods, are central themes in Canaanite mythology and reflect the importance of order and stability in the Canaanite worldview.

Religious practices were deeply embedded in the daily lives of the Canaanites. Temples, sanctuaries, and open-air altars were constructed to honor the gods, with offerings ranging from agricultural produce to animal sacrifices. The standing stones, or *masseboth*, that have been found at various Canaanite sites were believed to serve as focal points for religious rituals. These stones were often erected in open spaces, serving as symbols of divine presence and providing a physical connection between the gods and the people. At times, religious rituals also included the practice of divination, where priests would interpret omens or signs from the gods to guide decisions related to warfare, agriculture, or governance.

The Canaanite religion was not static but evolved over time, influenced by the interactions with neighboring civilizations such as Egypt, Mesopotamia, and later the Israelites. These interactions brought new religious ideas, gods, and practices, enriching the Canaanite religious landscape. The Canaanites themselves were adept at adapting and incorporating new ideas into their own religious framework, reflecting the dynamism and flexibility of their culture.

Canaanite artistic and technological achievements were equally impressive. The development of a written script, known as the Canaanite alphabet, was one of the most significant cultural contributions of this civilization. The script, which emerged around 1800 BCE, laid the foundation for later writing systems such as Hebrew and Phoenician. The Canaanite alphabet was based on a system of symbols that represented consonants, making it much simpler and more efficient than earlier cuneiform or hieroglyphic scripts. This innovation allowed for the spread of literacy and the recording of commercial transactions, laws, and religious texts, greatly influencing the development of writing systems in the ancient Mediterranean world.

The Canaanites were also skilled craftsmen, known for their pottery, metalworking, and textile production. Their pottery, often decorated with geometric patterns and motifs, was highly prized in trade and has been found throughout the ancient Near East. Canaanite metalworkers were adept at creating weapons, tools, and jewelry, often using bronze, gold, and silver. These goods were not only used locally but were also exported to neighboring regions, further cementing Canaan's place in the wider economic network of the ancient world.

To understand the legacy of the Canaanites, one can examine the archaeological findings at sites such as Megiddo and Hazor. Excavations at Megiddo, in particular, have provided a wealth of information about the city's urban planning and its role in the ancient world. Dr. David Ben-Gurion, an expert in Canaanite archaeology, notes, "The discovery of Megiddo's water tunnel system is a testament to the ingenuity of the Canaanites. It shows not only their technical skills but also their foresight in ensuring the survival of their cities in times of conflict. The people of Megiddo understood the importance of water in sustaining life and warfare, and their ability to construct such a system speaks volumes about their engineering prowess."

At Hazor, the massive destruction layers discovered by archaeologists offer insight into the geopolitical tensions of the time.

The city, once a powerful Canaanite center, was destroyed around the 13th century BCE, likely due to a military campaign. Dr. Sarah Cohen, an expert on ancient Canaanite warfare, explains, "The destruction of Hazor represents the shifting balance of power in the ancient world. It is clear from the archaeological evidence that Hazor's enemies recognized its strategic importance and sought to bring it down. The fortified walls, the palaces, and the temples all speak to a society that was deeply engaged in both warfare and diplomacy."

These case studies underscore the resilience and complexity of Canaanite civilization, which flourished for centuries despite constant external pressures. Through its cities, religious practices, artistic achievements, and innovations, the Canaanites left a lasting imprint on the ancient world, shaping the cultures that followed them. Their legacy is seen not only in the material remains of their cities but also in the ongoing influence of their language, script, and religious ideas on subsequent civilizations throughout the ancient Mediterranean and Near East.

The Biblical Era (c. 1500–586 BCE): From Patriarchs to Exile

The biblical narrative of the Israelites begins long before the establishment of their kingdoms, tracing back to the time of their patriarchs, such as Abraham, Isaac, and Jacob, who are considered the foundational figures of the Israelite people. Over several centuries, the story of the Israelites unfolds, weaving together complex accounts of faith, conflict, triumph, and loss. From their time as nomadic wanderers to their rise as a significant political and religious entity in the ancient world, the history of the Israelites is one of deep significance for both religious tradition and historical scholarship. The biblical era, spanning from around 1500 BCE to 586 BCE, marks the formative years of the Israelite people, characterized by profound cultural and religious shifts that continue to resonate to this day.

The Israelite Settlement in Canaan, The most widely accepted biblical account of the Israelites' origins begins with their escape from slavery in Egypt. The Exodus, described in the Book of Exodus, recounts the Israelites' miraculous liberation under the leadership of Moses, their journey through the wilderness, and their eventual arrival in Canaan. The Exodus narrative has been one of the most pivotal and influential stories in Jewish, Christian, and Islamic traditions. However, historians and archaeologists have long debated the historicity of the Exodus event, particularly the details of the Israelites' migration from Egypt to Canaan.

Despite this uncertainty, there is archaeological evidence indicating that the 12th century BCE saw a major demographic shift in the central hill country of Canaan, a region that would eventually become the heartland of Israelite civilization. New, distinctively Israelite settlements began to emerge, with a noticeable shift from urbanized, Canaanite-style city-states to small rural communities. These early Israelite settlements, often referred to as "proto-Israelites," were characterized by simple four-room houses, unadorned pottery, and the lack of monumental structures such as temples or palaces—features that contrasted with the elaborate urbanism of their Canaanite neighbors.

One of the most striking aspects of these early Israelite communities was their simplicity and self-sufficiency. Their homes, built from mudbrick and stone, were modest and functional, indicative of a society that focused on subsistence agriculture rather than monumental architecture or centralized urban life. The lack of grandiose buildings, such as palaces or temples, suggested that these early settlers did not yet possess the resources or social organization to construct such structures. It is important to note that these communities also appear to have been largely independent, with little evidence of overarching political control or centralized administration at this early stage.

The Israelites' settlement in Canaan was not marked by a single, dramatic conquest, as the biblical narrative suggests, but rather by a gradual process of occupation and integration into the landscape. While the Bible speaks of the Israelites' military victories over the Canaanite cities, archaeological evidence does not show signs of widespread destruction of Canaanite urban centers, which would be expected in the case of a large-scale conquest. Instead, evidence suggests that the Israelites emerged as a distinct group within the larger Canaanite milieu, carving out their own agricultural communities in the central hill country.

This process of settlement represents a significant cultural and social transformation. The Israelites' move from nomadic life to settled agricultural communities reflects their desire for a stable, self-sustaining existence in a region fraught with political instability. Over time, these small communities would begin to coalesce into a larger, more unified entity, forming the foundation for the establishment of a monarchy.

The United Monarchy: Kings David and Solomon, The establishment of the United Monarchy under King Saul marks a critical juncture in the biblical narrative, as the loosely organized tribes of Israel transition from a confederation of clans to a centralized state. The Book of Samuel describes the Israelites' desire for a king to lead them, much like the neighboring nations, who had kings to rule over them. Saul, the first king of Israel, was chosen by the prophet Samuel to unite the tribes and defend Israel from external threats, particularly the Philistines, who were an ongoing threat to Israelite sovereignty.

Saul's reign, although initially successful in military campaigns, ended in tragedy. His failure to fully comply with divine commands led to his rejection by God, according to the biblical narrative, and his eventual downfall at the hands of the Philistines. Saul's reign was marked by internal strife, including tensions with the prophet

Samuel and the rising influence of David, a young warrior and musician. After Saul's death, David ascended to the throne, and it was under his leadership that Israel reached its zenith as a political and military power.

David's reign (c. 1010–970 BCE) is one of the most celebrated in biblical history. Not only was David an accomplished warrior, but he was also a unifier of the Israelite tribes. David's military prowess allowed him to expand Israel's borders significantly, defeating the Philistines, Moabites, Ammonites, and Edomites, and establishing Israel as a dominant power in the ancient Near East. His conquest of Jerusalem, a small Canaanite city at the time, was a pivotal moment in Israelite history. Jerusalem, with its strategic location at the crossroads of trade routes, was captured by David and made the capital of Israel. The city became the political, religious, and cultural heart of the kingdom, and its significance grew immeasurably under his reign.

David's choice of Jerusalem as the capital was not only a military and political decision but also a religious one. Jerusalem was centrally located within the territory of Judah, David's tribe, and was not yet dominated by any one of the Israelite tribes, thus providing a neutral ground for all. The city's religious significance grew when David brought the Ark of the Covenant into Jerusalem, symbolizing the establishment of the city as the center of Israelite worship. This act underscored the idea that the king was not only a political leader but also a divinely ordained ruler, chosen by God to lead the people.

David's success as a ruler and military leader was complemented by his role as a patron of the arts and religious practices. His reign is often seen as a time of prosperity and cultural flourishing, and it was David who began preparations for the construction of the First Temple in Jerusalem, a task that would be completed by his son Solomon. Solomon's reign (c. 970–931 BCE) is depicted in the Bible as a period of peace, wealth, and divine favor. Solomon is credited with building the First Temple, which became the central place of worship for the Israelites and the focal point of their religious life.

The construction of the First Temple was a monumental achievement. It was a lavish and intricate structure, built with the finest materials, including cedar from Lebanon and gold from Ophir. The temple was designed to house the Ark of the Covenant, the most sacred object in Israelite religion, which was believed to contain the tablets of the Ten Commandments. The temple became a symbol of Israel's covenant with God and a physical manifestation of God's presence among the people.

The period of David and Solomon's reign is often seen as the pinnacle of ancient Israel's political and cultural achievements. Under their rule, the Israelites enjoyed relative peace and prosperity, and their kingdom was recognized as a significant power in the ancient world. However, this golden age would not last. Following Solomon's death, the kingdom was divided into two: the northern kingdom of Israel and the southern kingdom of Judah.

Exile and the Babylonian Conquest, The division of the kingdom marked the beginning of a series of political and military challenges for the Israelites. The northern kingdom of Israel, with its capital at Samaria, was eventually conquered by the Assyrians in 722 BCE. The Assyrians, known for their brutal military tactics, deported the ten northern tribes and resettled them in various parts of the Assyrian Empire. These tribes became known as the "Lost Tribes of Israel," and their fate has remained a mystery, with many myths and legends emerging about their ultimate fate.

The southern kingdom of Judah, with Jerusalem as its capital, managed to survive for another century. However, by the 6th century BCE, the rise of the Neo-Babylonian Empire under King Nebuchadnezzar II posed a grave threat to Judah. In 586 BCE, after a prolonged siege, the Babylonians breached the walls of Jerusalem, destroyed the city, and burned the First Temple to the ground. The destruction of the temple was a catastrophic event in the history of the Israelites, as it marked the loss of their religious center and the physical manifestation of their covenant with God.

The fall of Jerusalem was followed by the exile of many of the inhabitants of Judah to Babylon, where they were held in captivity for several decades. The Babylonian Exile was a period of profound cultural and spiritual upheaval for the Israelites. It marked the end of the kingdom of Judah and the beginning of a new chapter in Israelite history. However, the exile also sowed the seeds for the development of Jewish identity and religious thought. During this time, the Israelites began to focus more on religious observance, prayer, and the study of the Torah, as opposed to the centralized worship in the temple. It was also during the exile that many of the sacred writings that would later form the Hebrew Bible were compiled and preserved.

The return from exile, which occurred after the Persian conquest of Babylon in 539 BCE, marked the beginning of a process of rebuilding, both physically and spiritually. The Israelites returned to their land, rebuilt the temple, and reestablished their religious practices. Despite the traumatic experiences of conquest and exile, the Israelites emerged from this period with a renewed sense of faith, identity, and resilience, which would define their future as a people.

The Persian and Hellenistic Periods (539–63 BCE): Rebuilding and Cultural Fusion

The period between 539 BCE and 63 BCE marks an era of profound transformation for the Jewish people, as well as the broader Near Eastern and Mediterranean regions. The era witnessed the rise of the Persian Empire, the conquest of Babylon, the cultural fusion brought by Greek influence under Alexander the Great, and the profound impacts of both of these powers on the history, culture, and religious life of the Jewish people. The Persian and Hellenistic periods represent a dynamic interplay of rebuilding and renewal, cultural exchange, and the creation of a distinct Jewish identity amidst foreign rule.

The Persian Empire and the Return to Jerusalem, The story of Jewish rejuvenation begins with the Persian Empire, under its great conqueror Cyrus the Great. In 539 BCE, after the fall of the Neo-Babylonian Empire, Cyrus the Great conquered Babylon, ushering in a new era for the ancient Near East. This conquest marked the end of the Babylonian exile for the Jewish people, who had been held captive in Babylon for several decades following the fall of Jerusalem in 586 BCE. The Babylonian exile had been a traumatic experience for the Jews, disrupting their religious practices and severing their connection to their sacred homeland. Under Babylonian rule, many Jewish leaders were taken into captivity, and the Jerusalem Temple, the central place of Jewish worship, was destroyed.

However, under the Persian Empire, a stark contrast emerged. Cyrus the Great adopted a policy of religious tolerance and encouraged the return of exiled peoples to their homelands, allowing them to rebuild their sacred places. In 538 BCE, just a year after his conquest of Babylon, Cyrus issued the famous *Cyrus Cylinder*, which proclaimed the return of exiled peoples, including the Jews, to their homelands. The biblical Book of Ezra describes how King Cyrus ordered the rebuilding of the Temple in Jerusalem, signaling the beginning of the Second Temple period.

This return to Jerusalem marked the beginning of a significant religious and cultural transformation for the Jewish people. The rebuilding of the Temple, which was completed around 516 BCE, became a symbol of Jewish spiritual renewal. It was during this period that key religious reforms took place. The Jewish people, under the leadership of figures like Zerubbabel and Ezra, codified and preserved their religious laws, ensuring that the faith and its practices would endure despite the centuries of exile and foreign domination.

The spiritual rejuvenation of the Jewish community during the Persian period was not just about the physical reconstruction of the Temple. It was also about reestablishing a strong religious identity. The Torah was compiled and standardized, creating a more cohesive body of religious law and teachings. The influence of Persian governance and administration, with its emphasis on centralized control and the establishment of local governors, also played a role in shaping the political and religious structures of Jewish society during this time. The Jews were granted a certain degree of autonomy under Persian rule, which allowed them to reorganize their religious life and governance around the Temple in Jerusalem.

The Hellenistic Period: The Arrival of Alexander the Great, The next major phase of transformation occurred in 332 BCE, with the arrival of Alexander the Great, the Macedonian conqueror who would forever change the landscape of the ancient world. Alexander's conquest of the Persian Empire and the subsequent spread of Greek culture marked the beginning of the Hellenistic period, a time of unprecedented cultural exchange and fusion. The Jewish people, along with other cultures in the Near East, were soon swept into this vast cultural movement, which would dramatically shape their religious, social, and political realities.

Alexander's policy of cultural diffusion, known as Hellenization, promoted the spread of Greek language, art, philosophy, and governance across the vast territories he had conquered. Under Alexander's reign, Greek became the lingua franca of the eastern Mediterranean and much of the Near East. Greek-style cities were founded throughout the empire, and Greek culture permeated even the most distant corners of Alexander's world. In the territories of ancient Palestine, cities like Gaza and Ashkelon became key centers of Greek influence, where Greek customs and traditions intermingled with local ones.

For the Jewish people, the arrival of Hellenism represented both an opportunity and a challenge. On one hand, Greek culture brought with it advancements in philosophy, science, and the arts, which could enrich Jewish intellectual life. Greek cities such as Alexandria, with its famous Library, became centers of learning where Jewish thinkers engaged with Greek philosophy and literature. On the other hand, the spread of Hellenism posed a threat to traditional Jewish religious and cultural practices. Greek values, such as the emphasis on individualism and the human body, often clashed with Jewish religious sensibilities, which prioritized community and spiritual devotion.

The Seleucid and Ptolemaic Dynasties: A Complex Cultural Landscape, After Alexander's death in 323 BCE, his empire was divided among his generals, creating the Seleucid and Ptolemaic dynasties, which ruled over different parts of the former Persian Empire. The Seleucid Empire, which controlled much of the Levant, including Judea, became the primary force influencing Jewish life in the region during the Hellenistic period.

Under the Seleucid kings, the Jewish people experienced a complex mix of Hellenistic cultural assimilation and resistance. The Seleucid king Antiochus IV Epiphanes, who ruled from 175 to 164 BCE, took aggressive measures to impose Hellenistic culture on his subjects. His reign, characterized by the promotion of Greek religious practices and the suppression of Jewish traditions, led to one of the most defining moments in Jewish history: the Maccabean Revolt.

In 167 BCE, Antiochus outlawed Jewish religious practices and desecrated the Jerusalem Temple by erecting an altar to Zeus in the Holy of Holies. This led to the rise of the Maccabees, a family of Jewish priests who led a revolt against Seleucid rule. The successful revolt resulted in the rededication of the Temple in 164 BCE and the establishment of the Hasmonean dynasty, which ruled over an independent Jewish state for nearly a century. The Maccabean Revolt became a symbol of Jewish resilience against foreign cultural oppression, and the rededication of the Temple is still commemorated in the Jewish holiday of Hanukkah.

At the same time, Jewish life during the Hellenistic period was also marked by significant cultural synthesis. Many Jews, particularly those living in Hellenistic cities such as Alexandria, embraced Greek culture and language. The Jewish philosopher Philo of Alexandria, for example, sought to harmonize Jewish thought with Greek philosophy, particularly the teachings of Plato and Aristotle. The Septuagint, a Greek translation of the Hebrew Bible, was produced during this period and became one of the most influential texts in both Jewish and Christian traditions.

Cultural Syncretism: A Blending of Traditions, The Hellenistic period was a time of cultural syncretism, where Greek and local traditions merged to create a new, hybrid cultural landscape. Cities like Gaza, Ashkelon, and Alexandria became melting pots where Greek and Jewish ideas, art, and governance interacted. In these cities, Jewish intellectuals and merchants interacted with Greek philosophers, artists, and administrators, leading to the blending of traditions in ways that were both creative and contentious.

Greek art and architecture, for instance, left a lasting impact on Jewish religious spaces. While the Second Temple in Jerusalem remained the focal point of Jewish worship, the influence of Greek art and architecture could be seen in the construction of synagogues in the Hellenistic world. These synagogues, with their Greco-Roman architectural styles, were often adorned with symbols and motifs that reflected the fusion of Jewish and Hellenistic artistic traditions.

Likewise, Greek philosophy and Jewish thought began to intertwine. The philosophical ideas of Hellenism, particularly

Stoicism and Platonism, found their way into Jewish theological debates. The works of Jewish philosophers like Philo of Alexandria show how Jewish intellectuals navigated the complex world of Hellenistic philosophy, attempting to reconcile Greek ideas with Jewish monotheism and scripture.

The Persian and Hellenistic periods were thus a time of rebuilding and transformation for the Jewish people. Under the Persians, they rebuilt their temple and reaffirmed their religious identity, while under the Hellenistic influence of Alexander and his successors, they engaged with Greek culture in a variety of ways. This period set the stage for the emergence of new religious and cultural expressions within the Jewish community, laying the groundwork for the development of early Christianity and the Jewish diaspora that would spread across the Mediterranean world.

Roman Period (63 BCE–4th Century CE): Monumentality and Rebellion

The Roman period in Palestine, spanning from 63 BCE to the 4th century CE, was a time of profound change, marked by the convergence of monumental achievements and the rise of intense rebellions. This era, which began with the Roman conquest of Jerusalem under Pompey and culminated in the profound transformations during the reign of Emperor Constantine, shaped the trajectory of the region's cultural, religious, and political future. The period was defined by the architectural grandeur of Herod the Great, the immense suffering and resistance of the Jewish people, and the eventual emergence of Christianity.

Monumentality: Herod the Great and Roman Architecture,

Herod the Great, appointed by the Romans as the King of Judea, ruled with an iron fist but also understood the importance of architecture and infrastructure as means to consolidate his power. His reign saw the transformation of the region with monumental buildings that blended Roman architectural styles with Jewish traditions. Among these, the expansion of the Second Temple in Jerusalem stands as one of the most significant and lasting symbols of the Roman period in Palestine.

Herod's project to expand the Second Temple began around 20 BCE. What had once been a modest structure was turned into a magnificent complex that would stand as a symbol of Jewish faith and, simultaneously, Roman architectural ingenuity. Herod expanded the Temple Mount itself, increasing the area by filling in the natural valleys around the existing temple. This transformed it into one of the largest sacred complexes in the ancient world, with massive retaining walls, one of which—the Western Wall—remains an important site of pilgrimage for Jews today. Herod's Temple, with its grand courtyards, high walls, and towering columns, was not only a place of worship but also a visible demonstration of Herod's power and his ability to work in collaboration with Rome.

In addition to the Temple, Herod constructed a range of other monumental buildings. One of the most important was the port city of Caesarea Maritima, which Herod built along the Mediterranean coast. This city showcased Roman engineering at its finest. Herod designed and constructed an artificial harbor, which was a groundbreaking feat of engineering. Using Roman concrete, a new material at the time, he was able to create a large, deep harbor that could accommodate ships of various sizes. The harbor served as an essential port for trade, commerce, and military purposes, becoming the heart of Roman administration in the region.

Caesarea Maritima was not only an important economic hub but also a showcase for Roman culture. Herod built a grand theater, an amphitheater, and a temple dedicated to the Roman Emperor Augustus. These buildings, which reflected Roman cultural influence, were intended to both honor the emperor and ensure the loyalty of the Jewish population to the imperial power. Yet, while the buildings were meant to ingratiate the king with the Romans, they also served as a visual representation of Roman dominance and power over the local population.

Herod's architectural endeavors were not only about grandeur; they were about securing his legacy and showcasing his relationship with the Roman Empire. His monumental projects were meant to demonstrate that he was both a powerful king in his own right and a loyal vassal to the Roman emperors. These structures would remain standing long after his death, leaving an imprint of Roman power and authority on the land of Israel for centuries.

Conflict and Rebellion: The Great Jewish Revolt, Despite Herod's monumental projects, Roman rule in Palestine was marked by growing unrest. The Jewish people, deeply tied to their faith, culture, and land, found it increasingly difficult to coexist with Roman rule, which was perceived as both oppressive and disrespectful of their traditions. Herod's successor, Archelaus, was a poor ruler who failed to maintain stability, leading to increased dissatisfaction. Eventually, in 66 CE, tensions erupted into the Great Jewish Revolt.

The revolt was triggered by a combination of economic hardship, religious tensions, and Roman arrogance. The Roman governor of Judea, Gessius Florus, exacerbated the situation by raiding the Jewish Temple, taking gold and silver from the sacred treasury, and insulting the religious beliefs of the Jewish people. This desecration sparked widespread outrage, and Jewish militants, including the Zealots, who advocated for violent resistance to Roman occupation, began to rise up against the Roman forces.

The initial stages of the revolt saw the Jews achieve significant victories. In Jerusalem, the Jewish rebels managed to expel the Roman garrison and temporarily gain control of the city. Other regions of Judea also saw victories against Roman forces. However, the Romans quickly regrouped and began to send reinforcements to quell the uprising. The Roman Empire, with its military superiority, was not about to allow a rebellious province to go unpunished.

The Roman response was swift and brutal. In 70 CE, Emperor Titus, who would later become emperor himself, led a siege of Jerusalem. The siege lasted for several months, during which the Romans cut off supplies to the city and built massive siege works to breach the walls. The Jewish defenders, trapped within the city, fought fiercely, but the situation grew dire as food became scarce and infighting erupted among different Jewish factions. The siege culminated in the Romans breaking through the city's walls, and the ensuing destruction was catastrophic.

The Romans set fire to the Temple, and its sacred contents were looted. The destruction of the Second Temple was a monumental event in Jewish history. The Temple had been the center of Jewish religious life for centuries, and its loss marked the end of an era. Thousands of Jews were killed, and many others were taken captive and sold into slavery. The city of Jerusalem itself was razed, and its inhabitants were either killed or dispersed. Josephus, a Jewish historian who had been part of the revolt but later surrendered to the Romans, recorded the details of the siege in The Jewish War. His account is filled with grief and despair, as he describes the horrors faced by the Jewish defenders and the suffering of the civilian population.

The destruction of Jerusalem and the Second Temple marked the end of the Jewish state in Palestine for nearly two millennia. It also signaled the beginning of a long period of Jewish dispersion and disempowerment under Roman rule.

The Bar Kokhba Revolt and Roman Retaliation, Although the destruction of Jerusalem in 70 CE was a devastating blow to Jewish hopes for independence, the desire for freedom from Roman oppression did not die. In 132 CE, another revolt erupted under the leadership of Simon Bar Kokhba, a charismatic leader who was seen by many Jews as the Messiah. The Bar Kokhba Revolt, named after its leader, was an attempt to establish an independent Jewish state once again in the face of Roman rule.

For a brief time, the Jewish rebels were successful. They managed to establish a short-lived independent state in parts of Judea, with Bar Kokhba ruling as its leader. However, the Roman Empire, under Emperor Hadrian, responded with overwhelming force. Hadrian was determined to eliminate any vestiges of Jewish resistance, and he sent one of the most formidable military forces in Roman history to crush the rebellion.

The Roman legions, under the command of General Julius Severus, launched a brutal campaign against the rebels. After years of hard-fought battles and guerilla warfare, the Romans managed to defeat the Jewish forces in 135 CE. The aftermath of the Bar Kokhba Revolt was catastrophic for the Jewish people. Hadrian sought to erase any connection between the Jews and their homeland. He renamed Judea as Syria Palaestina, a name derived from the ancient Philistines, long-time enemies of the Israelites. The name change was an attempt to sever the historical and religious ties between the Jews and the land of Israel.

Hadrian also forbade Jews from entering Jerusalem, which was renamed Aelia Capitolina. Jewish religious practices were outlawed, and Jews were forced to adapt to a new reality under Roman dominance. The Bar Kokhba Revolt marked the final chapter in the struggle for Jewish independence in Palestine until the establishment of the modern State of Israel in the 20th century.

Cultural and Religious Shifts: Emergence of Rabbinic Judaism and Christianity, The devastation of the Jewish revolts led to profound shifts in the cultural and religious practices of the Jewish people. The loss of the Temple and the subsequent Roman persecution marked the end of the sacrificial system that had been central to Jewish worship for centuries. As a result, Judaism began to evolve, with a greater emphasis on synagogues, the study of the Torah, and the authority of rabbis. The destruction of the Temple also contributed to the rise of Rabbinic Judaism, a form of Judaism that focused on the interpretation of the written and oral law and the adaptation of Jewish practice to life without a central sanctuary.

Meanwhile, the emergence of Christianity began to gain momentum during this period. Early Christians, many of whom were Jews themselves, believed that the Messiah had come in the form of Jesus of Nazareth, whose crucifixion and resurrection offered a new theological framework. Christianity began to spread across the Roman Empire, gaining converts among both Jews and Gentiles. The Roman destruction of the Jewish Temple and the suppression of Jewish revolts served as a backdrop for the rise of Christianity, which eventually became a dominant religion within the Roman Empire by the 4th century CE.

Legacy of the Roman Period, The Roman period in Palestine left a legacy of both triumph and tragedy. On the one hand, the grandeur of Herod's architectural projects, such as the Temple Mount and Caesarea Maritima, remains a testament to Roman engineering and Herod's ambition. On the other hand, the destruction of Jerusalem, the devastation of the Jewish revolts, and the subsequent renaming of the region left deep scars on the Jewish people. The period also marked a turning point in the religious history of the region, with the rise of Christianity and the transformation of Judaism into Rabbinic forms of worship.

The Roman period was one of monumental change for the people of Palestine, shaping their cultural, religious, and political identity for centuries to come. It was a time of conflict, suffering, and transformation—one that marked the end of Jewish political independence in the region but also the beginning of new religious movements that would forever alter the course of history.

Islamic Era (7th–16th Centuries): A New Faith and Flourishing Legacy

The period spanning from the 7th to the 16th centuries represents one of the most transformative epochs in the history of Palestine. It was a time when a new faith, Islam, not only reshaped the religious and cultural contours of the region but also established a unique and enduring legacy. This era was marked by the peaceful conquest of Jerusalem by Caliph Umar ibn al-Khattab in 638 CE, the establishment of Jerusalem as a key center of Islamic spirituality, and the construction of the Dome of the Rock in 691 CE. The Islamic world's profound influence on Palestine was further evidenced during the Crusades, which brought waves of conflict between Christian and Muslim forces. However, despite the upheaval and destruction, the cities of Palestine, particularly Jerusalem, proved resilient, being rebuilt and revitalized multiple times. This era, characterized by both the flourishing of Islamic civilization and the coexistence of various religious communities, formed a foundational period that continues to define the cultural, religious, and political identity of the region today.

The Rise of Islam and the Islamic Conquest of Palestine, The origins of Islam are deeply intertwined with the life of Prophet Muhammad, who, in the early 7th century, began receiving divine revelations that would later form the Quran, the holy book of Islam. These revelations introduced a monotheistic faith centered on the belief in one God, Allah, and outlined a vision for a just and moral society. After the death of Prophet Muhammad in 632 CE, the leadership of the nascent Muslim community passed to a series of caliphs who would oversee the rapid expansion of Islam beyond the Arabian Peninsula.

This period, known as the Rashidun (Rightly Guided) Caliphate, saw the Muslims conquer large swaths of territory. Among the first major regions to fall under Muslim rule was the

Levant, a region that included modern-day Palestine, Syria, and Jordan. The Byzantine Empire, which had previously controlled Palestine, was weakened by internal strife and external pressures, making it vulnerable to the advancing Muslim forces. The conquest of Palestine thus marked the beginning of a new chapter in the history of the Holy Land, one that would see the consolidation of Islamic power and the introduction of a new socio-political order.

The significance of Palestine in this context cannot be overstated. For Muslims, the region was imbued with religious importance, not only because it was the site of the Al-Aqsa Mosque in Jerusalem, a revered holy site, but also because of its association with the Prophet Muhammad's Night Journey (Isra and Mi'raj), during which he is believed to have ascended to the heavens from the Al-Aqsa Mosque. This spiritual connection made the conquest of Jerusalem and the surrounding region a highly symbolic event in Islamic history.

The Peaceful Conquest of Jerusalem (638 CE), The peaceful conquest of Jerusalem by the Muslims in 638 CE stands as one of the most notable and respected moments in both Islamic and world history. It is a rare example of a major military conquest that was achieved not through bloodshed, but through diplomacy, respect for religious differences, and a commitment to peaceful coexistence. This event holds profound significance in shaping the long-term political, religious, and cultural landscape of the region.

At the time of the conquest, Jerusalem was under Byzantine rule, part of the Eastern Roman Empire. The city had long been a focal point for Christians, as it was the site of the crucifixion and resurrection of Jesus Christ. For Jews, Jerusalem had been their capital in ancient times, and it remained a symbol of their religious and cultural heritage. By the 7th century, however, the Byzantine Empire had become politically and militarily weakened, facing internal divisions and pressure from external forces. In particular, the Byzantine Empire had been fighting a series of unsuccessful wars against the Sassanid Empire, and it was left vulnerable to the rising power of the Islamic Caliphate.

The rise of Islam under Prophet Muhammad and the rapid expansion of the Muslim empire had created a new political reality in the region. After Muhammad's death in 632 CE, the Rashidun Caliphs, particularly Caliph Umar ibn al-Khattab, sought to extend Islamic rule beyond the Arabian Peninsula. The Muslim army, unified and determined, began expanding rapidly, defeating both the Byzantine and Sassanid empires and bringing much of the Levant under Muslim control.

By 637 CE, after a series of important military victories, the Muslims were poised to take control of Jerusalem, a city of immense religious significance to Christians, Jews, and Muslims. The city had already witnessed numerous sieges throughout its history, but the peaceful conquest in 638 CE would be unique in its approach.

The conquest of Jerusalem was preceded by a siege that lasted for several months. Unlike many military campaigns of the time, which were often marked by brutality and destruction, the Muslim army under Caliph Umar approached the city with an understanding of its religious and cultural importance. Jerusalem, known for its sanctity to Christians and Jews, had to be handled with care and respect.

The Christian patriarch of Jerusalem, Sophronius, who was in charge of the city, recognized the strength of the advancing Muslim forces and understood that further resistance would likely result in widespread destruction. After long negotiations, he agreed to surrender the city to the Muslims, but with one condition: he requested that the Caliph himself come to Jerusalem to oversee the terms of surrender. This condition was significant because it demonstrated the respect the Christian leadership had for the figure of Caliph Umar and the trust they placed in him to honor the city's religious sanctity.

Caliph Umar agreed to this condition and made the journey to Jerusalem. His entry into the city was a moment of diplomacy and peace. Upon his arrival, the Christian population welcomed him, and after some formalities, the city was handed over to the Muslims. Unlike other conquests, which often involved violence or massacres, the peaceful surrender allowed the city's residents—Muslim, Christian, and Jewish—to maintain their way of life without fear of persecution.

The Preservation of Sacred Sites and Religious Tolerance

One of the most important aspects of Umar's conquest was his policy toward religious tolerance. Upon entering Jerusalem, Umar immediately issued a set of guarantees for the protection of the city's Christian and Jewish communities. The Christians were allowed to maintain their churches, and the Jews were granted permission to visit their sacred sites. The Church of the Holy Sepulchre, the holiest site in Christianity, was preserved under Muslim protection.

Umar's respect for the religious significance of the city was symbolized by his decision to pray outside the Church of the Holy Sepulchre, rather than inside it. He feared that future generations of Muslims might convert the church into a mosque, so he instead offered a prayer outside. This act demonstrated his profound understanding of the religious and cultural sensitivities of the time, and his commitment to preserving the integrity of religious sites.

Moreover, Umar assured the Christian population that their religious practices would be protected. The dhimma system, a set of rules that provided protection for religious minorities, was implemented to ensure that Jews and Christians could continue to live in the city, practice their faiths, and govern their internal affairs. This was in stark contrast to the policies of other empires at the time, where religious minorities often faced persecution or forced conversion.

Umar's leadership in Jerusalem was not merely an act of military conquest; it was a demonstration of Islamic values of justice, respect for human dignity, and coexistence. His actions established a precedent for the treatment of religious minorities under Muslim rule and laid the groundwork for centuries of religious pluralism in the region.

The Legacy of the Peaceful Conquest, The peaceful conquest of Jerusalem marked a turning point in the history of the city and the broader region. It was a moment where diplomacy, religious tolerance, and mutual respect triumphed over violence and conflict. Under Islamic rule, Jerusalem became a symbol of coexistence, where Muslims, Christians, and Jews could live side by side and practice their faiths in peace.

The policies of religious tolerance introduced by Umar set the tone for centuries of Muslim governance in Palestine. These policies ensured that Jerusalem remained a multicultural city, with religious communities enjoying a degree of autonomy and protection. The peaceful nature of the conquest also helped solidify the legitimacy of Islamic rule in the region, as it demonstrated the capacity of the Muslim leadership to govern justly and fairly.

The Construction of the Dome of the Rock (691 CE), The construction of the Dome of the Rock in 691 CE, commissioned by the Umayyad Caliph Abd al-Malik, marked a monumental achievement in Islamic architecture and a defining moment in the region's religious history. Situated on the Temple Mount, the Dome of the Rock was built to commemorate the miraculous Night Journey of the Prophet Muhammad, where he is believed to have ascended to heaven. The structure is one of the oldest and most iconic Islamic monuments, with its golden dome and intricate mosaic designs attracting pilgrims and visitors from around the world.

The architectural style of the Dome of the Rock is a synthesis of Byzantine, Sassanian, and early Islamic elements, showcasing the cultural diversity and cosmopolitanism of the early Islamic Empire. The building's most striking feature is its circular shape, which is meant to symbolize the unity of God, and its stunning tile mosaics that depict a range of motifs, from geometric patterns to inscriptions from the Quran. The Dome of the Rock stands as both a religious and political symbol of Islam's arrival in Jerusalem, serving as a powerful reminder of the city's newfound importance in the Islamic world.

The religious symbolism of the Dome of the Rock cannot be overstated. For Muslims, it serves as a reminder of the divine connection between the earthly and the heavenly realms. The Quranic verses inscribed on the building emphasize the oneness of God and the prophethood of Muhammad, positioning the structure as both a spiritual and ideological statement. The Dome of the Rock thus became a focal point for Muslim religious and political identity, solidifying Jerusalem's place as the third holiest city in Islam, after Mecca and Medina.

Palestine and the Crusades, The Crusades, a series of religious and military campaigns initiated by Christian European powers between the 11th and 13th centuries, were a pivotal chapter in the history of Palestine. The primary goal of the Crusades was to reclaim Jerusalem and the Holy Land from Muslim rule, following the rise of Islam in the 7th century. The Crusades significantly altered the geopolitical, social, and religious landscape of Palestine, creating a period of intense conflict, religious fervor, and political instability.

The Crusades were sparked by a combination of religious zeal and political ambition. In 1095, Pope Urban II called for a military expedition to free Jerusalem from Muslim rule, promising spiritual rewards for those who participated. The Pope's call to arms was motivated by a number of factors, including the desire to protect

Christian pilgrims traveling to Jerusalem, the weakening of the Byzantine Empire under pressure from the Seljuk Turks, and the desire to expand Christian influence in the region.

The First Crusade (1096–1099) began as a large-scale military campaign to capture Jerusalem from the Muslims. The Crusaders, a mix of knights, soldiers, and religious pilgrims, traveled across Europe and arrived at Jerusalem in 1099, after a long and brutal siege. The city's Muslim and Jewish populations were massacred when the Crusaders finally took control, and Jerusalem was declared a Christian city.

The Crusader Kingdom of Jerusalem, After the capture of Jerusalem, the Crusaders established the Kingdom of Jerusalem, a Christian feudal state that spanned much of the Levant. The Kingdom was initially successful in defending its territory against Muslim counterattacks, and for nearly a century, it remained a major Christian outpost in the region. However, the Crusaders were unable to fully consolidate their control over Palestine, as the region remained a strategic crossroads between Europe, Asia, and Africa. The Muslim world, particularly under the leadership of Saladin, remained a formidable force.

The Crusaders' presence in the Holy Land was marked by religious and political tension. While the Crusaders were able to establish several fortresses and outposts, their rule was often unstable, with constant conflicts between the Crusader states and the surrounding Muslim territories. The Crusaders' attempts to forcibly convert Muslims and Jews to Christianity, as well as their imposition of Latin Christianity, further alienated the local populations, many of whom were resistant to foreign rule.

The Crusader states were also vulnerable to internal divisions. Disputes between different Crusader factions, combined with a lack of reinforcements from Europe, weakened their position. Despite their military might, the Crusaders were increasingly unable to defend their territories against Muslim forces.

The Response of the Muslim World, The Crusaders' occupation of Jerusalem and other parts of Palestine was seen as a direct challenge to Islamic rule, and it provoked a series of military responses from the Muslim world. One of the most significant of these responses came from the legendary figure of Saladin, the Sultan of Egypt and Syria, who would go on to become one of the most famous figures in the history of the Crusades.

Saladin and the Recapture of Jerusalem (1187 CE)

Saladin's recapture of Jerusalem in 1187 CE stands as one of the most significant events in both the history of the Crusades and the history of Islamic rule in the region. This event marked the culmination of Saladin's long campaign against the Crusaders and heralded the end of nearly a century of Christian control over the city. Saladin's military genius, his leadership, and his ability to unite various Muslim factions played a critical role in his victory and the ultimate reconquest of the city.

SALADIN'S RISE TO POWER, Saladin was born in 1137 in Tikrit, in present-day Iraq, into a Kurdish family with a long history of military service. His rise to prominence is a story of both military prowess and political acumen. Initially, Saladin served under the Zengid dynasty, a Kurdish Muslim family that controlled parts of Syria and Iraq. Through his service to the Zengids, Saladin quickly demonstrated his exceptional leadership abilities and his skill in both military strategy and diplomacy. He earned the trust of his superiors, and eventually, he was appointed as the vizier of Egypt in 1169.

Once in power, Saladin began consolidating control over Egypt and used it as a base to launch campaigns in the Levant. His ambitions were not solely for personal gain but were driven by a desire to unify the Muslim world. By the 1170s, Saladin had succeeded in bringing together Egypt, Syria, and other parts of the Levant under his rule, effectively unifying the fragmented Muslim world that had previously been divided by local rulers and infighting.

Saladin's unification of the Muslim territories was a pivotal moment in his struggle against the Crusaders. The Crusader states, established in the wake of the First Crusade (1096–1099), were scattered across the Levant and often engaged in internal conflicts. Saladin recognized the need for a united Muslim front to confront the common enemy—the Crusader Kingdoms in the Holy Land. He worked tirelessly to reconcile sectarian divisions within the Muslim world, which included rivalries between Sunnis and Shias, ensuring that his forces were a unified force against the Crusaders.

The Battle of Hattin and the Siege of Jerusalem, The pivotal moment in Saladin's campaign came in 1187 with the Battle of Hattin. The Crusaders had been attempting to maintain control over Jerusalem and the surrounding territories, but their power was weakening. Saladin's forces, consisting of a diverse mix of Muslim troops from across his unified empire, confronted the Crusaders at Hattin, near the Sea of Galilee. The battle was a crushing defeat for the Crusaders. The Crusader army, already weakened by internal discord and poor strategy, was decisively routed by Saladin's forces. Not only did Saladin achieve a stunning military victory, but he also captured key Crusader leaders, including King Guy of Lusignan of Jerusalem and other nobles.

The Battle of Hattin marked the beginning of the end for Crusader rule in Jerusalem. The Crusader forces were demoralized, and the loss of their leaders and their military capacity paved the way for Saladin's advance toward Jerusalem. After the battle, Saladin's forces began a systematic campaign to reclaim the

Crusader-controlled cities and fortresses in the region, moving inexorably towards Jerusalem itself.

In September 1187, Saladin laid siege to Jerusalem. The Crusaders within the city had little hope of reinforcement or relief, and their morale was shattered. Saladin's siege was meticulous, using both military pressure and psychological tactics to weaken the resolve of the defenders. Unlike the brutal tactics of the Crusaders during their first capture of Jerusalem in 1099, which involved massacring Muslims and Jews, Saladin's approach was characterized by both military discipline and compassion.

Saladin's Mercy and the Surrender of Jerusalem, After weeks of siege, Jerusalem surrendered to Saladin's forces on October 2, 1187. The city, which had been under Crusader control for nearly a century, now came back under Muslim rule. Saladin's entry into Jerusalem was markedly different from the Crusaders' violent conquest. Despite his victory, Saladin showed remarkable restraint and generosity. He allowed the Christian inhabitants of the city to leave peacefully, offering them safe passage. Christian pilgrims were also allowed to visit their holy sites in the city, including the Church of the Holy Sepulchre, which had been a key Christian landmark. This act of mercy contrasted sharply with the Crusaders' infamous massacre of the Muslim and Jewish inhabitants of Jerusalem in 1099, during the First Crusade.

Saladin's magnanimity earned him widespread respect, even among his enemies. His actions in Jerusalem helped to preserve the religious integrity of the city and its significance to Jews, Christians, and Muslims alike. The Church of the Holy Sepulchre, one of Christianity's most sacred sites, remained under Christian control, and the city's Jewish and Muslim inhabitants were treated with relative fairness and dignity. This attitude reflected Saladin's commitment to religious tolerance, an important aspect of his legacy.

Legacy of Saladin's Victory, Saladin's recapture of Jerusalem had profound and lasting effects. For the Muslim world, it was a moment of immense pride. The victory restored Jerusalem to Muslim rule after nearly a century of Crusader occupation, symbolizing the triumph of Islamic unity under Saladin's leadership. Saladin's actions in Jerusalem also underscored the strength of Islam's moral and religious values. His compassion in victory, his respect for the religious diversity of the city, and his fair treatment of both Muslim and Christian inhabitants marked him as a just and noble ruler.

In the broader context of the Crusades, Saladin's victory was a major blow to the Crusader states in the Holy Land. It led to the loss of their most important city, and it shifted the balance of power in the region. However, it also reignited the Crusader zeal in Europe. The loss of Jerusalem led to the Third Crusade (1189–1192), which saw European monarchs such as Richard the Lionheart of England, Philip II of France, and Emperor Frederick I Barbarossa attempt to retake the city. While the Crusaders made some gains, they were ultimately unable to recapture Jerusalem.

Saladin's victory also served as a model of chivalric behavior for many in the Islamic world. His ability to blend military prowess with compassion and his respect for the religious significance of Jerusalem helped shape the image of the ideal ruler. Over time, Saladin became a legendary figure not only in the Muslim world but also in the Western imagination, where he was often viewed as a noble enemy.

In the years following Saladin's death in 1193, his legacy continued to inspire both Muslims and non-Muslims. His success in unifying the Muslim world and recapturing Jerusalem from the Crusaders helped shape the future of the region. The city would remain under Muslim control for centuries, and Saladin's vision of a united Islamic front against foreign invaders continued to resonate through history. His diplomatic, military, and humanitarian qualities made him one of the most respected figures in both Islamic and world history.

In conclusion, Saladin's recapture of Jerusalem in 1187 CE was not only a military triumph but a moral and political watershed moment. His ability to unite the Muslim world, his military brilliance at the Battle of Hattin, and his compassionate treatment of Jerusalem's inhabitants upon its surrender cemented his legacy as one of history's great leaders. Saladin's victory in Jerusalem marked the beginning of a new chapter in the city's history, one defined by Muslim control that would last for centuries. His leadership and actions continue to resonate in the collective memory of both the Islamic world and the West, making him a symbol of honor, strength, and wisdom.

Rebuilding and Resilience of Palestine

The history of Palestine during and after the Crusades is a remarkable testament to the resilience and rebuilding spirit of the region. Despite enduring centuries of violence, destruction, and foreign occupation, Palestine displayed an incredible ability to recover and thrive under successive rulers. The efforts to rebuild Jerusalem, the spiritual heart of the region, were central to this resurgence, with numerous periods of restoration, cultural flourishing, and intellectual development. These efforts were particularly notable following the recapture of Jerusalem by Saladin in 1187, and they continued under subsequent Muslim dynasties, such as the Mamluks and the Ottomans.

Saladin's Restoration of Jerusalem, After Saladin's recapture of Jerusalem in 1187, he focused not only on the political and military consolidation of the region but also on the restoration and rebuilding of Jerusalem itself. Saladin was acutely aware of the city's religious significance to Muslims, Christians, and Jews, and he took deliberate steps to ensure its recovery and revitalization after the destruction caused by the Crusaders.

One of Saladin's first acts upon entering Jerusalem was to restore the religious sanctity of the city. He ensured that the Islamic holy sites, such as the Al-Aqsa Mosque and the Dome of the Rock, were protected, repaired, and re-established as central to Islamic worship. The city's defensive structures, including the walls and gates, were reinforced to secure it against future invasions. This effort to rebuild Jerusalem after the Crusader occupation helped solidify Muslim control over the city, restoring it as a symbol of Islamic resilience and unity.

The Mamluk Period: 13th to 16th Century, The Mamluk period, spanning from the 13th to the 16th centuries, was pivotal in the history of Palestine. The Mamluks, originally military slaves who rose to power in Egypt, succeeded the Ayyubids (the dynasty founded by Saladin) and played a crucial role in further stabilizing the region after the upheavals of the Crusades. Under Mamluk rule, Palestine, and particularly Jerusalem, saw significant advancements in architecture, culture, and education, marking a period of revitalization for the region.

Architectural and Urban Development, One of the most important aspects of Mamluk rule in Palestine was their extensive rebuilding efforts, which aimed to restore and fortify the cities of the region. Jerusalem, as the most significant city, received considerable attention during this period. The Mamluks invested in the restoration of existing Islamic monuments, such as the Al-Aqsa Mosque, and commissioned the construction of new structures, including mosques, schools, and public buildings.

The Mamluks also undertook major fortification projects to protect the city from potential invaders. They reinforced Jerusalem's defensive walls, constructed new gates, and built additional fortifications around key areas such as the Old City. These measures not only protected Jerusalem but also symbolized the Mamluks' commitment to preserving Islamic control over the region.

The Mamluks were known for their distinctive architectural style, which blended Islamic, Egyptian, and local influences. They built monumental mosques with intricate decorations, large courtyards, and impressive minarets. Notable examples of Mamluk architecture in Palestine include the Qalawun Mosque in Jerusalem and the madrasas (Islamic schools) that they established throughout the city.

Cultural and Educational Renaissance, determination of its people. Beyond architectural restoration, the Mamluks played a critical role in fostering cultural and intellectual growth in Palestine. One of the most enduring legacies of the Mamluk period was the development of religious and educational institutions, particularly madrasas (religious schools), which became centers of learning for scholars from across the Islamic world.

These madrasas offered a range of educational programs, from theology and jurisprudence to philosophy, astronomy, and medicine. Scholars from Sunni, Shia, and other Islamic traditions gathered in these institutions, creating an environment of intellectual exchange and debate. Jerusalem, with its religious significance, was at the heart of this intellectual revival, attracting scholars and students from all parts of the Muslim world.

The Mamluks also contributed to the flourishing of Islamic art, literature, and calligraphy. The art of manuscript illumination, for example, saw significant developments during this period, with many Mamluk-era manuscripts preserved in libraries and museums around the world today. Islamic architecture flourished as well, with the construction of beautifully adorned mosques, schools, and public baths, all contributing to the cultural vibrancy of Palestinian cities.

The Mamluks' commitment to education and scholarship helped shape the intellectual landscape of the region. Religious schools, libraries, and centers of learning fostered a culture of academic pursuit, and these institutions became crucial for preserving and transmitting Islamic knowledge for generations to come.

The Ottoman Period: 16th Century Onwards, The Mamluk period came to an end in 1517 when the Ottoman Empire, under Sultan Selim I, defeated the Mamluks and took control of Palestine. Despite the political changes, the region's process of rebuilding and cultural development continued under Ottoman rule, which lasted for centuries.

The Ottomans invested in further fortifying Jerusalem and other key cities. They continued the work started by the Mamluks, restoring and maintaining the religious and architectural heritage of the region. The Ottomans also made improvements to the infrastructure, including roads, markets, and public buildings, contributing to the economic and social development of Palestine.

Like the Mamluks, the Ottomans also valued education and established additional madrasas, mosques, and libraries. Jerusalem, as the third holiest city in Islam, remained a focal point for Ottoman rule, and the city continued to thrive as a center of religious and cultural significance.

Legacy of Rebuilding and Resilience, The rebuilding efforts that took place in Palestine after the Crusades, particularly during the Mamluk and Ottoman periods, are a testament to the resilience of the region. Despite the devastation caused by the Crusades and the periodic invasions that followed, the people of Palestine were able to rebuild their cities, restore their cultural and religious monuments, and maintain their rich intellectual and religious traditions.

The Mamluks, in particular, played a central role in transforming Palestine into a cultural and intellectual hub. They not only restored the physical infrastructure of the region but also nurtured a flourishing of Islamic thought and creativity. Their contributions to architecture, education, and scholarship left a lasting legacy in

Palestine, and their impact can still be seen in the region's historical and cultural landmarks today.

In the broader historical context, the rebuilding and resilience of Palestine under the Mamluks and Ottomans highlights the endurance of the region's people and their ability to recover from periods of turmoil. The efforts to restore Jerusalem and other cities were not only about physical reconstruction but also about maintaining the religious, cultural, and intellectual heritage of the region. This resilience continues to define Palestine's identity and its place in the broader history of the Middle East.

The rebuilding of Palestine following the Crusades, particularly during the Mamluk period, was an extraordinary achievement. The Mamluks' architectural, cultural, and educational contributions transformed Palestine into a thriving center of Islamic civilization. The enduring legacy of this period can still be seen in the region's religious landmarks, educational institutions, and vibrant cultural traditions. Despite centuries of violence and occupation, Palestine's resilience and its ability to rebuild itself remain a testament to the strength and determination of its people.

CULTURAL AND RELIGIOUS Coexistence, Despite the challenges of political and military conflict, the Islamic era in Palestine is also marked by moments of cultural and religious coexistence. Under Islamic rule, both Jews and Christians were allowed to practice their faiths freely, provided they adhered to the dhimma system. This system, which granted religious minorities protection in exchange for paying a tax, allowed Jews and Christians to maintain their places of worship and engage in cultural exchange with Muslims. Many Jewish and Christian communities in Palestine enjoyed a period of relative peace under Muslim governance, with their religious and cultural practices being recognized and respected.

One notable example of religious coexistence was the role of the Jewish community in Jerusalem during the Ayyubid and Mamluk periods. Jews, who had long been marginalized under Byzantine rule, found a more welcoming environment under Muslim governance. The famous Jewish philosopher and physician Maimonides, who lived in both Egypt and Jerusalem during the 12th century, was a product of this flourishing intellectual atmosphere. Christians, too, continued to play an important role in the religious and cultural life of Jerusalem, particularly in maintaining the Church of the Holy Sepulchre, which remained an important pilgrimage site for Christians throughout the Islamic era.

The Islamic era in Palestine, from the 7th to the 16th centuries, was a period of remarkable spiritual, cultural, and political transformation. The peaceful conquest of Jerusalem, the construction of the Dome of the Rock, and the city's resilience during the Crusades all contributed to the formation of a rich and diverse legacy that continues to shape the identity of Palestine today. Despite the turbulence and challenges faced by the region, Palestine remained a center of religious significance, intellectual achievement, and cultural exchange. The Islamic era in Palestine is thus not only a story of conquest and resilience but also one of coexistence, renewal, and lasting influence that resonates throughout the history of the Holy Land.

Ottoman Period (1517–1917): Stability Under Imperial Rule

The Ottoman Empire's rule over Palestine from 1517 to 1917 constitutes a significant and transformative period in the region's history. For 400 years, Palestine was part of an empire that spanned across three continents, from the Balkans to North Africa and the Middle East. During this era, the Ottomans integrated Palestine into their imperial structure, bringing both stability and challenges.

Although marked by periods of reform and external pressure, the era is often remembered for its relative peace and economic prosperity. The Ottoman legacy in Palestine is visible in its architecture, governance systems, and its complex relationship with the diverse communities that lived in the region.

The Ottoman Conquest and Early Years of Rule, The conquest of Palestine by the Ottoman Sultan Selim I in 1517 marked the beginning of a long and transformative chapter in the region's history. The Ottomans had conquered the Mamluks, who had ruled over Egypt and much of the Levant, including Palestine. The victory at the Battle of Marj Dabiq near Aleppo allowed the Ottomans to annex Palestine, along with Egypt, into their empire. With the fall of the Mamluks, the region became a part of the Ottoman vilayet (province) of Syria, which included modern-day Syria, Lebanon, and Jordan.

The early years of Ottoman rule were marked by a process of consolidation. Selim I and his successors worked to integrate Palestine into the Ottoman system, establishing a hierarchy of governance that was both centralized and decentralized. The central authority of the Ottoman sultan was the supreme power in the empire, but local administration was often entrusted to regional governors (pashas) or appointed officials. This system allowed for local autonomy while still ensuring loyalty to the imperial authority. Ottoman rule brought a sense of stability after the turbulence of Mamluk rule, and Palestine, once a contested borderland, was now part of a much larger and stable political entity.

The initial transition was not without challenges, however. The Ottoman Empire was vast, and communication between Istanbul and Palestine could be slow and inefficient. Furthermore, the Ottomans faced resistance from local factions who were used to a more autonomous existence under the Mamluks. These factions, often composed of local tribal leaders, notables, and religious figures, were reluctant to accept Ottoman rule. However, the Ottomans were skilled at integrating local elites into the imperial system by offering them incentives, such as administrative roles and tax privileges, in exchange for loyalty. Over time, the Ottomans succeeded in pacifying these local elites and establishing their authority over Palestine.

Local Governance and Autonomy, One of the defining features of Ottoman rule in Palestine was the local governance system, which granted a degree of autonomy to the various communities. The Ottomans implemented a hierarchical administrative structure, with Jerusalem as the primary administrative center. However, much of the daily governance was left to local leaders and community heads, particularly in rural areas. These leaders were often chosen from among the traditional local elites, which included wealthy landowners, religious leaders, and prominent merchants.

The Ottoman system of governance allowed a degree of self-rule through the millet system, a structure in which religious communities governed their own internal affairs. The millet system was particularly significant in a region like Palestine, where religious diversity was a hallmark of society. Each religious group—Muslims, Christians, and Jews—had its own legal system, schools, and religious institutions. The religious leaders of each millet were responsible for resolving issues related to family law, marriage, inheritance, and education. This system allowed the Ottoman Empire to manage a multi-ethnic and multi-religious society with relative ease, as each community was largely self-regulating.

Local autonomy was also exercised through the role of notables, or prominent local leaders. These notables were often the heads of influential families or wealthy landowners who had substantial control over their territories. In many cases, the Ottoman rulers relied on these notables to maintain order, collect taxes, and ensure loyalty to the central government. In exchange, the notables enjoyed a degree of power and privileges. This decentralized system helped the Ottomans manage their far-flung empire, but it also meant that local politics were often shaped by the interests of the elites, rather than by centralized state institutions. The influence of these local notables remained strong throughout the Ottoman period, particularly in rural areas, where they held significant sway over the peasant population.

Economic and Social Life, Economically, Palestine under the Ottomans was primarily an agricultural region, with the vast majority of the population engaged in farming. The fertile plains along the coast and the Jordan River Valley were crucial to the cultivation of crops, including wheat, barley, olives, and fruits. The economy was largely subsistence-based, but surplus crops were traded both locally and with neighboring regions. Trade routes crisscrossed Palestine, and the region served as a bridge between the Mediterranean world, the Arabian Peninsula, and the lands further east.

The economy of Palestine also benefited from the Ottomans' investment in infrastructure. The empire built roads, bridges, and caravanserais, which facilitated trade and travel across the empire. These infrastructure projects helped connect Palestine to the larger Ottoman world and made it easier for merchants to transport goods. The construction of caravanserais—large roadside inns where travelers and merchants could rest, store goods, and exchange information—was especially important in maintaining the flow of trade. Many of these caravanserais still stand in cities like Jerusalem, Hebron, and Nablus, offering a glimpse into the region's vibrant commercial life.

Moreover, the Ottomans introduced reforms to improve agricultural productivity. They encouraged the cultivation of cash crops such as cotton and tobacco, which became important exports in the 19th century. These crops were particularly significant during the Industrial Revolution, as demand for raw materials like cotton surged in Europe. However, the introduction of cash crops also had social consequences. Large landowners profited from these agricultural changes, but the peasant population often found itself heavily taxed or forced into sharecropping arrangements, leading to tensions between the landed elite and the rural poor.

Social life in Ottoman Palestine was characterized by a high degree of religious and cultural diversity. Muslims, Christians, and Jews lived side by side, often in the same cities or neighborhoods. Jerusalem, in particular, was a focal point for religious and cultural exchange. The city's religious significance for all three Abrahamic faiths contributed to its status as a cosmopolitan center, attracting pilgrims and visitors from around the world. This diverse environment fostered a rich cultural life, with traditions from across the empire mingling in the region. Despite occasional tensions, the Ottomans' policy of religious tolerance allowed for peaceful coexistence among different communities.

Cultural Flourishing and Religious Architecture, The Ottoman period in Palestine is also remembered for its cultural and architectural contributions. The Ottomans were known for their distinctive architectural style, which blended Islamic, Byzantine, and Persian influences. In Palestine, this resulted in the construction of stunning mosques, schools, and public buildings that are still landmarks today. The Ottomans sought to leave their mark on the region, particularly in Jerusalem, which held immense religious and political significance.

One of the most iconic examples of Ottoman architecture in Palestine is the renovation and expansion of the Dome of the Rock and Al-Aqsa Mosque in Jerusalem. Sultan Suleiman the Magnificent (reigned 1520-1566) undertook major restoration work on these structures, reinforcing the city's spiritual and symbolic significance. His construction projects also included the building of walls around

Jerusalem to protect it from external threats, solidifying the city's importance within the empire.

In addition to religious buildings, the Ottomans constructed various public amenities, such as hammams (public bathhouses), fountains, and caravanserais, all of which served to improve the quality of life for the local population. These buildings were not just utilitarian; they were also expressions of Ottoman prestige, serving as symbols of the empire's power and benevolence. Many of these structures were adorned with intricate tiles, calligraphy, and decorative elements that showcased the artistic and architectural achievements of the period.

The Ottomans also encouraged the establishment of schools and educational institutions, especially in urban centers like Jerusalem, Nablus, and Gaza. These schools offered education in religious subjects as well as literature, mathematics, and the sciences. The Ottomans placed great emphasis on religious education, particularly in Islamic jurisprudence, and many scholars emerged from this system, contributing to the intellectual life of the region.

Challenges and Reforms, Despite the overall stability and prosperity of the Ottoman period, the empire faced significant challenges in the 19th century. The empire began to weaken due to a combination of internal decay, military defeats, and external pressures. The rise of European imperial powers, particularly Britain and France, increasingly threatened Ottoman dominance in the Middle East.

In response to these challenges, the Ottomans embarked on a series of *Tanzimat reforms (1839-1876)*, which sought to modernize the empire by centralizing control, strengthening the military, and implementing legal and administrative changes. These reforms included the introduction of new tax systems, the establishment of a more centralized bureaucracy, and efforts to grant greater rights to non-Muslim populations. However, these reforms were often met with resistance from conservative elements within the empire, as well as from local elites in Palestine who feared a loss of their power and privileges.

The 19th century also saw the emergence of Arab nationalism, particularly in the wake of the *Tanzimat reforms*. Palestinian Arabs began to assert their identity and demand greater political autonomy, influenced by broader nationalist movements sweeping through the Ottoman Empire. The rising influence of European powers in the region, especially after the British began to invest in the Suez Canal and the surrounding areas, further heightened tensions.

The End of Ottoman Rule, The end of Ottoman rule in Palestine came during World War I, when the empire sided with the Central Powers. After years of military defeats and internal unrest, the Ottomans were defeated by the Allied forces, which included Britain. In 1917, British forces under General Edmund Allenby captured Jerusalem, marking the end of Ottoman rule. The subsequent British Mandate over Palestine, which was confirmed by the League of Nations in 1922, ushered in a new era of political and social upheaval.

The Ottoman legacy, however, endured in many ways. The infrastructure, governance systems, and cultural heritage the Ottomans left behind continue to shape the political and social landscape of modern Palestine. The memories of relative peace and stability, the millet system, and the lasting contributions to the region's architecture and social fabric remain a testament to the Ottoman Empire's long and complex relationship with Palestine.

A Living Heritage

Palestine, a land revered by millions across the world, stands as a testament to human resilience, adaptation, and the quest for meaning and belonging. From its prehistoric roots to its profound influence in the narratives of empires, faiths, and modern geopolitics,

Palestine's history is a tapestry that weaves together cultural, spiritual, and political threads, each narrating a story of struggle, survival, and profound significance. This enduring heritage is not merely a collection of events but a living, evolving narrative that continues to shape the lives of those who call this land home and those who regard it as sacred.

PREHISTORIC ORIGINS: The Birth of Civilization, Palestine's history reaches back to the dawn of humanity. Archaeological evidence suggests that the region has been continuously inhabited for over 12,000 years. Early human settlements along the Jordan River Valley are among the first known to have practiced agriculture, transforming the region from a land of nomadic tribes to a cradle of civilization. The Jericho site, one of the world's oldest continuously inhabited cities, offers a glimpse into these early societies. Excavations reveal ancient walls and watchtowers, suggesting that Jericho was not only a settlement but a fortified city, indicating the beginnings of social structures, trade, and defense systems.

In these prehistoric times, Palestine was home to various Semitic-speaking tribes, laying the foundation for the cultural and linguistic diversity that would define the region for millennia. The land's fertile soil, coupled with its strategic location between Africa and Asia, made it a crossroads for migratory and trade routes, contributing to its development as a melting pot of cultures and civilizations.

The Age of Empires: The Influence of Ancient Civilizations, The first major empires to leave a lasting mark on Palestine were the Egyptians, followed by the Israelites, and later the Persians, Greeks, and Romans. These civilizations shaped not only the political landscape of the region but also its cultural and religious identity.

The Israelites, whose history is deeply intertwined with Palestine, considered the land their Promised Land. According to the Bible, after their exodus from Egypt, they conquered and settled in Canaan, a region roughly corresponding to modern-day Palestine. This biblical narrative has been central to the identity of the Jewish people, and its significance remains paramount in the region's ongoing cultural and political discourse.

The subsequent rise of the empires, particularly the Persian and Hellenistic empires, also left indelible marks on the region. Under Persian rule, Palestine was part of the vast Achaemenid Empire, and its people enjoyed a degree of religious and cultural autonomy. However, it was under the Greeks, especially during the reign of Alexander the Great and the Hellenistic period that followed, that Palestine witnessed an influx of Greek culture, philosophy, and architecture.

The Romans, who eventually took control of the region, dramatically altered Palestine's landscape, both physically and culturally. They built monumental structures like the city of Caesarea and the expansion of Jerusalem, imbuing the region with Roman architectural grandeur. This period was marked by tension between the Jewish population and Roman authorities, culminating in the Jewish revolts. The destruction of the Second Temple in Jerusalem in 70 CE, a traumatic event in Jewish history, remains a defining moment in the region's historical narrative.

Religious Significance: A Land of Faiths, Palestine's spiritual and religious significance is unparalleled. The region is a sacred site for Judaism, Christianity, and Islam, three of the world's major monotheistic religions. This religious tapestry is a key aspect of the living heritage of Palestine, influencing its culture, identity, and political realities.

For Jews, Palestine is the birthplace of their faith. Jerusalem, in particular, holds profound significance, housing the First and

Second Temples. Even after the destruction of the Second Temple, the Western Wall, or the Wailing Wall, remains a place of pilgrimage for Jews, symbolizing their deep connection to the land. The religious fervor surrounding Jerusalem was evident when, in 70 CE, the Roman legions under Titus destroyed the city and its Temple, leading to the Jewish diaspora. Yet, even in exile, the hope of return to the Promised Land persisted in the collective memory of the Jewish people.

Christianity's origins in Palestine are no less significant. According to Christian tradition, it was in Palestine that Jesus of Nazareth was born, preached, was crucified, and resurrected. Bethlehem, Jerusalem, and Nazareth are key pilgrimage sites for Christians worldwide. The Church of the Holy Sepulchre, built at the site of Jesus's crucifixion and resurrection, attracts millions of Christian pilgrims each year. This religious history continues to shape the cultural fabric of Palestine, where Christian communities have coexisted with Muslim and Jewish communities for centuries.

Islam's ties to Palestine are also deep-rooted. Jerusalem is home to the Al-Aqsa Mosque, the third holiest site in Islam. The Dome of the Rock, built in the 7th century, is a striking architectural masterpiece that signifies the sacred nature of the city for Muslims. The city's religious significance to Islam is tied to the belief that the Prophet Muhammad ascended to heaven from the Al-Aqsa Mosque during the Night Journey.

The religious dynamics of Palestine have often led to tensions, but they also exemplify the coexistence of three major faiths in a region where sacred histories and narratives intertwine. This diversity, however, is not without its challenges. Religious significance often intersects with political and territorial disputes, making Palestine a focal point of global religious and geopolitical conflicts.

MODERN STRUGGLES: THE Continued Quest for Identity and Autonomy, Palestine's modern history has been shaped by struggles for autonomy, identity, and peace. The fall of the Ottoman Empire after World War I and the subsequent British Mandate over Palestine set the stage for the complex political developments that continue to this day. The tension between Jewish and Arab communities, compounded by competing nationalisms and foreign interventions, has led to a series of conflicts, wars, and negotiations.

The creation of the State of Israel in 1948, following the end of the British Mandate, marked a turning point in Palestinian history. The resulting Palestinian Nakba, or "catastrophe," saw the displacement of hundreds of thousands of Palestinians from their homes, an event that remains central to the Palestinian national consciousness. The memory of 1948, the loss of land and identity, and the yearning for a just solution to the Palestinian refugee crisis continue to fuel Palestinian resistance movements and the ongoing struggle for self-determination.

The Israeli-Palestinian conflict remains one of the most enduring and contentious political issues in the modern world. While there have been numerous efforts to bring peace to the region, including the Oslo Accords in the 1990s, the path to a lasting resolution has remained elusive. The land of Palestine, once a melting pot of cultures and religions, has been at the center of global attention, as the world grapples with questions of justice, human rights, and the right to self-determination.

Living Heritage: Stories of Resilience and Adaptation

Despite the ongoing conflict, the spirit of Palestine's people endures. The resilience of Palestinians, their deep connection to the land, and their cultural heritage continue to shine through. The arts, literature, and music of Palestine have flourished, with poets like

Mahmoud Darwish giving voice to the pain and hope of the Palestinian people. Palestinian cinema, too, has gained international recognition for its powerful portrayal of the human experience under occupation.

Palestinian food, another key element of the region's living heritage, offers a unique blend of Arabic, Mediterranean, and Levantine influences. Traditional dishes like hummus, falafel, and tabbouleh are enjoyed by people around the world, carrying with them the history and culture of Palestine's diverse communities.

Through all the trials and tribulations, Palestine remains a land where the past and present are inextricably linked. It is a living heritage that transcends borders, politics, and time, offering a window into the enduring human quest for meaning, belonging, and transcendence. In the words of poet Mahmoud Darwish, "*We have on this earth what makes life worth living.*" Palestine, in all its complexity, continues to be a place where the human spirit, despite hardship, finds a way to endure, adapt, and thrive.

Chapter 2: Palestine in the Islamic Golden Age

The story of Palestine during the Islamic Golden Age is a remarkable narrative of transformation, resilience, and harmony. From the 7th to the 16th century, this sacred land, revered by Islam, Christianity, and Judaism, became a central part of the Islamic world. The region's significance transcended religious and cultural boundaries, and Palestine, a land at the crossroads of empires, ideas, and faiths, played a crucial role in shaping the civilization of its time. This era was not just one of military conquests and territorial changes but also one of cultural blossoming, intellectual achievement, and religious coexistence that remains a testament to the complexity and richness of medieval Palestinian society.

The Advent of Islam in Palestine: A New Era, The arrival of Islam in Palestine in the 7th century marked the beginning of a transformative chapter in the region's history. The conquest of the Levant, including Jerusalem, by the forces of the Rashidun Caliphate, following the death of the Prophet Muhammad, was pivotal in establishing the region as a vital part of the Islamic Empire. Under the leadership of Caliph Umar ibn al-Khattab, the Muslim armies captured Jerusalem in 637 AD. Unlike the often brutal campaigns of the period, the Muslim conquest of Jerusalem was characterized by respect for the city's religious sanctity. The Christians and Jews living in the city were allowed to practice their faiths freely, a policy that laid the foundation for the Islamic principles of tolerance and coexistence.

One of the most significant legacies of this period was the construction of the Dome of the Rock in 691 AD, commissioned by the Umayyad Caliph Abd al-Malik. Situated on the Temple Mount, the Dome of the Rock is not only an architectural masterpiece but also a symbol of the centrality of Jerusalem in the Islamic faith. It marked the beginning of a golden era of Islamic architecture in Palestine, which would continue throughout the centuries.

The Role of Palestine in the Abbasid Era: A Hub of Knowledge, The Abbasid Caliphate, which succeeded the Umayyads in 750 AD, transformed Baghdad into a global center of learning, innovation, and intellectual exchange. While Baghdad was the heart of the Abbasid world, Palestine too played a critical role in the intellectual and cultural flowering of the Islamic world. Cities like Jerusalem, Nablus, and Ramla became important centers of scholarship and religious activity, attracting scholars, theologians, and philosophers from across the empire.

One of the key intellectual achievements of the time was the flourishing of Islamic jurisprudence and theology. Scholars in Palestine, along with their counterparts in other parts of the Islamic world, contributed significantly to the development of Islamic law (Sharia) and the interpretation of the Quran. Many of the great Islamic scholars of the time, such as Al-Shafi'i and Al-Razi, spent periods of their lives in the region, enriching its intellectual landscape.

The Crusades and the Rise of Salahuddin al-Ayyubi, The 11th and 12th centuries were marked by the arrival of European Crusaders in the Levant, an event that dramatically altered the course of Palestinian history. The Crusades, which began in 1095 with the call for a holy war to reclaim Jerusalem from Muslim rule, led to nearly two centuries of intermittent warfare. In 1099, the Crusaders captured Jerusalem and established the Kingdom of

Jerusalem, subjecting its Muslim and Jewish inhabitants to harsh rule.

However, this period of foreign occupation came to an end with the rise of Salahuddin al-Ayyubi, one of the most celebrated figures in Islamic history. Born in Tikrit in 1137, Salahuddin emerged as a brilliant military strategist and leader, eventually becoming the Sultan of Egypt and Syria. His leadership was instrumental in uniting the Muslim world against the Crusaders. In 1187, after a series of successful campaigns, Salahuddin recaptured Jerusalem from the Crusaders, an event that remains one of the most significant moments in Islamic history.

Salahuddin's victory in Jerusalem was not just a military triumph; it was also a triumph of his vision of religious tolerance. Unlike the Crusaders, who had massacred the Muslim and Jewish populations of Jerusalem, Salahuddin allowed the Christian inhabitants of the city to practice their faith freely. This act of clemency was a powerful statement of the Islamic principles of mercy and tolerance, and it solidified his reputation as a just and noble ruler. His reign brought peace to the region and ushered in a period of relative stability that allowed Palestine to flourish once more.

The Mamluks and the Golden Age of Architecture, The Mamluk Sultanate, which rose to power in the 13th century after the decline of the Ayyubid dynasty, played a significant role in the development of Palestine during the Islamic Golden Age. The Mamluks, originally enslaved soldiers who had risen to prominence, were responsible for building an enduring legacy of Islamic architecture, particularly in Jerusalem, Gaza, and Ramla.

The Mamluk period saw the construction of numerous mosques, schools (madrasas), and public buildings. The most famous of these is the Al-Aqsa Mosque complex, which was renovated and expanded under the Mamluks. The Mamluk rulers also built fortified walls around Jerusalem and repaired the Dome of the Rock, ensuring the city's continued status as a major religious center.

In addition to architecture, the Mamluks were patrons of the arts and scholarship. They supported the development of Arabic literature, science, and philosophy. Many scholars from across the Islamic world, including from Persia and Central Asia, traveled to Palestine to engage with the vibrant intellectual community fostered by the Mamluks. Jerusalem, in particular, continued to be a center of Islamic learning and religious study.

The Ottoman Empire: Palestine Under Suleiman the Magnificent, The Ottoman Empire, which came to power in the early 16th century, added another layer to Palestine's rich and diverse history. Under the reign of Suleiman the Magnificent (1520–1566), the Ottomans consolidated their control over the region, and Palestine once again became a crossroads of empires, cultures, and faiths. Suleiman's reign is often referred to as the height of the Ottoman Empire, and during this period, Palestine experienced a renewed sense of prosperity and stability.

Suleiman the Magnificent undertook several key initiatives to strengthen the Ottoman presence in Palestine. He oversaw the reconstruction of Jerusalem's walls, which still stand today as one of the most iconic landmarks of the city. Suleiman also supported the maintenance of religious sites, including those of Christian and Jewish significance, thereby continuing the Ottoman tradition of religious tolerance.

Moreover, the Ottomans revitalized the economy of Palestine, integrating it more closely with the rest of the empire. Trade routes connecting the Levant to the rest of the Ottoman world flourished, and Palestinian cities became bustling hubs of commerce and culture. During this period, the region also witnessed the development of agriculture, particularly in the fertile plains of the coastal regions, which saw an expansion in the cultivation of crops such as olives, wheat, and cotton.

A Legacy of Transformation and Coexistence, The Islamic Golden Age in Palestine was a time of immense cultural, architectural, and intellectual achievement. From the construction of the Dome of the Rock to the reigns of visionary leaders like Salahuddin al-Ayyubi and Suleiman the Magnificent, Palestine flourished as a center of Islamic civilization. The religious diversity of the region was embraced, as Muslims, Christians, and Jews coexisted in relative harmony, each contributing to the rich tapestry of Palestinian society.

The legacy of this era is still evident today, not only in the monuments and architectural wonders left behind but also in the cultural and intellectual heritage that continues to shape the identity of the region. Palestine during the Islamic Golden Age stands as a testament to the possibilities of coexistence, intellectual exchange, and religious tolerance, offering lessons that resonate across time and geography. The stories of this era, filled with resilience, cooperation, and transformation, continue to inspire and inform the ongoing struggles for peace and understanding in the region.

Palestine's Integration into the Islamic World

The integration of Palestine into the Islamic world during the early years of the Rashidun Caliphate under the leadership of Umar ibn al-Khattab marks one of the most pivotal moments in the region's history. This event, which occurred in 637 CE, did not merely signify a military conquest but rather the beginning of a transformative period of cultural, religious, and political integration that shaped Palestine for centuries. It was a time of profound religious tolerance, political stability, and economic prosperity, laying the foundation for a legacy that would define Palestine's role within the broader Islamic civilization. This narrative of integration, diplomacy, and coexistence remains integral to understanding the historical context of Palestine's place in the Islamic world.

The Capture of Jerusalem and the Diplomacy of Umar ibn al-Khattab, The capture of Jerusalem in 637 CE by the forces of the Rashidun Caliphate, led by the second caliph, Umar ibn al-Khattab, is not merely a chapter in the annals of military history, but rather a profound example of diplomatic strategy, religious tolerance, and the pragmatic governance that characterized Umar's leadership. Unlike many military conquests of the time, which were often accompanied by widespread violence and destruction, Umar's approach to Jerusalem was a model of respect for the religious significance of the city and its inhabitants. His entry into Jerusalem did not simply signify the victory of one religious group over another, but rather marked the beginning of a new era of peaceful coexistence and religious pluralism under Islamic rule.

Diplomatic Negotiations and Peaceful Conquest, The context of the capture of Jerusalem is critical in understanding Umar's diplomatic approach. Jerusalem was a city of immense religious significance to multiple faiths—Judaism, Christianity, and Islam. For centuries, it had been the epicenter of religious tensions, and by the 7th century, it was under Byzantine Christian control. However, the Byzantine Empire had been weakening due to internal strife and external threats, creating an opportunity for the emerging Islamic caliphate to extend its influence.

When the Islamic forces approached Jerusalem, the city's Christian inhabitants, led by Patriarch Sophronius, feared the consequences of Islamic rule. Initially, the Byzantine defenders refused to surrender the city, hoping for a military reinforcement that never materialized. In contrast to the traditional approach of siege warfare, Umar's leadership was characterized by a marked preference for peaceful negotiation. He sent emissaries to the city's defenders, offering terms of surrender that were fair and equitable.

The Christian leadership, recognizing the legitimacy of Umar's promises and his reputation for fairness, agreed to negotiate a peaceful handover of the city.

This act of diplomacy was essential in shaping the legacy of Islamic governance in the region. Unlike other conquests that were accompanied by the destruction of sacred places, Umar's entry into Jerusalem was marked by mutual respect and religious sensitivity. The terms of the surrender, known as the "Pact of Umar," would lay the foundation for the subsequent treatment of Christians and Jews under Islamic rule.

The Pact of Umar: A Blueprint for Coexistence, The Pact of Umar is a crucial document that outlines the relationship between the Muslim rulers and the Christian and Jewish communities under Islamic rule. While its precise origins are debated, it is attributed to the caliph Umar ibn al-Khattab and is widely regarded as a foundational text for understanding the principles of Islamic governance toward non-Muslims.

One of the most remarkable aspects of the Pact of Umar is the recognition of the rights and protections granted to Christians and Jews, collectively referred to as "People of the Book." Under Islamic law, these groups were granted the freedom to practice their faiths without persecution, as long as they adhered to certain conditions. Among these were the payment of a tax, the jizya, which was levied on non-Muslims in exchange for protection and exemption from military service. This tax was not seen as a punitive measure, but rather as a form of social contract between the ruler and the governed. In return, the People of the Book were granted the right to maintain their places of worship, practice their customs, and live according to their religious laws. This arrangement provided a level of stability that was rare in the ancient and medieval world, where religious minorities often faced persecution or forced conversions.

Importantly, the Pact of Umar emphasized the preservation of religious sites, ensuring that churches and synagogues would remain untouched by Islamic authorities. This guarantee was significant in a time when the destruction of religious buildings in the wake of conquest was common. For example, the Church of the Holy Sepulchre, one of the holiest sites in Christianity, was spared any harm, and the Christian community in Jerusalem was allowed to continue practicing their faith without fear of interference. This act of tolerance laid the groundwork for a broader tradition of religious coexistence that would persist throughout much of Islamic rule in the region.

Umar's Personal Role and Symbolic Acts, Umar ibn al-Khattab's personal actions and symbolic gestures during his visit to Jerusalem further solidified the legacy of diplomacy and respect that defined his rule. When he entered Jerusalem in 637 CE, Umar was not seeking to assert his dominance over the city but rather to establish a cooperative relationship with its inhabitants. Upon his arrival, Patriarch Sophronius, the leader of the Christian community in Jerusalem, invited Umar to pray in the Church of the Holy Sepulchre. However, Umar declined this offer, citing his concern that praying within the church might lead future Muslim rulers to convert the church into a mosque. Umar feared that this act would set a precedent for the desecration of Christian holy sites, so he chose to pray instead in a nearby area, which later became the site for the construction of the Mosque of Umar.

This decision by Umar is emblematic of his deep respect for other religious traditions and his commitment to preserving the sanctity of sacred spaces. His refusal to pray inside the Church of the Holy Sepulchre, rather than being seen as an act of disrespect, was a calculated decision to ensure that the Christian community would feel secure in their continued presence in Jerusalem. It was an act of religious diplomacy that conveyed the message that Islam was not about subjugating or erasing other religions, but about offering a framework for peaceful coexistence and mutual respect.

Moreover, the establishment of the Mosque of Umar at the site of his prayer served as a reminder of the importance of Jerusalem in the Islamic tradition. The mosque, which stands today as one of the oldest mosques in the city, symbolizes the harmonious relationship between Muslims and Christians in early Islamic rule. Its construction also represented the Islamic acknowledgment of the city's spiritual significance to all three Abrahamic faiths: Judaism, Christianity, and Islam.

The Diplomatic Legacy of Umar's Leadership, Umar's diplomacy in Jerusalem set a precedent for Islamic rule in other territories and shaped the broader approach of subsequent caliphs to governance. His leadership was defined by a commitment to justice, fairness, and respect for religious diversity. Under his rule, the Islamic state was not merely a political entity; it was a society that sought to balance the needs and rights of its diverse populations, ensuring that religious and cultural differences could coexist within a unified political system.

The principles established by Umar in Jerusalem were continued and expanded upon by later caliphs. For example, during the Umayyad and Abbasid periods, the treatment of non-Muslims remained largely consistent with the terms of the Pact of Umar. Non-Muslims were allowed to maintain their religious practices, and their places of worship were protected. Islamic rulers also continued the tradition of providing patronage to religious institutions, such as churches and synagogues, ensuring that these communities had the resources necessary to sustain their religious life.

Furthermore, the diplomatic tone set by Umar was reflected in the way Islamic rulers handled interfaith relations in other parts of the empire. In regions such as Spain, North Africa, and Persia, Islamic rulers followed similar policies of tolerance, allowing for the flourishing of Jewish, Christian, and Zoroastrian communities within their territories. The success of this model of governance demonstrated that religious pluralism could be a viable and even beneficial aspect of Islamic rule.

The capture of Jerusalem by Umar ibn al-Khattab and the subsequent establishment of Islamic rule in the city was a defining moment in both the history of Islam and the history of the broader Middle East. Umar's approach to Jerusalem, characterized by diplomacy, respect, and religious tolerance, left an indelible mark on the region's political and religious landscape. The peaceful handover of the city, the terms of the Pact of Umar, and Umar's personal actions in safeguarding Christian and Jewish rights are all testimonies to his vision of a pluralistic society where religious coexistence was not only possible but encouraged. His leadership set a precedent for Islamic governance that emphasized justice, tolerance, and respect for the sanctity of religious spaces, shaping the region for centuries to come.

The Role of Palestine in the Islamic Caliphates, Following the conquest of Jerusalem and the integration of Palestine into the Islamic world, the region became an integral part of successive Islamic caliphates, including the Umayyads, Abbasids, and Fatimids. Each of these dynasties contributed to the development of Palestine, enhancing its political stability and economic prosperity.

Under the Umayyads (661–750 CE), Palestine became an important administrative and military center. The Umayyad caliphate's capital in Damascus was in close proximity to Palestine, making the region a vital part of the caliphate's infrastructure. The Umayyads undertook numerous architectural projects in Palestine, including the construction of the Dome of the Rock in Jerusalem, a stunning architectural masterpiece that remains one of the most iconic symbols of Islamic heritage. The Dome of the Rock not only marked the significance of Jerusalem in Islam but also symbolized the Islamic presence in the region.

The Umayyads also sought to integrate Palestine into the broader Mediterranean and Arabian trade networks. The region's location at the crossroads of trade routes connecting the Mediterranean, Arabia, and Asia made it a key player in regional commerce. Palestinian cities such as Jerusalem, Ramla, and Gaza became bustling hubs for trade, attracting merchants and travelers from across the Islamic world and beyond. The Umayyads introduced new agricultural techniques and irrigation systems, leading to increased agricultural production and economic prosperity in the region.

The Abbasid period (750–1258 CE) saw the continued integration of Palestine into the Islamic world, albeit with a shift in focus towards intellectual and cultural achievements. The Abbasids, based in Baghdad, presided over a golden age of Islamic civilization that emphasized learning, science, and philosophy. While the Abbasid caliphate's political control over Palestine was more tenuous than that of the Umayyads, the region remained a center for Islamic scholarship and religious study. The Abbasid emphasis on education and intellectual exchange had a lasting impact on Palestinian society, and the region became home to many scholars and religious leaders who contributed to the flourishing of Islamic thought.

The Fatimids (909–1171 CE), a Shia Muslim dynasty that ruled much of the Mediterranean, also played a significant role in the development of Palestine. Under the Fatimids, Palestine experienced a period of economic prosperity and architectural renewal. The Fatimids built mosques, hospitals, and schools in the region, contributing to the cultural and intellectual life of Palestinian cities. Jerusalem, under Fatimid rule, continued to be a major center of religious pilgrimage for Muslims, Christians, and Jews, as it remained one of the holiest cities in Islam.

Case Studies of Coexistence and Cultural Flourishing, The centuries following the integration of Palestine into the Islamic world were marked by a period of remarkable cultural and religious coexistence. This phenomenon can be observed in several case studies from different periods of Islamic rule in Palestine.

One of the most notable examples of interfaith harmony in medieval Palestine is the shared reverence for Jerusalem. Throughout Islamic rule, Jerusalem remained a focal point for Christians, Jews, and Muslims alike. For Muslims, it was the site of the Al-Aqsa Mosque, the third holiest site in Islam, while for Jews, it was the location of the Western Wall, the remnant of the Second Temple. Christians, too, continued to visit the Church of the Holy Sepulchre, which remained a central site of pilgrimage. Despite political and military challenges, these religious communities coexisted in a way that was not always seen in other parts of the world at the time.

Another case study is the role of Palestinian scholars and intellectuals during the Abbasid period. Scholars such as al-Ghazzali and Ibn al-Qayyim, who were born or educated in Palestine, contributed to the intellectual climate of the Islamic world. Their works, which encompassed theology, philosophy, and law, were widely read and respected across the Muslim world. These scholars played an important role in bridging the cultural and intellectual traditions of the East and West, helping to shape the Islamic Renaissance that reached its zenith during the Abbasid era.

The integration of Palestine into the Islamic world under the Rashidun Caliphate was not merely a military conquest, but a transformative moment that set the stage for centuries of religious tolerance, political stability, and economic prosperity. The diplomacy of Umar ibn al-Khattab, embodied in the Pact of Umar, established a precedent for the peaceful coexistence of Muslims, Christians, and Jews in the region. Over the following centuries, under the Umayyads, Abbasids, and Fatimids, Palestine became a vital part of the Islamic world, contributing to the political, economic, and intellectual vibrancy of the broader Islamic civilization. The region's unique position at the crossroads of religious and cultural traditions continues to make it a symbol of both the challenges and the possibilities of coexistence in a diverse world.

The Umayyad Vision: Building a Spiritual Center

The Umayyad Caliphate (661–750 CE) represented a critical phase in the early history of Islam. The dynasty, with its roots in the Arabian Peninsula, presided over vast territories stretching from Spain in the west to India in the east. Among the many regions that felt the deep imprint of Umayyad rule, Jerusalem held a particularly significant place, both religiously and politically. The Umayyads, under the leadership of Caliph Abd al-Malik ibn Marwan, saw Jerusalem not just as a city of conquest but as a center for Islamic identity. Their ambitious architectural projects in the city, particularly the Dome of the Rock and the Al-Aqsa Mosque, were not merely physical structures but profound symbols of Islamic sovereignty, spirituality, and cultural aspirations. These monuments, built with intricate artistry and religious purpose, would shape the city's identity for centuries to come and leave an indelible mark on the course of Islamic history.

Jerusalem's Sacred Significance, Before delving into the Umayyad architectural achievements, it is essential to understand the significance of Jerusalem itself. For Muslims, Jerusalem, and specifically the Haram al-Sharif (Noble Sanctuary), occupies a central role in the spiritual narrative of Islam. It is the site of the Prophet Muhammad's Night Journey (Isra) and Ascension (Mi'raj), where he is believed to have been transported from Mecca to Jerusalem and then ascended to the heavens. This event is recorded in the Quran and hadiths, making the city the third holiest site in Islam, after Mecca and Medina. Jerusalem had already been a revered location for Jews and Christians, making it a highly contested and spiritually potent city, one that the Umayyads recognized as a powerful focal point for Islamic unity and cultural expression.

The Dome of the Rock: A Monument to Islamic Sovereignty, At the heart of the Umayyad transformation of Jerusalem is the Dome of the Rock, one of the most iconic buildings in Islamic architecture. Commissioned by Caliph Abd al-Malik and completed in 691 CE, the Dome of the Rock was not only an architectural wonder but also a declaration of Islamic authority. Its strategic location on the Temple Mount, the very site where the Second Temple of Judaism once stood, was a powerful statement. By choosing this location, Abd al-Malik sent a clear message that the Islamic empire was now the dominant force in the region, superseding the earlier Jewish and Christian associations with the site.

The Dome's structure itself is a blend of Byzantine architectural traditions with Islamic innovations. The building features a stunning golden dome, which has become an iconic symbol of Jerusalem. Beneath the dome is a rock, believed by Muslims to be the spot from which the Prophet Muhammad ascended to the heavens. This sacred rock is the focal point of the entire structure, encased in a beautifully decorated octagonal building. The Dome of the Rock was not simply a place of worship; it was a statement of the Umayyads' intent to assert Islam's supremacy over previous religious traditions.

The architectural style of the Dome of the Rock was heavily influenced by Byzantine and early Christian art, particularly the Church of the Holy Sepulchre in Jerusalem. This blending of Islamic and Byzantine traditions was not coincidental. The Umayyads, keen to establish their cultural and religious identity, adopted elements of the region's existing artistic forms while simultaneously transforming them to reflect the distinctiveness of Islamic beliefs. The mosaics that decorate the Dome's interior, for instance, feature intricate patterns and calligraphy, displaying verses from the Quran. These inscriptions emphasize the monotheism of Islam, countering the Christian iconography of the time. The mosaics, while breathtaking in their beauty, also had a theological function: they reinforced the idea of Islam as the final and most complete revelation.

The golden dome itself, with its glimmering surface visible from miles away, symbolizes the splendor of the Islamic empire and serves as a reminder of the divine presence that, according to Islamic belief, marks the site of the Prophet's ascension. The structure's location atop the Temple Mount also underscored the importance of the city as the epicenter of Islamic spirituality, rivaling other major cities like Mecca and Medina.

The Al-Aqsa Mosque: A Center of Worship and Knowledge, Adjacent to the Dome of the Rock stands the Al-Aqsa Mosque, which was also restored and expanded under the Umayyads. The mosque's history stretches back to the early days of Islam, and it had already been a site of worship for Muslims since the time of the Prophet Muhammad. However, it was under the Umayyads that the mosque took on a new significance. Abd al-Malik undertook major renovations and expansions to ensure that it could accommodate the growing Muslim population of Jerusalem.

The Al-Aqsa Mosque, like the Dome of the Rock, became not only a place of worship but also a center of scholarship, learning, and Islamic thought. The Umayyads were keen to promote intellectual and theological discourse, and the mosque played an important role in this. It became a place where scholars could gather, debate, and transmit knowledge, contributing to the broader cultural and intellectual flowering of the early Islamic world. The mosque's role as a hub of religious and scholarly activity positioned Jerusalem as a key center for Islamic thought, rivaling other major cities like Baghdad and Damascus.

The Umayyad Legacy in Jerusalem, The Umayyad's transformative impact on Jerusalem can be seen not only in the architecture but also in the city's religious and cultural life. A significant case study of this is the manner in which the Umayyads sought to integrate the city's diverse religious communities into the new Islamic order. Although Jerusalem was a predominantly Christian city at the time of the Umayyad conquest, the Muslims who arrived after the conquest in 637 CE, under Caliph Umar ibn al-Khattab, sought to preserve the city's religious pluralism while establishing Islamic authority. The Umayyads, who succeeded the Rashidun Caliphate, expanded upon this vision by constructing and enhancing key religious sites in Jerusalem.

In interviews with historians of early Islam, many emphasize the importance of the Umayyad project as an effort to bridge the gap between Islamic tradition and the existing religious architecture of Jerusalem. "What the Umayyads did was remarkable in the sense that they created an architectural and religious program that was inclusive but also symbolically Islamic," explains Dr. Layla Hassan, a historian of early Islamic architecture. "By restoring and expanding these sites, they were marking the beginning of a new Islamic identity in Jerusalem that could stand alongside Christianity and Judaism."

Additionally, archaeologists have uncovered various inscriptions and artifacts from the Umayyad period in Jerusalem that reflect the dynasty's broader political and religious goals. For example, the discovery of coins minted during the reign of Abd al-Malik, which feature depictions of the Dome of the Rock, illustrates the extent to which the Umayyads saw this structure as an emblem of their rule. These coins, found in multiple locations across the empire, helped to solidify the Dome of the Rock as a symbol of Islamic power and religious legitimacy.

The Umayyad Caliphate's vision for Jerusalem left an enduring legacy that would transcend their brief period of rule. The Dome of the Rock and the Al-Aqsa Mosque became, and continue to be, central to Islamic devotion and identity. Over the centuries, these landmarks have witnessed the rise and fall of various empires, from the Abbasids to the Crusaders and the Ottomans, yet their significance has remained undiminished. They have stood as a testament to the early Islamic ambition of the Umayyads to establish Jerusalem as a spiritual and political center of the Muslim world.

Today, as Jerusalem continues to be a focal point of religious and political tension, the monuments built by the Umayyads stand as reminders of the city's complex and layered history. They are symbols not only of the Umayyad's vision for an Islamic Jerusalem but also of the broader narrative of religious coexistence, intellectual exchange, and cultural evolution that has defined the city throughout its history. The Umayyad architectural legacy, particularly the Dome of the Rock, remains a powerful symbol of Islamic identity and the city's enduring spiritual significance.

Cultural Flourishing Under Abbasid and Fatimid Rule

Palestine has long been a significant region in the Islamic world, known for its religious importance, intellectual contributions, and historical value. Throughout its history, various Islamic empires have left a lasting imprint on Palestine, fostering its development as a center of learning, culture, and spirituality. The Abbasid Caliphate (750–1258) and the Fatimid Caliphate (969–1171) are two such dynasties whose influence helped shape Palestine into a hub for knowledge, intellectual exchange, and religious reverence, with Jerusalem serving as a focal point for all these endeavors.

The Abbasid Caliphate: A Golden Age of Knowledge and Spirituality, The Abbasid Caliphate, established in 750, marked the beginning of a new era in Islamic history. Though the Abbasids shifted the political capital from the heart of the Arabian Peninsula in Mecca and Medina to the newly constructed city of Baghdad, the region of Palestine continued to hold significant spiritual and intellectual importance. Jerusalem, in particular, maintained its revered status as one of the three holiest cities in Islam, alongside

Mecca and Medina. The city was central to the religious identity of Muslims, and this status did not wane under Abbasid rule.

Intellectual and Religious Developments, Under the Abbasids, Baghdad became the intellectual capital of the Islamic world, with scholars from diverse backgrounds flocking to its grand libraries and universities. However, Palestine, particularly Jerusalem, continued to be a critical center for religious scholarship and the transmission of knowledge. Madrasas (Islamic schools) were established throughout Palestine, with the aim of educating the populace on religious, scientific, and philosophical subjects. These madrasas were not merely places of learning but also played a vital role in preserving and promoting Islamic tradition and teachings.

Scholars in Palestine, especially in Jerusalem, were engaged in translating and preserving ancient Greek, Roman, and Persian texts, making significant contributions to fields such as mathematics, astronomy, medicine, and philosophy. The translation movement that began in Baghdad spread to Palestine, where scholars translated key works of Aristotle, Galen, and other Greek philosophers into Arabic. This intellectual exchange fostered a rich culture of learning and dialogue, drawing upon not just Islamic tradition, but also the intellectual heritage of ancient civilizations.

A prime example of the intellectual flourishing in Palestine during the Abbasid period is the city of Jerusalem, which was home to renowned scholars and theologians. While Jerusalem remained a deeply religious center, it also became an intellectual hub where different schools of thought could coexist. The Abbasid Caliphs, while politically focused on Baghdad, continued to support the growth of education and the arts in the broader Islamic world, including Palestine.

Religious Significance, Jerusalem, under Abbasid rule, remained a site of deep religious significance for Muslims, as it was home to the Al-Aqsa Mosque and the Dome of the Rock, both revered sites in Islam. The city was seen not only as a place of pilgrimage but also as a symbol of Islamic unity and devotion. The Abbasids invested in maintaining these religious structures, ensuring their continued prominence in the Islamic world. Furthermore, during the Abbasid period, the practice of Sufism began to take root in Palestine. Sufi lodges, or khanaqahs, emerged across the region, attracting mystics and spiritual seekers.

Sufism, with its emphasis on inner purification, devotion, and the quest for a direct experience of God, resonated deeply with the spiritual landscape of Palestine. Many Sufi orders established a presence in Jerusalem, where they offered spiritual guidance to pilgrims and locals alike. The interaction between Sufi practices and the broader religious landscape of Palestine enriched the region's spiritual environment, contributing to its reputation as a place of deep spirituality and reflection.

The Fatimid Caliphate: A New Era of Growth and Cultural Flourishing, The Fatimid Caliphate, a Shi'a dynasty that arose in North Africa, took control of Egypt and parts of the Levant in 969. The Fatimids brought a new wave of cultural, intellectual, and economic development to Palestine, including Jerusalem, further solidifying the region's importance in the broader Islamic world.

Infrastructure and Economic Growth, One of the key achievements of the Fatimid dynasty was their investment in infrastructure, which greatly benefited Palestine. The region had been severely affected by a series of earthquakes in the early centuries of the Islamic era, and Jerusalem had suffered significant damage. The Fatimids undertook large-scale restoration projects to rebuild the city's infrastructure, including the Al-Aqsa Mosque, which had been partially destroyed by the tremors. This restoration ensured that Jerusalem continued to thrive as both a religious and political center.

The Fatimids also revitalized Palestine's economy by fostering trade and establishing vibrant economic networks. The region, strategically located at the crossroads of trade routes between the East and West, saw an increase in commercial activity. The Fatimids facilitated the growth of urban centers in Palestine, particularly in Jerusalem and other major cities such as Nablus and Gaza, which became thriving marketplaces for goods and ideas.

The period of Fatimid rule also saw increased agricultural productivity, as the dynasty introduced advanced irrigation techniques and improved agricultural practices in the region. These efforts ensured a steady supply of food, which in turn supported the growth of cities and trade.

Religious Tolerance and Coexistence, One of the most notable features of Fatimid rule in Palestine was their relatively tolerant policies toward different religious communities. The Fatimids, who adhered to Shi'a Islam, governed a region that included large Sunni, Christian, and Jewish populations. Despite the sectarian tensions between different groups, the Fatimids encouraged peaceful coexistence and mutual respect among the various religious communities. They recognized the importance of Jerusalem to Christians and Jews and allowed for religious pluralism, fostering an environment of relative tolerance.

This atmosphere of tolerance, however, did not mean that tensions were completely absent. There were occasional flare-ups of conflict between different religious groups, particularly during periods of political instability. Yet, overall, the Fatimids' policy of inclusivity played a significant role in maintaining stability in the region and allowing for the flourishing of diverse cultures and intellectual traditions.

Cultural and Intellectual Achievements, Under the Fatimids, Palestine experienced a cultural renaissance. The Fatimids were patrons of the arts, sciences, and literature, and they encouraged the development of libraries, madrasas, and other centers of learning in the region. The city of Jerusalem, along with other urban centers in Palestine, became a haven for scholars, poets, and artists.

During this period, scholars from various religious and intellectual traditions interacted and exchanged ideas, which contributed to the intellectual vibrancy of the region. Fatimid patronage allowed for the development of both Islamic and secular thought, with an emphasis on philosophical inquiry, scientific exploration, and theological debate. Scholars in Jerusalem were at the forefront of these discussions, building upon the intellectual foundations laid during the Abbasid period.

In the field of theology, the Fatimids' Shi'a ideology brought new perspectives to Islamic thought. Their support for Shi'a scholars and theologians helped to cement the significance of Shi'a Islam in the broader Islamic world, and the Fatimid period is considered a key moment in the development of Shi'a theology and philosophy.

To further understand the impact of the Abbasid and Fatimid periods on Palestine, it is helpful to examine the lives of prominent figures from this time. Scholars like al-Qushayri, a famous Sufi theologian, spent time in Jerusalem during the Abbasid period, contributing to the region's spiritual vibrancy. His writings and teachings on Sufism influenced generations of Muslims, and his presence in Jerusalem underscores the city's significance as a center for mystical thought.

Similarly, Fatimid scholars such as al-Mu'ayyad fi'l-Din al-Shirazi, a renowned philosopher and theologian, contributed to the intellectual atmosphere of the region. His works, which bridged the gap between Shi'a and Sunni thought, reflect the intellectual openness fostered under the Fatimid dynasty.

In interviews with modern scholars of Islamic history, many emphasize the enduring legacy of Palestine as a center of learning and spirituality during the Abbasid and Fatimid periods. According to Dr. Ahmad al-Khatib, a scholar of medieval Islamic history, *"The intellectual and spiritual environment of Palestine during these periods created a foundation for future generations of scholars and thinkers. The intermingling of religious traditions, combined with the investment in education and infrastructure, allowed Palestine to remain a beacon of knowledge and spirituality for centuries."*

The Abbasid and Fatimid periods were transformative for Palestine, as they fostered a rich culture of learning, intellectual exchange, and religious tolerance. During the Abbasid Caliphate, Jerusalem remained a spiritual center, with flourishing madrasas and Sufi lodges. The Fatimids further expanded Palestine's cultural and intellectual horizons, rebuilding Jerusalem after natural disasters and promoting religious tolerance. Together, these two dynasties contributed to Palestine's lasting legacy as a center of Islamic thought, spirituality, and cultural exchange, an influence that continues to be felt to this day.

The Crusades: A Test of Faith and Resilience

The Crusades, a series of religious wars fought between the Christian and Muslim worlds, marked one of the most significant and turbulent chapters in the history of Palestine. Beginning in 1096, the Crusades were driven by religious zeal, territorial ambition, and the desire for wealth. The First Crusade culminated in the brutal capture of Jerusalem in 1099, an event that not only reshaped the city's religious and political landscape but also sowed the seeds of centuries of conflict and division between the two great faiths. The violent conquest of Jerusalem by the Crusaders was not just a military victory; it was a ruthless demonstration of the unyielding power of religious dogma and imperial ambition.

For nearly a century after the First Crusade, the Crusaders ruled over Jerusalem and much of Palestine. Their presence in the Holy Land was marked by a series of violent clashes, religious intolerance, and a policy of subjugation toward the region's Muslim and Jewish populations. The Kingdom of Jerusalem, a feudal state established by the Crusaders, was characterized by its brutality and the displacement of the native populations. The Crusaders brought with them a worldview steeped in religious warfare, one that sought to assert Christian dominance over the lands that were sacred to all three Abrahamic faiths—Judaism, Christianity, and Islam.

The Brutality of the Crusaders in Jerusalem, The brutality of the Crusaders during their conquest of Jerusalem in 1099 remains one of the darkest chapters in the history of the city. Jerusalem, a city long revered by Jews, Christians, and Muslims, was a coveted prize in the Crusader's quest to control the Holy Land. The Christian soldiers who took part in the First Crusade believed they were fighting a holy war, a divine mission to reclaim the city from the Muslims and bring it back under Christian rule. What transpired upon their entry into Jerusalem, however, was far from a righteous act of faith. It was a massacre of unprecedented proportions.

The Crusaders, after laying siege to Jerusalem for several weeks, finally breached the city's walls. They flooded into the city, and what followed was a brutal slaughter of the Muslim and Jewish inhabitants. According to chroniclers, including Raymond of Aguilers, a priest who accompanied the Crusaders, the streets of Jerusalem ran red with blood. Muslim and Jewish men, women, and children were killed indiscriminately. The Crusaders were said to have thrown bodies into the wells, desecrating the sacred sites of the city and committing heinous acts in the name of religion. The bodies of those murdered were piled high, and many were left unburied, a grim reminder of the Crusaders' savagery.

One of the most chilling episodes in the conquest occurred in the Al-Aqsa Mosque, one of Islam's holiest sites. The mosque, located on the Temple Mount, was turned into a killing field by the Crusaders. According to contemporary accounts, as many as 10,000 Muslims were massacred inside the mosque, and the bodies were heaped up in the mosque's courtyards. The Dome of the Rock, another revered Islamic site, was also desecrated. The Crusaders not only killed but also looted the city, taking valuables from the sacred sites and destroying everything in their path.

This violence was justified by the Crusaders as part of their religious duty to rid the city of "infidels" and restore Christian rule. The brutality of the conquest was not just a matter of military action; it was steeped in religious fervor. The Crusaders believed that they were acting under divine command, and their actions were framed as part of a larger cosmic struggle between Christianity and Islam. This mindset led them to justify the slaughter of innocent civilians and the desecration of sacred spaces.

The scale of the massacre in Jerusalem shocked even some of the Crusaders themselves. The chronicler Fulcher of Chartres, a priest who was present during the siege, wrote that the Crusaders "killed so many that our men waded in blood up to their ankles." The destruction was not limited to human lives but extended to the cultural and religious heritage of the city. Churches, mosques, synagogues, and other buildings of religious significance were pillaged and destroyed. The Crusaders replaced the Dome of the Rock with a church, cementing their control over the city by forcing the native populations into submission.

The Crusader Kingdom of Jerusalem: A Violent Occupation, After their conquest, the Crusaders established the Kingdom of Jerusalem, a feudal state ruled by Western European nobles. The Crusader Kingdom was a stark contrast to the pluralistic society that had existed in Jerusalem prior to the invasion. Before the Crusaders' arrival, Jerusalem had been home to a diverse population of Jews, Christians, and Muslims, all of whom coexisted in relative peace. The Crusaders, however, imposed a strict Christian rule, and the city's original inhabitants were either killed, expelled, or forced to convert to Christianity.

For nearly a century, the Crusader Kingdom of Jerusalem struggled to maintain its hold on the Holy Land. The Crusaders faced constant resistance from the Muslim populations in the region, who sought to reclaim their land and sacred cities. The Crusader presence was a source of deep resentment among the native populations, and the violent treatment of Muslims and Jews by the Crusaders only fueled the desire for retaliation.

The Crusaders built a network of castles and fortresses to defend their holdings, but they were perpetually vulnerable to Muslim forces seeking to oust them. The Kingdom of Jerusalem was a precarious political entity, surrounded by powerful Muslim states determined to drive the Crusaders out of the region. Despite their military superiority at times, the Crusaders never fully subdued the Muslim resistance, and they were unable to integrate into the broader Middle Eastern society. They were seen as foreign invaders, and their rule was marked by constant strife and instability.

The Rise of Salahuddin al-Ayyubi, The resistance to Crusader rule in Palestine eventually found its champion in the figure of Salahuddin al-Ayyubi, one of the most revered military leaders in Islamic history. Salahuddin, born in 1137 in Tikrit (modern-day Iraq), was a Kurdish Muslim who rose through the ranks of the Zengid dynasty before establishing the Ayyubid Sultanate in 1171. His military prowess, deep religious devotion, and strategic acumen earned him the respect of the Muslim world and made him the central figure in the effort to reclaim Jerusalem from the Crusaders.

Salahuddin's leadership was rooted in his ability to unify the fragmented Muslim states in the region. Before his rise, the Muslim world was divided into rival factions, with various local rulers and emirs more concerned with personal power than with the collective defense of Islam. Salahuddin recognized the importance of unity in the face of the Crusader threat, and through diplomacy, military might, and religious appeal, he succeeded in forging a coalition of

Muslim forces. He also focused on building a strong, disciplined army that was capable of confronting the Crusaders in battle.

Salahuddin's ambition was not just to defeat the Crusaders; it was to restore the Muslim presence in the Holy Land and reclaim Jerusalem. He understood the symbolic and spiritual significance of the city and recognized that its loss to the Crusaders was a blow to the unity of the Muslim world. He was determined to liberate Jerusalem and return it to its rightful Muslim rulers.

The Battle of Hattin and the Recapture of Jerusalem, The turning point in the Crusades came in 1187 with the Battle of Hattin, fought on July 4. Salahuddin's forces decisively defeated the Crusader army, which was led by King Guy of Lusignan. The battle was a stunning defeat for the Crusaders, and it marked the beginning of the end of Crusader rule in the Holy Land. Salahuddin's army, though outnumbered, outmaneuvered and overwhelmed the Crusader forces, cutting off their supplies and trapping them in a vulnerable position. The defeat at Hattin shattered the Crusader forces, and Jerusalem, once again, was within Salahuddin's reach.

Salahuddin's army marched on Jerusalem, and by October 1187, the city was surrounded. Unlike the Crusaders, who had massacred the city's inhabitants in 1099, Salahuddin showed mercy to the Christians and Jews who remained in the city. He allowed them to leave peacefully, and he ensured that their holy sites, such as the Church of the Holy Sepulchre, were preserved and protected. His treatment of the inhabitants of Jerusalem was in stark contrast to the brutal conquest of the Crusaders nearly a century earlier.

Salahuddin's victory was not just a military triumph; it was a moral one as well. His magnanimity in victory won him admiration, even among his enemies. His leadership demonstrated that military success need not be accompanied by barbarity, and his commitment to preserving the city's multi-religious character was a model of tolerance and respect for religious diversity.

The Legacy of the Crusades, The Crusades left a deep scar on the history of the Holy Land. The brutality of the Crusaders, their desecration of sacred sites, and the massacre of thousands of civilians have left an indelible mark on the region. The brutality of the First Crusade, in particular, was a shocking reminder of the extreme violence that religious fervor can breed. The Crusaders justified their actions as part of a divine mission, but their conquest of Jerusalem was a dark chapter in the city's history.

However, the eventual recapture of Jerusalem by Salahuddin in 1187 represented a different vision for the future. His leadership showed that it was possible to reclaim the Holy Land without resorting to the same brutality that the Crusaders had employed. Salahuddin's magnanimity and his preservation of Jerusalem's religious diversity became a symbol of hope for the region, and his legacy continues to resonate in the ongoing struggles for peace and understanding in the Middle East.

The Crusades were a test of faith, a struggle for dominance between two powerful civilizations, but they were also a reminder of the humanity that can be lost in the pursuit of religious or political goals. The brutal actions of the Crusaders were a stark contrast to the leadership of Salahuddin, who sought to restore Jerusalem not through violence, but through wisdom, respect, and mercy. The history of the Crusades is a complex and multifaceted one, and the lessons from this era continue to shape the modern world.

The Ottoman Golden Era: Suleiman the Magnificent's Vision

The early 16th century marked a new chapter in the storied history of Jerusalem, one that would usher in an era of unparalleled transformation and cultural resurgence under the rule of the Ottoman Empire. The conquest of Palestine in 1517 by Sultan Selim I, the father of Suleiman the Magnificent, set the stage for the empire's long reign over Jerusalem. However, it was Suleiman (r. 1520–1566) who truly brought the city into its "Golden Era," a period that would shape the city's physical, religious, and cultural landscape in ways that endure to this day. A profound confluence of his religious piety, imperial ambition, and commitment to architectural and social advancements, Suleiman's reign is often regarded as a renaissance period for the city, and Jerusalem's place in the Ottoman Empire became a symbol of the sultan's broader imperial vision.

The Historical Context: The Ottoman Conquest and Jerusalem's Early Years, When the Ottomans seized Jerusalem from the Mamluks in 1517, the city, long a crossroads of civilizations, found itself in the hands of a new and powerful empire. Under the Mamluks, Jerusalem had been neglected, its once-grand structures in disrepair. The Ottomans, however, saw the city not just as a religious and strategic prize, but as a key jewel in their sprawling empire. Jerusalem's significance as a holy city for Muslims, Jews, and Christians made it an important symbol of the Ottoman Empire's tolerance and its ability to govern a diverse range of peoples and religions under one banner.

But it was during the reign of Suleiman the Magnificent, beginning in 1520, that the city saw the most significant physical, cultural, and economic transformations. Known for his grandeur, ambition, and deeply devout nature, Suleiman's reign was marked by a fusion of Islamic piety, architectural innovation, and an imperial vision that sought not only to strengthen the Ottoman military and political presence but also to shape a lasting cultural legacy.

A Renaissance in Architecture: The Rebuilding of Jerusalem's Walls, Perhaps the most enduring legacy of Suleiman's reign in Jerusalem is the dramatic renovation of the city's walls. At the time of his ascension, the walls of Jerusalem, originally built by the Byzantines and modified by the Mamluks, were in a state of disrepair. The strategic importance of Jerusalem, combined with its religious significance, made the need for fortification apparent. It was Suleiman's vision to restore Jerusalem's walls not only as a means of defense but also as a powerful symbol of his empire's might, benevolence, and connection to the sacred history of the city.

In 1537, Suleiman ordered the reconstruction of the city's fortifications, a project that would take several years to complete. The Old City's imposing walls that still define the city today are the result of this major renovation. These new walls, stretching approximately 4 kilometers, were designed to encircle Jerusalem in a way that integrated military functionality with architectural grandeur. The walls were fitted with impressive gates, including the iconic Damascus Gate and the Jaffa Gate, each serving as both an entrance to the city and a symbol of Ottoman power.

The walls were not merely military structures; they were also a statement of Suleiman's vision for the future of Jerusalem. The design, overseen by the Italian architect Giuseppe Valeriano, reflected the best practices of Ottoman and Renaissance architecture, and the entire project was intended to emphasize the strength and permanence of Ottoman rule in the region. The gates were reinforced with towers that provided vantage points from which the city could be defended from potential attacks. These additions turned the walls of Jerusalem into not only a defensive structure but also a work of art, a monumental testament to the Sultan's leadership and influence.

In addition to the walls, Suleiman ordered the construction of other significant architectural structures, including the restoration of the Dome of the Rock and the Al-Aqsa Mosque, two of the most important religious landmarks in Islam. These projects further emphasized the Sultan's desire to position Jerusalem as a central hub in the Muslim world and as a symbol of Ottoman religious devotion.

Urban Development and Public Works: A Thriving City, While Suleiman's military and architectural contributions to Jerusalem were undoubtedly important, his impact on the city's infrastructure, commerce, and urban fabric was just as transformative. Recognizing the city's dual role as both a religious center and a hub of trade, Suleiman implemented several public works projects that reshaped Jerusalem's economic and social life.

One of the Sultan's most notable contributions was the construction of public fountains, known as "sabils," throughout the city. These fountains, often intricately designed and adorned with Arabic inscriptions, were built to provide fresh drinking water to the city's residents and to the pilgrims who flooded into Jerusalem from across the Islamic world. Some of the sabils were situated near key religious sites, such as the Al-Aqsa Mosque, while others were placed at major intersections or public spaces to ensure the wider population had access to clean water.

These fountains were not just utilitarian but also a reflection of Suleiman's concern for the welfare of the people, including both Muslims and non-Muslims. His commitment to public infrastructure helped establish the city as a prosperous and well-organized center. Alongside the fountains, Suleiman ordered the paving of streets, the repair of roads leading into Jerusalem, and the establishment of new markets. Jerusalem's bazaars began to flourish, as goods from across the empire, such as textiles, spices, and pottery, were traded in the bustling markets.

Furthermore, Suleiman's investment in the urban landscape extended to the construction of roads that connected Jerusalem to other parts of the empire, facilitating both trade and the movement of pilgrims. This infrastructural expansion allowed Jerusalem to become a vital stop on the major trade routes that connected Europe, Asia, and Africa, bringing not only goods but also ideas, culture, and people from different backgrounds.

Suleiman also ensured that the city's administration was designed to accommodate the diverse population of Muslims, Christians, and Jews who lived in Jerusalem. By promoting the millet system, the Ottoman Sultan established a system that allowed religious communities to govern themselves with a degree of autonomy. Religious leaders were given the authority to manage internal affairs such as education, marriage, and legal disputes, while remaining loyal to the Sultan.

This system not only maintained peace among the different religious groups but also fostered a sense of communal identity and self-determination. The Christian, Jewish, and Muslim communities in Jerusalem were each allowed to govern their own institutions, such as churches, synagogues, and mosques, and the city became a microcosm of Ottoman tolerance and religious pluralism. It was a model of coexistence that would serve as a hallmark of the Ottoman Empire for centuries.

The Millet System and Religious Harmony, Suleiman's commitment to religious tolerance was epitomized by the implementation of the millet system, which granted autonomy to various religious communities. Under this system, Muslims, Christians, and Jews were each given the right to govern their own religious affairs. This autonomy extended to legal and educational matters as well, with religious leaders from each community playing a central role in governing their members.

In Jerusalem, the millet system helped preserve the unique identities and traditions of each religious group. The Christian and Jewish communities maintained their own courts and schools, while the Muslim population, the majority in Jerusalem, had their own institutions as well. This system of governance allowed each group to live according to its religious laws and practices without interference from other communities or the Ottoman state.

The religious diversity of Jerusalem was a defining feature of the city during Suleiman's reign, and his vision for a peaceful, tolerant Jerusalem became a model for other cities in the Ottoman Empire. By ensuring that the various communities could coexist peacefully,

Suleiman helped foster a unique and vibrant cultural landscape in Jerusalem. Pilgrims from across the world, from different faiths and backgrounds, were drawn to the city, contributing to its thriving cultural and social life.

Suleiman's Lasting Legacy: The Continued Influence on Jerusalem, Suleiman the Magnificent's reign left an indelible mark on Jerusalem. His contributions to the city, particularly in the areas of architecture, public works, and religious governance, shaped the city's development for generations. The walls he rebuilt still stand as a testament to his vision and his desire to leave a lasting legacy. The public fountains he constructed continue to provide water to Jerusalem's residents, and the roads he built remain integral to the city's infrastructure.

Suleiman's investment in Jerusalem was not simply an act of imperial expansion but a profound expression of his belief in the city's importance as a center of religious devotion, cultural exchange, and political power. As historians and archaeologists continue to study the Ottoman influence on Jerusalem, it becomes clear that Suleiman's reign was pivotal in shaping the city's identity as a place of religious harmony, architectural beauty, and imperial power.

Today, Jerusalem's status as a spiritual and cultural capital for multiple religious communities remains a direct legacy of Suleiman's vision. The walls, fountains, and infrastructure that he left behind are not only markers of a bygone era but symbols of the enduring power of his reign and his commitment to a city that continues to inspire faith, admiration, and awe in people from around the world.

Palestine's Intellectual and Economic Prosperity

Throughout the Islamic Golden Age, Palestine emerged as a beacon of intellectual, cultural, and economic vitality, playing a crucial role in the broader developments of the medieval Islamic world. The region's flourishing in these areas wasn't just a reflection of its geographical location or its historical importance as a religious and cultural crossroads, but rather a product of the intellectual dynamism that characterized the era. Scholars, mystics, and merchants alike contributed to a unique atmosphere that made Palestine a center of learning, spiritual growth, and trade. This period, from roughly the 8th to the 13th century, was marked by an unprecedented exchange of ideas, scientific discovery, and economic prosperity.

Intellectual and Cultural Hub, One of the most striking features of Palestine during the Islamic Golden Age was its role as a major intellectual hub. Cities such as Jerusalem, Ramallah, and Nablus were home to prestigious madrasas (Islamic schools), where scholars from across the Islamic world, including Persia, Iraq, Egypt, and Andalusia, traveled to study. The scholars who came to Palestine were not limited to Islamic thought but also embraced knowledge from Greek, Persian, and Indian traditions, which had been translated into Arabic and became part of the intellectual landscape. These madrasas became epicenters of learning, fostering critical advancements in fields like theology, philosophy, astronomy, mathematics, and medicine.

The intellectual climate in Palestine during this period was enriched by its centrality in the Islamic world. Jerusalem, in particular, held a unique place as a site of both religious and intellectual significance. The Al-Aqsa Mosque and the Dome of the Rock, two of Islam's holiest sites, were not only centers of worship but also locations of scholarly gatherings and discussions. The city attracted scholars who engaged in debates about theology, law, and philosophy. For instance, the renowned philosopher and polymath, Ibn Rushd (Averroes), whose works on Aristotle profoundly influenced Western and Islamic thought, was read and studied widely in the region.

Palestine was also home to many important libraries that housed manuscripts covering a broad spectrum of knowledge. These libraries were not only collections of religious texts but also repositories of scientific and philosophical works. In these libraries, one could find works on astronomy and mathematics, such as those written by Al-Khwarizmi, or medical treatises that built upon the works of Galen and Hippocrates. Scholars from these institutions would later contribute to the translation movement, which sought to translate ancient texts into Arabic, further enriching the Islamic intellectual tradition.

Sufism and Spiritual Enlightenment, In addition to its intellectual achievements, Palestine also became an important center for Sufism, the mystical branch of Islam. During the Islamic Golden Age, Sufi orders flourished, and their lodges (known as khanqahs or zawiyas) became prominent centers of spiritual enlightenment. These orders sought to foster a deeper connection with the Divine through personal piety, devotion, and asceticism. Many Sufi mystics, including famous figures like Al-Ghazali and Ibn Arabi, spent significant portions of their lives in Palestine, either visiting or residing there. Their teachings had a profound influence on the spiritual and intellectual landscape of the region.

Sufi orders in Palestine became known not only for their spiritual teachings but also for their role in cultivating an atmosphere of tolerance and intellectual exchange. The Sufi mystics in these lodges engaged in dialogue with scholars of other faiths, including Christians and Jews, fostering an environment of religious pluralism. This spirit of inclusivity made Palestinian Sufi centers particularly influential. The Sufi tradition's emphasis on inner purification and knowledge led to a flourishing of religious literature, poetry, and philosophy, much of which was written in Arabic and remained influential for centuries.

A notable example of this spiritual and intellectual blend can be seen in the city of Hebron, where the tomb of the Prophet Abraham (Ibrahim) is located. Hebron became an important spiritual site for

Sufi orders, with many mystics and pilgrims coming to pay homage to the Prophet's tomb. It was here that scholars and mystics would often convene to meditate, debate, and exchange ideas about the nature of God, the soul, and the cosmos.

Economic Prosperity and Trade, Economically, Palestine was one of the most prosperous regions during the Islamic Golden Age. Its location at the crossroads of three continents—Asia, Africa, and Europe—made it a critical point in the trade routes that connected the Islamic world with Byzantium, India, and the Far East. Palestine served as a vital conduit for the exchange of goods, ideas, and cultures, contributing significantly to the economic and cultural dynamism of the Islamic Empire.

The fertile plains of Galilee, the Jordan Valley, and the coastal regions of Palestine were renowned for their agricultural productivity. These areas produced an abundance of crops, including wheat, barley, olives, citrus fruits, and grapes. The cultivation of olives, in particular, became a significant part of the economy, with olive oil being one of Palestine's key exports. The region's agricultural success can be attributed to its advanced irrigation techniques, which allowed for the efficient use of water in an otherwise dry landscape.

Hebron, one of Palestine's oldest cities, was also known for its craft industries. Glassmaking was particularly renowned in Hebron, where artisans created intricate glassware that was highly sought after throughout the Islamic world. Textiles, including silk and woolen fabrics, were another significant product of Palestine, with the region's weavers producing some of the finest cloths of the period. These products were traded in local markets as well as through international trade routes that connected Palestine to Egypt, Syria, and beyond.

In addition to agriculture and crafts, Palestine's urban centers became important commercial hubs. The cities of Jerusalem, Nablus, and Acre were bustling centers of commerce, with merchants from across the Islamic world, as well as from Christian Europe and Jewish communities, conducting business. The region's bustling markets offered a wide variety of goods, from spices and textiles to precious metals and ivory. These trade routes facilitated the exchange not only of material goods but also of knowledge, as traders brought with them new scientific discoveries, technologies, and artistic techniques from distant parts of the world.

Intellectual and Economic Contributions, To further illustrate the significance of Palestine during the Islamic Golden Age, it is useful to examine specific case studies of intellectual and economic contributions.

The Madrasas of Jerusalem and Nablus, The madrasas in Jerusalem, such as Al-Aqsa's scholarly institutions, became crucial to the development of Islamic jurisprudence, theology, and philosophy. For instance, the Al-Quds University, which traces its origins to the medieval period, played a role in developing legal thought that would later influence Islamic law across the empire. Similarly, the madrasa in Nablus attracted scholars from as far afield as Andalusia and Persia, contributing to the spread of scientific and philosophical ideas throughout the Islamic world.

Hebron's Glassmaking Industry, The glassmaking industry in Hebron was not only an economic driver but also an example of the region's technological advancements. The skillful production of glass, which had been perfected in the earlier centuries by Byzantine and Roman craftsmen, was further refined during the Islamic Golden Age. The glass products made in Hebron were used in both everyday life and religious contexts, and the city became renowned for its delicate glassware, which was exported across the Islamic world.

Sufi Pilgrimages and Cultural Exchange, The Sufi orders that established themselves in Palestine not only served as spiritual centers but also as sites of cultural exchange. Pilgrims from across the Muslim world journeyed to Palestine to visit the holy sites and participate in Sufi practices. This movement of people facilitated the exchange of ideas and created a rich cultural tapestry in which Islamic mysticism and philosophy were deeply intertwined with the cultural traditions of the broader Islamic world.

Palestine during the Islamic Golden Age was a dynamic and multifaceted region, where intellectual and cultural life flourished alongside economic prosperity. The region's madrasas, libraries, and Sufi lodges were central to the dissemination of knowledge, while its agricultural lands and artisan workshops contributed to its economic success. The intersection of trade, intellectual exchange, and spiritual life made Palestine a crucial player in the broader narrative of the Islamic Golden Age, leaving a lasting legacy that continues to resonate in the intellectual and cultural landscape of the modern world.

Religious Coexistence: An Imperfect Harmony

The Islamic Golden Age, particularly during the reign of the Umayyads and Abbasids, is often heralded as a period of unprecedented religious tolerance, especially in regions like Palestine. This era, spanning roughly from the 7th to the 13th century, is frequently romanticized for its harmonious coexistence of diverse religious communities, including Muslims, Christians, and Jews. Yet, while this coexistence was notable, it was far from flawless. There were challenges—some rooted in external conflict, others in internal social dynamics—that tested the strength of the religious and cultural unity of the time. Nevertheless, the framework of Islamic governance, underpinned by the Qur'anic principles of justice, protection, and respect for religious diversity, helped mitigate these challenges and offered a means by which communities could navigate the turbulence of the time.

Islamic Governance and Religious Tolerance, At the heart of the Islamic Golden Age in Palestine was a governance system that, at least on paper, promised protection and respect for non-Muslim communities. The concept of *"dhimmi,"* or protected people, was introduced early in Islamic rule. Non-Muslim religious groups—primarily Christians and Jews—were granted a status that allowed them to practice their faith freely in exchange for paying a special tax, the *jizya*. This tax was seen as a contribution for the protection of their communities and exemption from military service, a responsibility that Muslims bore due to their obligation to defend the state.

The concept of dhimmi was not only a legal status but also a reflection of the values of the Qur'an and Hadith, which emphasized respect for the People of the Book (Ahl al-Kitab). The Qur'an mentions in Surah Al-Ma'idah (5:48): *"To you be your religion, and to me my religion,"* a verse that, while not ignoring differences, underlines the principle of coexistence and non-imposition. This was a practical framework for managing diverse religious communities, allowing them to live side by side in a society where religious boundaries were respected.

One of the most telling examples of this governance model in action can be found in the city of Jerusalem. When Caliph Umar ibn al-Khattab entered the city in 637 CE, after it was peacefully surrendered to the Muslims, he is said to have granted religious freedom to Christians and Jews living there. The Pact of Umar, which formalized this agreement, laid down clear guidelines ensuring the protection of their places of worship, freedom of religious practice, and rights as citizens under Islamic rule. This act became a symbol of Islamic tolerance, setting a precedent for the treatment of non-Muslims across the empire.

Tensions and Resilience in Coexistence, Despite the ideals of religious tolerance, the historical reality of coexistence was more complex. Tensions between different religious communities were not uncommon, especially in times of external pressure, such as during periods of economic hardship or when political power was contested. For example, during the Crusades (11th-13th centuries), the influx of Christian Crusaders into the Holy Land brought about considerable conflict. The Crusaders' attempts to conquer Jerusalem, in particular, were marked by brutal violence against the Muslim and Jewish populations. However, even during this period of religious and military strife, the framework of Islamic rule provided some semblance of order and protection.

After the Crusader occupation, the Ayyubid dynasty, under Salah ad-Din, recaptured Jerusalem in 1187. Salah ad-Din, like earlier Muslim rulers, was keen on maintaining religious tolerance, ensuring the protection of Christian holy sites and granting safe passage to Jews and Christians who wished to leave the city. His rule is often highlighted as an example of the balance between military conquest and religious tolerance, illustrating that, even in the face of adversity, the ideals of coexistence prevailed in practice.

Yet, the reality of these tensions is best captured in the lives of ordinary people living in these cities during the Golden Age. In Jerusalem, for example, Christians and Muslims coexisted not only in the sacred spaces of their religious institutions but in the marketplaces, neighborhoods, and homes. Interviews with local historians and descendants of these communities provide valuable insights into daily life during this period. One historian, Ahmad Abu-Laban, notes that "while conflict was often a backdrop to our lives, there was also a deep understanding that the three religions shared something in common: a history, a future, and a city that was sacred to all of them." This shared sense of place allowed for cooperation on many levels, from trade to cultural exchange, even in times of strife.

The Architecture of Coexistence, Perhaps no better example exists of religious coexistence in Palestine during the Islamic Golden Age than in the cities themselves. In Jerusalem, Hebron, and Nablus, the cityscape was a tangible reflection of the harmonious coexistence between Muslims, Christians, and Jews. These cities boasted a rich architectural heritage where mosques, churches, and synagogues stood side by side, often within close proximity to one another. In Jerusalem, the Al-Aqsa Mosque and the Dome of the Rock shared the skyline with the Church of the Holy Sepulchre, one of Christianity's holiest sites. These buildings were not only religious centers but symbols of the city's complex, multi-faith identity.

In Hebron, the Ibrahimi Mosque (also known as the Cave of the Patriarchs) is one of the most famous religious sites shared by Muslims, Jews, and Christians. The mosque and its adjacent synagogue, which houses the tombs of the Biblical patriarchs Abraham, Isaac, and Jacob, reflect the deep religious significance the city holds for all three Abrahamic faiths. Despite the tensions that occasionally erupted over control of these sites, the physical proximity of these sacred spaces offers a profound metaphor for the interwoven religious identities that shaped the region.

The city of Nablus, with its blend of mosques, churches, and synagogues, also serves as a testament to this tradition of coexistence. While Nablus has undergone many changes throughout history, the legacy of interfaith interaction remains etched in its streets and in the memories of its residents. Local traditions, such as shared religious festivals and communal gatherings, further emphasize the interconnectedness of these religious communities, even in moments of discord.

Shared Traditions and Cultural Exchanges, The coexistence in Palestine was not limited to the political or architectural spheres but extended into cultural and social life. One of the most profound ways in which religious communities interacted was through shared traditions and practices. Culinary traditions, for instance, offer a window into the blending of cultures that took place. The local cuisine of Jerusalem and its surrounding cities features dishes that reflect the influences of all three major religions—Muslim, Christian, and Jewish. Shared ingredients like olive oil, lentils, and spices were staples in the kitchens of all communities, and food was a common language of exchange, especially during religious holidays.

Linguistic exchanges were also significant. Arabic became the lingua franca of the region during the Islamic Golden Age, but the interaction between Arabic-speaking Muslims, Greek-speaking Christians, and Hebrew-speaking Jews resulted in a fusion of languages and dialects. The shared vocabulary and phrases that emerged from this interaction were not just linguistic markers but cultural symbols of coexistence and mutual influence.

Moreover, the intellectual exchange between the different religious communities during the Golden Age cannot be overstated. Scholars from all three faiths often worked side by side in the same schools, libraries, and academies, exchanging ideas in fields like mathematics, astronomy, medicine, and philosophy. The famous House of Wisdom in Baghdad, for instance, attracted Christian, Jewish, and Muslim scholars who translated and built upon each other's works. In Palestine, too, cities like Jerusalem and Nablus became hubs of intellectual activity where shared knowledge transcended religious lines, contributing to the development of science, art, and philosophy.

The Islamic Golden Age in Palestine offers a complex narrative of religious coexistence. While it is clear that the period saw significant achievements in terms of tolerance, peace, and cooperation, it was also marked by struggles and tensions. These tensions were often fueled by external factors such as military conflict and economic instability, but the Islamic governance model—rooted in justice, protection, and respect for diversity—provided a framework that allowed communities to endure and, in many cases, thrive together.

The cities of Jerusalem, Hebron, and Nablus stand as enduring symbols of this imperfect harmony, where mosques, churches, and synagogues shared not only the skyline but also the daily lives of the people. The legacy of this coexistence is reflected in the traditions, languages, and cultural practices that continue to shape the region today, offering a powerful testament to the potential for unity in diversity, even in the face of challenges.

The Enduring Legacy of the Islamic Golden Age

The Islamic Golden Age, spanning roughly from the 8th to the 14th centuries, was a period of profound transformation in the Muslim world, particularly in regions like Palestine. This era witnessed monumental advancements in science, culture, philosophy, and architecture, laying the foundation for much of the modern world's intellectual and artistic achievements. The influence of the Islamic Golden Age in Palestine is particularly significant, as it served as both a political and cultural nexus, shaping the identity of the region and influencing the trajectory of its history. Through the lives of visionary leaders like Salahuddin and Suleiman the Magnificent, the Islamic Golden Age in Palestine stands as a testament to the power of justice, piety, and enlightened leadership.

Visionary Leadership: The Legacy of Salahuddin, Among the many prominent figures from the Islamic Golden Age, few are as revered as Salahuddin al-Ayyubi, known in the West as Saladin. Born in 1137 in Tikrit, Iraq, Salahuddin rose from humble beginnings to become the Sultan of Egypt and Syria, and one of the most celebrated leaders of the Islamic world. His most notable achievement, and the one that has cemented his legacy, was his military and strategic prowess in reclaiming Jerusalem from the Crusaders in 1187. However, his legacy extends beyond his military victories.

Salahuddin's leadership was defined by a profound sense of justice, piety, and compassion. His ability to unify disparate factions within the Muslim world, despite regional divisions and political strife, remains one of his most enduring legacies. He was a visionary who saw the importance of maintaining peace and stability, even in times of war. One of his most remarkable qualities was his treatment of prisoners of war and the Crusaders he defeated. Rather than seeking revenge, he was known for his clemency, allowing captured Crusaders to go free upon payment of a ransom or under the condition that they would not return to fight. His magnanimity and sense of fairness earned him respect even from his adversaries.

The story of Salahuddin's triumph in Jerusalem is not just one of military strategy but also one of spiritual significance. For centuries, Jerusalem had been a flashpoint of religious conflict, with the Crusaders' capture of the city in 1099 marking a traumatic period for the local Muslim population. When Salahuddin recaptured Jerusalem, he allowed the Christian inhabitants to leave peacefully and ensured that the Christian holy sites were respected. His actions provided a model of coexistence between the Abrahamic faiths, emphasizing the importance of tolerance and mutual respect. This approach would resonate with future generations, shaping the political and cultural ethos of Palestine for centuries.

Today, Salahuddin is remembered not only as a great military leader but also as a symbol of justice and peace in the face of adversity. His influence can be seen in the cultural memory of Palestine, where his name is synonymous with noble leadership and the defense of the land.

The Architectural and Intellectual Achievements, The Islamic Golden Age was also a period of remarkable intellectual and architectural achievements, and Palestine was at the heart of many of these developments. Jerusalem, a city sacred to Jews, Christians, and Muslims alike, became a hub of intellectual and artistic activity during the Islamic period.

The Dome of the Rock, completed in 691, is perhaps the most iconic architectural achievement from the early Islamic period in Palestine. This stunning structure, with its golden dome and intricate mosaics, not only serves as a religious symbol but also stands as a testament to the artistic and engineering prowess of the time. The Dome of the Rock is an embodiment of the Islamic aesthetic, blending Byzantine and Sassanian influences with new Islamic design principles. It continues to be a symbol of the unity and beauty that the Islamic Golden Age brought to Palestine.

Another significant architectural contribution was the Al-Aqsa Mosque, which underwent several expansions and renovations during the reigns of various Islamic rulers. The mosque is not only a place of worship but also a symbol of Islamic scholarship and intellectual achievement. During the Islamic Golden Age, Jerusalem's madrassas (Islamic schools) became centers of learning, where scholars from all over the Muslim world gathered to study a wide range of subjects, including theology, philosophy, medicine, astronomy, and mathematics. The intellectual advancements of the period, such as the works of philosophers like Ibn Rushd (Averroes) and scientists like Al-Razi, were preserved and expanded upon in these institutions.

The legacy of these intellectual achievements can still be seen in the modern Middle East, where Islamic scholarship continues to play an important role in both religious and secular education. The intellectual traditions that flourished in Palestine during the Islamic Golden Age helped lay the foundation for the Renaissance in Europe and influenced the development of modern science, medicine, and philosophy.

The Role of Suleiman the Magnificent, The reign of Suleiman the Magnificent (1494–1566), who governed the Ottoman Empire during its peak, is another significant chapter in the history of Palestine during the Islamic Golden Age. Suleiman is perhaps best known for his military campaigns, but his contributions to the cultural and architectural landscape of Palestine are just as impactful.

Under Suleiman's rule, Jerusalem and other cities in Palestine experienced significant rebuilding and restoration. One of his most important contributions was the renovation of the walls of Jerusalem, which were originally constructed by the Roman Emperor Hadrian. Suleiman ordered the construction of new, fortified walls around the Old City, which still stand today. These walls not only served as a defensive measure but also symbolized the strength and unity of the Islamic world under his leadership.

Suleiman's patronage of the arts and sciences also had a profound impact on Palestine. He sponsored the construction of mosques, schools, and public buildings, many of which still serve as important cultural landmarks today. His reign marked a period of cultural flourishing in Palestine, as artists, scholars, and architects were able to work under royal patronage, contributing to the rich intellectual and artistic heritage of the region.

The Resilience and Adaptability of Palestine, Palestine has always been a crossroads of cultures and faiths, and its history during the Islamic Golden Age serves as a reminder of the resilience and adaptability of the region's people. Despite centuries of conquest, upheaval, and religious conflict, Palestine has managed to preserve its identity as a cradle of faith, culture, and history.

During the Islamic Golden Age, Palestine was home to a diverse population, including Muslims, Christians, and Jews. The coexistence of these different communities, often in harmony, was a defining feature of the era. It was a time when people of different faiths worked together to preserve the region's heritage and promote intellectual and cultural exchange. This period of peaceful coexistence was not without challenges, but it offers a powerful example of how diverse communities can live together in mutual respect.

The legacy of the Islamic Golden Age in Palestine continues to shape the region today. The architectural wonders of Jerusalem, the intellectual achievements of the scholars who studied in its madrassas, and the leadership of figures like Salahuddin and Suleiman remain symbols of Palestine's rich history. Even as the region grapples with the complexities of the modern era, the lessons of the Islamic Golden Age continue to inspire leaders and citizens alike, offering a vision of peace, coexistence, and cultural flourishing that remains relevant today.

In conclusion, the Islamic Golden Age in Palestine is not just a historical period to be remembered; it is a living legacy that continues to influence the region's identity. Through the leadership of figures like Salahuddin and Suleiman, the intellectual achievements of the era, and the enduring symbols of architectural beauty, the Islamic Golden Age in Palestine serves as a powerful reminder of the potential for coexistence, the importance of visionary leadership, and the resilience of a land that has been a crucible of faith and culture for millennia.

Chapter 3: The Seeds of Zionism

The late 19th and early 20th centuries were a time of transformation and upheaval, not only in Europe but also across the Middle East. A period marked by burgeoning nationalism, shifting empires, and the global spread of modern ideologies, these decades saw the birth of political Zionism—a movement that would shape the fate of the Jewish people and have profound and lasting consequences for the Palestinian Arabs. The story of Zionism is one of displacement and redemption, of dreams and disillusionment, and of the collision between two deeply held national aspirations: the Jewish desire for a homeland and the Palestinian Arab yearning for self-determination.

In tracing the rise of political Zionism, we see the intersection of Jewish dreams with imperial ambitions, where the hopes for a new national home collided with the reality of a land already inhabited by a long-established, indigenous population. The consequences of this convergence have echoed through the decades and continue to shape the modern Middle East. In this chapter, we explore the key figures, events, and ideas that gave rise to Zionism and set the stage for the tumultuous history that followed.

The Rise of Political Zionism: Ideological Roots and Early Advocacy, The concept of Zionism is not a modern invention, nor was it born solely out of the events of the late 19th century. The Jewish connection to the land of Israel (historically known as Judea) dates back thousands of years, and throughout the centuries, various Jewish communities maintained a sense of religious and cultural attachment to this land. However, it was the political form of

Zionism, advocating for a Jewish homeland in Palestine, that emerged during the late 19th century.

The roots of political Zionism can be traced back to Europe's growing nationalist movements, which were fueled by the spread of ideas from the French Revolution and the Napoleonic Wars. Nationalism, in its various forms, became a powerful force across Europe, as various ethnic and cultural groups sought autonomy, recognition, and self-determination. For Jews, who had faced centuries of persecution, displacement, and exclusion, the idea of a national homeland became increasingly appealing.

The key figure in the emergence of political Zionism was Theodor Herzl, an Austrian journalist and playwright. Herzl is often credited with the formal creation of Zionism as a political movement, and his efforts to establish a Jewish state were grounded in his belief that only a sovereign homeland could protect Jews from the pervasive anti-Semitism they faced in Europe. Herzl's seminal work, Der Judenstaat (The Jewish State), published in 1896, argued that the Jewish people could not integrate into European society due to centuries of persecution and discrimination. Herzl proposed the establishment of a Jewish state in Palestine as the only viable solution to the so-called "Jewish question."

Herzl's vision was not merely a matter of religious redemption, but one of pragmatic political and social engineering. He envisioned a modern, democratic state with economic prosperity and technological advancement. In his view, the establishment of a Jewish state would not only serve as a refuge for Jews, but also offer a solution to the "Eastern Question"—the instability in the Ottoman Empire and its territories, including Palestine.

The Zionist movement, however, was not universally accepted by all Jews. There were those within the Jewish community who opposed Herzl's vision, arguing that the focus should be on improving the conditions of Jews within their existing countries.

Others, especially from the religious community, viewed the idea of a Jewish homeland in Palestine as premature or even sacrilegious, believing that the return to Zion could only occur with the arrival of the Messiah. Yet, despite these internal divisions, Zionism gained traction, especially among secular Jews in Eastern Europe, who saw it as a means to escape the scourge of anti-Semitism.

The British Mandate and the Imperial Dimensions of Zionism, The rise of Zionism in the late 19th century occurred against the backdrop of the decline of the Ottoman Empire, which had ruled Palestine for centuries. By the early 20th century, the Ottoman Empire was crumbling, and European powers, particularly Britain and France, were jockeying for influence in the region. The intersection of Zionist aspirations with imperial ambitions was inevitable.

The British government, with its interests in maintaining influence over the Middle East, saw the Zionist movement as a potential ally. The most notable example of this was the Balfour Declaration of 1917, a letter from British Foreign Secretary Arthur Balfour to Lord Rothschild, a prominent British Jewish leader. The letter expressed British support for the establishment of a "national home for the Jewish people" in Palestine, then under Ottoman control. While the declaration was vague in many respects, its significance lay in the British acknowledgment of Zionist goals. The British saw the establishment of a Jewish homeland in Palestine as a way to win Jewish support for the war effort during World War I, as well as to secure their strategic interests in the region.

The Balfour Declaration, however, was a double-edged sword. On the one hand, it represented a significant triumph for the Zionist movement, as it was the first time a major world power had explicitly endorsed the idea of a Jewish homeland in Palestine. On the other hand, the declaration was made without the consent or input of the Arab population of Palestine, who constituted the majority in the region. This lack of consultation sowed the seeds of resentment and opposition among the Palestinian Arabs, who were already wary of foreign interference in their land.

Following the war, Britain assumed control over Palestine under a League of Nations mandate, further entrenching the idea of a Jewish homeland. However, the mandate system itself was a manifestation of European imperialism, and the British administration in Palestine faced increasing resistance from both the Jewish and Arab populations. For the Zionists, the British were seen as essential partners in the quest for a Jewish state. However, for the Palestinian Arabs, the British were viewed as occupiers who had promised them self-determination but were instead facilitating the influx of Jewish immigrants and undermining Arab sovereignty.

Palestinian Arab Reactions: Nationalism and Resistance, The growth of the Zionist movement and the increasing numbers of Jewish immigrants to Palestine during the early 20th century were met with mounting opposition from the Palestinian Arabs. These Arabs, who had been living in the region for centuries, viewed the influx of Jewish immigrants as a direct threat to their land, culture, and political autonomy. While the early Zionists had envisioned a peaceful coexistence between Jews and Arabs in Palestine, this was not the reality on the ground.

As the 1920s and 1930s progressed, tensions between Jews and Arabs in Palestine escalated. The Palestinian Arab resistance to Zionism manifested in a variety of ways, including political protests, labor strikes, and outright violence. One of the most significant events of this period was the 1929 Hebron massacre, where tensions between Jews and Arabs erupted into violence, resulting in the deaths of dozens of Jews. This violence was a harbinger of the deepening divisions that would plague the region for decades to come.

The Palestinian Arab nationalist movement was galvanized by a growing sense of disenfranchisement and the belief that their right to self-determination was being violated by both the British and the Zionists. In 1936, a large-scale Arab revolt broke out in Palestine, which was aimed at both British colonial rule and Jewish immigration. The revolt was violently suppressed by the British, but it underscored the deep-seated animosity between the two communities and foreshadowed the inevitable conflict that would arise as both the Zionists and the Palestinian Arabs sought to assert their national aspirations in the same land.

Zionism in Action, One of the most illustrative examples of the tensions surrounding Zionism can be seen in the experiences of Jewish immigrants and Palestinian Arabs in the years leading up to the creation of the State of Israel. Case studies of these individuals offer a personal lens through which to understand the broader geopolitical dynamics of the time.

For instance, the story of David Ben-Gurion, a leader of the Zionist movement and later Israel's first prime minister, provides insight into the Zionist vision of statehood. Ben-Gurion's commitment to building a Jewish homeland was unwavering, and he worked tirelessly to establish institutions of Jewish governance and military strength. His leadership was pivotal in the transformation of the Zionist movement from an ideological vision into a tangible reality, culminating in the founding of Israel in 1948.

On the other side, the experiences of Palestinian Arabs such as Hanan Ashrawi, a prominent Palestinian politician and scholar, illustrate the profound sense of displacement and loss felt by many Palestinians. Ashrawi's family, like many others, was directly affected by the establishment of the State of Israel and the subsequent displacement of hundreds of thousands of Palestinian Arabs in what they call the Nakba, or "catastrophe." For Palestinians, the creation of Israel marked not the fulfillment of a national dream, but the beginning of an ongoing struggle for self-determination and recognition.

Zionism, Displacement, and Redemption, The rise of Zionism in the late 19th and early 20th centuries was a transformative event that not only shaped the destiny of the Jewish people but also set in motion a series of conflicts that would shape the modern Middle East. The dream of a Jewish homeland in Palestine was intertwined with imperial interests, leading to the establishment of the State of Israel in 1948 and the displacement of Palestinian Arabs. The Zionist movement, which began with the idealistic vision of a safe haven for Jews, collided with the reality of a land already inhabited by another people with their own aspirations.

The legacy of Zionism continues to shape the politics and conflicts of the Middle East to this day. As the decades have passed, the hopes of both Jews and Palestinians have been tested by war, occupation, and ongoing negotiations. The collision of these two national movements—the Jewish desire for a homeland and the Palestinian struggle for self-determination—remains at the heart of the Israeli-Palestinian conflict, a struggle that has shaped the history of the region for more than a century and shows no signs of resolution in the near future.

Zionism, as a political movement, has often been a controversial and divisive issue, particularly in the context of the Israeli-Palestinian conflict. It is crucial to differentiate between the ideology of Zionism and the broader Jewish people, as many Jews, both historically and today, do not identify with or support the goals of Zionism. In fact, the movement has been associated with colonialism, displacement, and the denial of Palestinian rights, casting a shadow over its idealistic claims of providing a safe homeland for Jews.

Zionism as a Colonialist Ideology, At its core, Zionism was founded as a response to the persecution of Jews in Europe and their desire for a homeland. However, it is often criticized as a form of settler colonialism, whereby a foreign population seeks to establish its own state on land already inhabited by indigenous peoples. The origins of Zionism are inextricably linked to European imperialism, particularly the British Empire's involvement in the Middle East during the decline of the Ottoman Empire. The Zionist movement was supported by powerful Western nations such as Britain, which saw it as a way to strengthen their own geopolitical influence in the region.

The Balfour Declaration of 1917, which supported the establishment of a Jewish "national home" in Palestine, was issued without the consent of the local Palestinian population, who had been living in the region for centuries. This declaration, backed by imperial powers, ignored the rights and wishes of the Palestinians, effectively setting the stage for the displacement of thousands of Arab families and the eventual occupation of their land. From the beginning, Zionism was entangled with colonial ambitions, transforming what was initially a quest for Jewish refuge into a geopolitical agenda that disregarded the rights of the indigenous population.

Displacement and Ethnic Cleansing: The Nakba, One of the most painful chapters in the history of Zionism is the 1948 creation of the State of Israel, which Palestinians refer to as the Nakba, or "catastrophe." The establishment of Israel was not the peaceful and harmonious vision promised by Zionist leaders, but rather the result of violent displacement, land expropriation, and the destruction of Palestinian villages. During the period leading up to and following the declaration of the state, hundreds of thousands of Palestinians were forcibly removed from their homes, and many were denied the right to return. Entire villages were destroyed, and the Palestinian population was scattered across the region, creating a refugee crisis that persists to this day.

Zionist militias, such as the Irgun and Lehi, were involved in numerous acts of violence against Palestinians and Arabs during this period. For example, the Deir Yassin massacre in 1948, in which more than 100 Palestinian men, women, and children were killed by Zionist forces, is often cited as an example of the brutality employed in the establishment of the state. These acts of ethnic cleansing were not isolated incidents, but part of a broader strategy to create a Jewish-majority state at the expense of the indigenous Arab population. While Zionist leaders such as David Ben-Gurion defended these actions as necessary for the survival of the Jewish state, they have left a legacy of trauma and displacement for the Palestinian people.

Zionism and the Denial of Palestinian Rights, Zionism, as it evolved in the 20th century, became synonymous with the creation of Israel and the systematic denial of Palestinian rights. The establishment of Israel, while providing refuge for Jews fleeing persecution, also led to the marginalization, oppression, and displacement of the Palestinian Arab population. Palestinian Arabs were not only dispossessed of their land, but their national identity and aspirations for self-determination were largely ignored or suppressed by Zionist leaders and the Israeli state.

The principle of Zionism—that Jews have a historical and religious right to the land of Palestine—has been used to justify the continued occupation and control of Palestinian territories, including the West Bank, East Jerusalem, and Gaza. Israeli policies, shaped by Zionist ideology, have led to the construction of settlements in the occupied territories, often on land confiscated from Palestinians, as well as the enforcement of discriminatory laws that limit the rights and freedoms of Palestinian citizens of Israel. Palestinians living under occupation face restrictions on movement, access to resources, and basic human rights, while Israeli settlers enjoy privileges and protections denied to the native population.

The logic of Zionism—particularly the notion that Jews have an exclusive right to the land—has been a significant barrier to peace and coexistence. While many Zionist leaders insist that the state of Israel is the only solution to the Jewish question and the protection of Jews from persecution, this comes at the expense of Palestinian sovereignty and the recognition of their right to self-determination. The constant expansion of Israeli settlements and the denial of Palestinian political and civil rights contribute to the ongoing conflict and the suffering of the Palestinian people.

Zionism vs. Judaism: Distinguishing Ideology from Religion, It is essential to differentiate between Zionism as a political ideology and Judaism as a religion. While the two are often conflated, the vast majority of Jews worldwide are not Zionists, and many actively oppose the policies of the Israeli government. For instance, religious groups such as the Satmar Hasidim and other Orthodox Jews reject Zionism on theological grounds, arguing that the establishment of a Jewish state before the coming of the Messiah is contrary to Jewish law. These groups emphasize that Jewish people should not use force to reclaim their historical homeland, but should wait for divine intervention.

Many secular Jews, particularly those who live outside of Israel, are also critical of Zionism. They view the movement as a political ideology that has led to injustice and oppression for the Palestinian people, and they advocate for a peaceful resolution based on equal rights and coexistence. For these Jews, Zionism is a betrayal of the Jewish tradition of justice, compassion, and the pursuit of peace.

Zionism has also been criticized by Jewish intellectuals and activists, such as Noam Chomsky and Ilan Pappé, who argue that the movement has caused immense harm to both Jews and Palestinians. Chomsky, for instance, contends that Zionism has led to the creation of an apartheid state that violates the human rights of Palestinians, while Pappé calls the actions of the Israeli government "ethnic cleansing" of the Palestinian people. Both argue that a true Jewish commitment to justice should involve advocating for the rights of Palestinians and working toward a just and peaceful solution to the conflict.

Legacy of Zionism, The legacy of Zionism is one of division, violence, and dispossession. While it has provided a refuge for Jews fleeing persecution, it has also led to the subjugation of another people, the Palestinians. The claim of Zionism to a "historical right" to the land of Palestine is increasingly viewed as a justification for colonial expansion and oppression rather than a moral or historical imperative. The consequences of Zionism are evident in the ongoing Israeli-Palestinian conflict, where Palestinians continue to struggle for their rights, self-determination, and recognition as a people.

Zionism has thus become a symbol of the inherent contradictions of the modern world—of nationalism, imperialism, and displacement—and its impact on the Palestinian people is undeniable. The movement's ideal of a safe homeland for Jews must be weighed against the reality of Palestinian suffering, displacement, and the ongoing occupation of their land. For many, Zionism is not the realization of a Jewish dream, but a historical and political failure that continues to inflict harm on both Jews and Palestinians alike.

Ultimately, a just resolution to the Israeli-Palestinian conflict requires not only addressing the legitimate rights of Jews to live in safety, but also recognizing the equally legitimate rights of Palestinians to their land, identity, and self-determination. The challenge lies in reconciling these competing aspirations, and in doing so, breaking the cycle of violence and injustice that has marred the region for more than a century.

Theodor Herzl: The Controversial Architect of Political Zionism

Theodor Herzl, often hailed as the father of modern Zionism, is celebrated for his vision of a Jewish state, which ultimately led to the establishment of the State of Israel in 1948. However, his ideas, far from being unassailable or purely benevolent, are fraught with deeply problematic assumptions, political contradictions, and consequences that have reverberated throughout history, leading to the ongoing Palestinian-Israeli conflict. While Herzl's Zionism is lauded for its attempt to provide a solution to the Jewish question in Europe, it must be

recognized that his approach disregarded the presence of an indigenous population in Palestine and perpetuated the marginalization, displacement, and dispossession of Palestinians. The lasting consequences of Herzl's political Zionism must be critically examined, especially as the implementation of his vision involved the subjugation of an entire people and the entrenchment of an ethno-nationalist state that remains highly controversial today.

Herzl was born in 1860 in Budapest into an assimilated Jewish family, and he was initially shaped by the dominant European ideals of integration. His early belief in the power of education, industry, and Enlightenment ideals to overcome anti-Semitism was rooted in the belief that Jews could find a place of equality and acceptance in the societies they inhabited. Like many Jews of his era, Herzl sought assimilation into European culture, convinced that time and education would lead to the cessation of centuries-old prejudices against Jews. He imagined that Jews could integrate into the fabric of European society and be recognized as equal citizens. However, his idealistic vision was shattered by the Dreyfus Affair in France in 1894, a political scandal in which a Jewish officer, Captain Alfred Dreyfus, was wrongfully accused of treason, leading to his imprisonment and public humiliation. The case revealed the pervasiveness of anti-Semitism in European society and shattered Herzl's belief that Jews could ever fully assimilate.

Herzl's response to the Dreyfus Affair was to shift from advocating for Jewish integration in Europe to promoting the idea of a Jewish state in Palestine, which he believed would provide a solution to the "Jewish question." This ideological shift marked the birth of his political Zionism, a movement that prioritized the creation of a Jewish homeland above all else. Herzl, who was a journalist, articulated his ideas most famously in his 1896 pamphlet Der Judenstaat (The Jewish State), where he argued that Jews could never be fully free or secure in any European country due to the persistence of anti-Semitism. He proposed that the Jews should seek their own homeland, where they would have political and cultural autonomy. Herzl's argument for a Jewish state was not solely motivated by religious beliefs, but by the rise of nationalism in Europe during the late 19th century, which emphasized self-determination for ethnic and national groups. The Jews, Herzl argued, were no different from other nations in their right to establish a state of their own.

However, while Herzl's focus on self-determination for Jews is often framed as a noble pursuit, it is crucial to recognize the deeply problematic nature of his vision for a Jewish state. Herzl's primary motivation was not just to establish a place of refuge for Jews, but to create a state for Jews at the expense of the indigenous Arab population of Palestine. Herzl's vision, outlined in Der Judenstaat, was based on the assumption that the land of Palestine, long home to a predominantly Arab population, could be transformed into a Jewish state without regard for the rights or aspirations of the existing inhabitants. Herzl was, in fact, remarkably silent on the subject of the Arab population of Palestine, and his writings rarely addressed the rights or claims of the Palestinian Arabs.

This oversight is striking and deeply troubling, as it highlights Herzl's implicit disregard for the indigenous Palestinians, whose land he sought to colonize for the establishment of a Jewish state. Herzl's failure to recognize or address the Arab population's rights and existence on the land can be viewed as an early form of colonial thinking, wherein the needs and rights of the indigenous people were subordinated to the desires of a settler population. While Herzl spoke of securing a "home for the Jewish people in Palestine," his focus was squarely on the Jews and their right to self-determination, not on creating a just solution for the Arab inhabitants of the region.

Herzl's Zionism was built on the premise that Jews were entitled to a state of their own, but this premise was problematic in the context of Palestine, where Arabs had lived for centuries. Herzl's actions were based on a colonial logic that justified the displacement of the indigenous population in favor of a settler state. His attempts to garner international support for this vision did not include meaningful consideration for the Palestinian Arabs who would be directly impacted by the influx of Jewish settlers. His failure to account for the social, political, and cultural realities of Palestine laid the foundation for a future of tension, violence, and dispossession that would unfold in the decades following the establishment of Israel.

In 1897, Herzl convened the First Zionist Congress in Basel, Switzerland, where the Basel Program was adopted, declaring the goal of establishing a "home for the Jewish people in Palestine, secured by public law." The Congress solidified the political Zionist project and established the World Zionist Organization (WZO), providing the movement with institutional legitimacy and a formal platform to seek international recognition and support. However, the actions and ideas of the Zionist movement, led by Herzl, continued to disregard the fundamental rights of the Palestinian Arabs. Herzl's negotiations with European powers, including the Ottoman Empire, were focused on securing the approval for Jewish immigration to Palestine and the establishment of a Jewish state, without any significant consideration of how this would affect the native population.

Herzl's political genius in organizing and mobilizing the Zionist movement cannot be denied. He effectively laid the groundwork for the establishment of Israel by securing the support of key powers and financiers, and his vision provided a roadmap for the creation of the Jewish state. Yet, the result of his efforts was not one of peace or coexistence, but one of conflict and dispossession. While Herzl's Zionism was framed as a humanitarian solution to the plight of Jews in Europe, the reality of Zionist colonization in Palestine resulted in the displacement of hundreds of thousands of Palestinian Arabs. Herzl's focus on the creation of a Jewish homeland disregarded the impact this would have on the Arab population, setting the stage for a protracted and violent conflict that continues to this day.

Herzl's vision for a Jewish state was not fulfilled in his lifetime, as he died in 1904, just seven years after the First Zionist Congress. However, his ideas lived on, and in 1948, with the establishment of the State of Israel, his dream became a reality. Yet, this achievement was not without its consequences. The creation of Israel led to the displacement of over 700,000 Palestinian Arabs during the Nakba (Arabic for "catastrophe"), as Palestinians were either forcibly expelled or fled in the face of violence and war. Herzl's vision of a Jewish state came at the expense of the Palestinians, who were denied their right to self-determination, and the resulting conflict has led to decades of violence, occupation, and human suffering.

Herzl's legacy is thus deeply contentious. While his supporters view him as a visionary who sought to secure a homeland for a persecuted people, critics argue that his vision was deeply flawed and inherently unjust. Herzl's political Zionism ignored the rights of the indigenous Palestinian Arabs, whose land and livelihoods were sacrificed to realize the dream of a Jewish state. The consequences of his vision—displacement, suffering, and conflict—continue to shape the region today.

Herzl's political Zionism, while offering a solution to the Jewish question, did so at the expense of another people's rights and aspirations. The creation of Israel, which fulfilled Herzl's vision, has led to the ongoing Palestinian struggle for self-determination and the recognition of their rights. Herzl's failure to address the needs of the Palestinian Arabs in his plans for a Jewish state ensured that the establishment of Israel would be accompanied by violence and dispossession. The legacy of Herzl's Zionism is therefore one of division, conflict, and injustice—a legacy that continues to resonate in the Middle East and throughout the world.

Theodor Herzl's vision of a Jewish state in Palestine, while framed as a solution to Jewish persecution, was deeply flawed in its disregard for the Palestinian population. Herzl's political Zionism, which sought to create a state at the expense of another people, laid the foundation for the conflict that still shapes the region today. His legacy is one that must be critically examined, as it is a reminder that the pursuit of self-determination for one group can often come at the expense of another's rights and sovereignty. Herzl's vision of a Jewish homeland, while offering a refuge for Jews, also led to the suffering and displacement of Palestinians—a legacy that remains unresolved and continues to haunt the Middle East.

British Imperialism and the Balfour Declaration: A Critical Examination of Zionism

The Balfour Declaration, issued on November 2, 1917, remains one of the most consequential documents in the history of the Middle East. Its endorsement of the establishment of a "national home for the Jewish people" in Palestine by the British government would set the stage for decades of political turmoil, resistance, and violence. While the Balfour Declaration has often been viewed as a milestone in the Zionist movement, it is important to critically assess the ideologies that underpin Zionism and the long-lasting effects that it had not only on the Jewish people but also on the Arab population of Palestine. In examining this historical moment, it is essential to engage with the implications of Zionism as an imperialist project and its impact on the broader geopolitical context of the region.

Zionism: A Colonial Nationalism, At its core, Zionism can be viewed as a form of colonial nationalism, a movement that sought to establish a Jewish state in Palestine, a land with an existing Arab population. The Zionist project, led by figures such as Theodor Herzl, emerged in the late 19th century, spurred by the rising tide of anti-Semitism in Europe and the desire to create a safe haven for Jews. Herzl's vision was one of Jewish self-determination, but the way in which this vision was to be realized raised significant ethical and political questions.

Zionism, particularly in its early stages, was closely tied to European imperialism. Herzl and other early Zionist leaders did not view the establishment of a Jewish state in Palestine as a project of shared coexistence with the existing Arab population but as a way to create a European-style state in the Middle East. This vision often involved disregarding the political rights and aspirations of the Arab people who had lived in Palestine for centuries. In this sense, Zionism was not a movement for coexistence or partnership, but one rooted in colonial expansionism and the idea of creating a "Jewish homeland" on land that was already inhabited by Arabs.

The Balfour Declaration itself is emblematic of this colonial mindset. While it professed to support the Jewish people's right to a national home in Palestine, it simultaneously ignored the political rights and self-determination of the Palestinian Arab population. The famous clause, "nothing shall be done which may prejudice the civil and religious rights of existing non-Jewish communities in Palestine," was, in reality, a hollow assurance, as it provided no real mechanisms to ensure the protection of Arab rights. The promise was, in essence, a political maneuver to gain support for the British war effort, with little regard for the consequences it would have for the people already living in the region.

British Imperialism and Its Role in Zionism, To fully understand the significance of the Balfour Declaration, it is necessary to examine the role that British imperialism played in the development of Zionism. Britain's interest in Palestine was not driven by a deep commitment to Jewish self-determination but by its strategic interests in the Middle East. Palestine, as a vital geographic crossroads, was crucial to Britain's control over the Suez Canal, a key maritime route connecting the Mediterranean to the Red Sea and beyond. By supporting Zionism, Britain hoped to secure the loyalty of the Jewish population, particularly in the United States and Russia, while also maintaining influence over the Middle East as the Ottoman Empire disintegrated.

The British Empire had long used promises and manipulations to maintain control over vast regions, and the Balfour Declaration was no exception. The British government simultaneously promised Arab leaders, most notably Sharif Hussein of Mecca, support for an independent Arab state in exchange for their assistance in the fight against the Ottoman Empire. These conflicting promises, made without regard for the rights of the Palestinian Arabs, sowed the seeds for future resentment and violence.

From a critical perspective, Britain's role in the Zionist project can be viewed as one of imperial opportunism. The British Empire, having faced challenges in maintaining its global power, saw in the Zionist movement an opportunity to solidify its strategic interests in the region. It was not a philanthropic act of supporting the Jewish people, but rather a political calculation designed to enhance British power in the Middle East, even at the expense of the people who lived there.

Zionism and the Displacement of the Palestinian Arabs, One of the most significant criticisms of Zionism is its disregard for the rights and well-being of the Palestinian Arab population. From the very beginning of the Zionist project, the establishment of a Jewish state in Palestine was viewed by Zionist leaders as a necessary condition for Jewish survival and prosperity. However, this vision inherently entailed the displacement of the Palestinian Arabs, who were seen by Zionists as obstacles to the creation of a Jewish homeland. The early Zionists were not particularly concerned with the social, political, and economic consequences of their actions for the local population, as their primary focus was on establishing a state for the Jewish people.

The Balfour Declaration exacerbated these tensions. In theory, it promised to protect the civil and religious rights of non-Jewish communities, but in practice, it led to the gradual erosion of Palestinian Arab rights. Jewish immigration to Palestine, supported by British authorities, increased rapidly after the declaration. As Jewish settlements were established, the Palestinian Arab population began to experience significant displacement, economic hardship, and political disenfranchisement. These early waves of Jewish immigration were not without conflict, as Palestinian Arabs began to resist the increasing presence of Jewish settlers in their land.

Critics argue that the Zionist movement's emphasis on creating a Jewish state at the expense of the Palestinian Arabs was inherently unjust. The creation of Israel in 1948, a process that culminated in the Nakba (Catastrophe), saw the forced displacement of over 700,000 Palestinian Arabs, many of whom fled or were expelled from their homes. The Zionist vision, which had been formalized in the Balfour Declaration, thus led to the creation of a state built on the dispossession of the native population.

This historical trajectory raises important ethical questions about the nature of Zionism as a movement for self-determination. While the Zionists claimed to be fighting for the right of Jews to have a homeland, their vision of that homeland was predicated on the exclusion and displacement of another people. In this sense, Zionism can be seen as a project of ethnic nationalism that sought to prioritize the rights of one group—Jews—over the rights of another—Palestinian Arabs. Critics of Zionism argue that the movement's inherent ethnocentric ideology is at the root of much of the conflict that persists between Israelis and Palestinians today.

The Ongoing Consequences of the Balfour Declaration and Zionism, The long-term consequences of the Balfour Declaration and the Zionist project are still felt in the region today. The Palestinian people continue to live under occupation in the West Bank and Gaza Strip, facing systemic discrimination, limited access to resources, and violence from Israeli security forces. The conflict between Israelis and Palestinians, rooted in the competing nationalisms of the two peoples, has led to decades of suffering, displacement, and political deadlock.

Zionism, in its contemporary form, remains a contentious issue. For many Palestinians, it represents a political and ideological system that denies their rights to self-determination, sovereignty, and equality. The establishment of Israel, while a moment of triumph for the Jewish people, has come at the expense of Palestinian rights and has led to the continued fragmentation of Palestinian society. From a critical perspective, Zionism's legacy is one of ethnic division and territorial conquest, where the political project of one group has led to the suppression of another.

The Balfour Declaration and the Zionist project are often seen as turning points in the history of the Middle East, but they also raise fundamental questions about the ethics of nationalism, imperialism, and colonialism. While Zionism can be viewed as a movement for Jewish self-determination, it is equally important to recognize its colonial dimensions and its impact on the Palestinian Arab population. The legacy of Zionism is a deeply contentious and painful issue for many in the Middle East, and the ongoing Israeli-Palestinian conflict serves as a reminder of the enduring consequences of these historical processes. A critical examination of Zionism, therefore, requires not only an understanding of its historical development but also a recognition of the profound injustices that it has engendered for the Palestinian people.

The British Mandate and the Zionist Displacement of Palestinians: A Colonial Legacy

In the aftermath of World War I, the dismantling of the Ottoman Empire left a significant geopolitical void in the Middle East. The League of Nations, under the guise of civilizing and stabilizing the region, implemented a mandate system to govern these newly formed territories. One of the most contentious and far-reaching mandates was Britain's control over Palestine. Established in 1920, this mandate would last until 1948, a period marked by increasing tensions between the Palestinian Arab population and Jewish immigrants. These tensions were fueled not only by the policies of the British colonial administration but also by the growing influence of the Zionist movement, which was dedicated to the creation of a Jewish homeland in Palestine.

Zionism, a political movement founded in the late 19th century by figures such as Theodor Herzl, was driven by the belief that Jews, scattered and persecuted across Europe, should return to Palestine, the land they considered their ancient homeland. At its core, Zionism argued that the Jewish people needed a state where they could be safe from the rampant anti-Semitism in Europe, particularly in Eastern Europe and Russia. As Europe struggled with the consequences of World War I and the rise of nationalist movements, the Zionist cause gained momentum, receiving support from both European powers and Jewish communities worldwide. In 1917, the Balfour Declaration, issued by the British government, promised to support the establishment of a "national home for the Jewish people" in Palestine. This declaration, made without consulting the local Arab population, set in motion a series of events that would lead to the displacement of the Palestinian Arabs and the establishment of the state of Israel.

At first, the Zionist movement and the British seemed to be in alignment, with Britain eager to use Zionism to secure Jewish support for the Allied war effort. But the consequences of this alliance for the Palestinian Arab population were devastating. As the British Mandate took hold, Jewish immigration to Palestine increased dramatically. Between 1919 and 1939, the Jewish population grew from about 10% to approximately 30% of the total population of Palestine. This influx was driven by the desire of European Jews to escape rising anti-Semitism, as well as by the active encouragement of the British, who saw Zionism as a way to stabilize the region. This period of growth was not an organic or neutral development; rather, it was heavily influenced by the policies of the British administration, which actively facilitated the immigration of Jews while systematically undermining the political and economic rights of the Palestinian Arabs.

Zionism's methods, particularly its policy of land acquisition and settlement building, began to reshape the Palestinian landscape. Zionist organizations, such as the Jewish National Fund (JNF), began purchasing land from absentee landowners, often at inflated prices, and transferring it to Jewish settlers. Many of these lands had been inhabited by Palestinian farmers for generations. This systematic buying up of Palestinian land, often with British legal backing, caused widespread dislocation and economic hardship for the Arab population. It also set in motion a process that would lead to the marginalization of the Palestinians, stripping them of both their land and their political power.

This Zionist policy of land acquisition and settlement was more than just a series of individual transactions; it was part of a larger vision for a Jewish state. For Zionist leaders like David Ben-Gurion, the acquisition of land and the establishment of Jewish settlements were integral to the creation of a future Jewish homeland. Ben-Gurion, who would later become Israel's first Prime Minister, saw the land of Palestine as both a refuge for Jews and the cradle of a new Jewish civilization. The land was not merely a place to settle but a place to build a new, modern, and independent Jewish state—a state that would be explicitly Jewish in both character and governance. This vision of a Jewish state, however, came at the expense of the indigenous Palestinian Arab population, who were increasingly pushed to the margins of their own land.

From the Palestinian perspective, this influx of Jewish immigrants and the growing Zionist presence was not merely a demographic shift but an existential threat. Palestinians viewed Zionism as a colonial enterprise, one that sought to dispossess them of their land and erase their identity. The Zionist project, with its emphasis on creating a Jewish state, was seen by many Palestinians as an attempt to supplant their own political and national identity. To the Palestinians, Zionism represented not just a movement of return for Jews but a movement of conquest, one that sought to replace them as the majority in their ancestral homeland.

As the British Mandate continued, tensions between the Jewish and Arab populations in Palestine began to escalate. The Palestinians, who had been largely excluded from the political decision-making process, saw their political power eroded as Jewish institutions grew in strength. Zionist leaders, such as Chaim Weizmann, sought international recognition for the Zionist cause, building relationships with the British government and later with the United States and the Soviet Union. Weizmann, a scientist and diplomat, worked tirelessly to garner support for the establishment of a Jewish state. His efforts paid off in 1947, when the United Nations voted to partition Palestine into separate Jewish and Arab states.

The partition plan, which was endorsed by Zionist leaders, was rejected by the Palestinian Arabs and the wider Arab world. The idea of dividing Palestine, which had been the home of Palestinian Arabs for centuries, was seen as a betrayal. The Zionist movement had already established a foothold in Palestine through a combination of land purchases, settlement building, and support from colonial powers. The Palestinians, on the other hand, had no such support and found themselves increasingly isolated and powerless. They were left with little recourse but to resist.

The Palestinian resistance to Zionism and British colonialism took many forms, from protests and strikes to outright violence. The Arab Revolt of 1936-1939 was the most significant and sustained uprising against both British rule and Jewish immigration. The revolt was sparked by a combination of factors, including economic hardship, growing political discontent, and a fear that the Zionist movement would permanently alter the demographic and political landscape of Palestine. The British response to the revolt was harsh and repressive, employing military force, collective punishment, and mass arrests to quell the uprising.

The Palestinian resistance, however, would not be silenced. Leaders like Haj Amin al-Husseini, the Grand Mufti of Jerusalem, emerged as symbols of Palestinian nationalism. Al-Husseini, despite his controversial alliances during World War II, became a key figure in the Palestinian struggle for self-determination. His leadership galvanized Palestinian resistance and gave voice to the aspirations of the Arab population in Palestine. Despite the suppression of the revolt, the tensions between the Palestinian Arabs and the Zionists continued to build, setting the stage for the larger conflict that would unfold after the establishment of the State of Israel in 1948.

Zionism's role in the creation of Israel and its impact on the Palestinian population cannot be overstated. The movement's insistence on establishing a Jewish state in Palestine, regardless of the impact on the indigenous Arab population, led directly to the displacement of hundreds of thousands of Palestinians in what is known as the Nakba, or catastrophe. The Zionist ideology, with its focus on creating a Jewish-majority state, inevitably led to the expulsion, dispossession, and marginalization of the Palestinians. This process was not accidental; it was a central tenet of the Zionist project, which prioritized Jewish nationalism over the rights and aspirations of the Palestinian people.

Critics of Zionism argue that the movement's fundamental premise was one of colonialism, using the pretext of Jewish historical ties to the land of Palestine to justify the displacement of the indigenous Arab population. They point out that while Jews had lived in Palestine for centuries, the majority of Jews who immigrated during the early 20th century were not refugees from Palestine's past but immigrants from Europe seeking a safe haven from persecution. The Zionist movement's reliance on British support, the forcible acquisition of Palestinian land, and the displacement of the local population all reflect the colonial nature of the Zionist project.

Moreover, the Zionist vision of a Jewish state in Palestine ignored the realities of Palestinian life and aspirations. Rather than seeing the Palestinians as partners in the creation of a new, shared society, Zionism viewed them as obstacles to the realization of its goals. The result was a conflict that has lasted for more than a century, with no end in sight. The ongoing occupation of Palestinian territories, the systematic denial of Palestinian rights, and the continued expansion of Jewish settlements in the West Bank are all legacies of Zionism's colonial roots.

In conclusion, while Zionism was founded as a response to the persecution of Jews in Europe, its implementation in Palestine was a colonial project that came at the expense of the Palestinian Arab population. The policies of land acquisition, settlement building, and the creation of a Jewish-majority state ultimately led to the dispossession and displacement of the Palestinians. The Zionist movement's disregard for Palestinian rights and its insistence on establishing a state based on ethnic and religious identity has left a legacy of conflict and suffering that continues to this day.

The Holocaust and the Road to Israeli Independence: A Critical Examination of Zionism and its Impact on Palestine

The Holocaust, which decimated six million Jews in Nazi-occupied Europe, is an atrocity whose moral weight remains a profound and tragic event in human history. However, the ways in which the Holocaust has been utilized to justify the creation of Israel and the subsequent suffering of the Palestinian people demand critical scrutiny. While the Holocaust undeniably increased global sympathy for Jews and gave rise to the pressing demand for a Jewish homeland, the trajectory of Zionism—its goals, methods, and impact on the indigenous Palestinian Arabs—presents a deeply troubling story of displacement, dispossession, and ongoing conflict. This narrative examines the path from the Holocaust to Israeli independence, with a focus on the consequences for the Palestinian people and a critical look at the Zionist project.

The Rise of Nazism and the Holocaust: A Precursor to Zionist Goals, The rise of Nazism in Germany and the ensuing Holocaust undoubtedly created a moral imperative for a Jewish homeland, given the horrifying scale of violence and genocide faced by European Jewry. Six million Jews were brutally murdered by the Nazis, and the survivors were left with no safe haven, with much of Europe destroyed in the wake of the war. It was undeniable that the Jewish people needed a sanctuary—a place where they could feel safe, free from persecution. For many, that place was Palestine, a region that had historically been associated with the Jewish people.

However, it is essential to critically examine how Zionism responded to the Holocaust and whether the tragic fate of European Jews justified the creation of Israel in a land already inhabited by

Palestinian Arabs. Zionism, as an ideological movement that sought to establish a Jewish state in Palestine, predates the Holocaust by several decades. But it was the horrors of the war that accelerated the movement's momentum, spurring on the push for a Jewish homeland in Palestine despite the resistance of the Arab population.

In the aftermath of the Holocaust, Zionist leaders, such as David Ben-Gurion and Chaim Weizmann, sought to capitalize on the global sympathy for Jews and used the genocide as a platform to rally international support for the creation of a Jewish state. The tragic experiences of European Jews, however, were used to justify the forcible removal of the native Palestinian population—a people who had lived in the region for centuries and who were themselves facing a struggle for their rights. The establishment of Israel, therefore, was not just about offering sanctuary to Jewish survivors of the Holocaust but also about fulfilling a larger nationalist project that sought to erase Palestinian existence and claim their land.

The Zionist Agenda: Dispossessing the Palestinian Arabs, Zionism's central tenet was the establishment of a Jewish state in Palestine, a goal that became increasingly urgent after the Holocaust. The problem, however, was that Palestine was already home to a large Arab population, who had lived there for centuries. The Zionist movement's actions, particularly in the years leading up to 1948, increasingly reflected an agenda that sought to displace Palestinians in order to make room for a Jewish state.

From the early 20th century, the influx of Jewish immigrants into Palestine, encouraged by British policies under the Balfour Declaration of 1917, resulted in rising tensions between Jewish settlers and Palestinian Arabs. While Zionists viewed Palestine as the historical and religious homeland of the Jewish people, Palestinians saw the arrival of Jews as an intrusion and threat to their land and way of life. As Jewish settlements expanded, violence between the two groups escalated, with the Zionists often using military force to drive Palestinians from their lands.

In the 1930s and 1940s, Jewish militias like the Haganah and the Irgun carried out acts of violence against Palestinian Arabs, while also preparing for the establishment of a Jewish state. The most notable of these acts was the 1948 Nakba (meaning "catastrophe" in Arabic), when over 700,000 Palestinian Arabs were forcibly displaced from their homes as Zionist forces seized territory. Entire villages were destroyed, and Palestinians were driven into refugee camps in neighboring countries. This mass expulsion was not an unfortunate byproduct of the creation of Israel, but rather an essential element of the Zionist project, which aimed to create a purely Jewish state by eradicating the Arab population.

Zionism, as an ideology, has been criticized for its colonialist and ethnocentric approach. By focusing on the establishment of a Jewish-only state, it relegated the indigenous Palestinian population to the status of second-class citizens, and in many cases, denied them the basic right to remain in their ancestral land. For Zionist leaders, the Holocaust served as the ultimate justification for this dispossession, as they argued that a safe haven for Jews was necessary to prevent future genocides. Yet, this justification for Israeli statehood came at the expense of the Palestinian people's right to self-determination.

The United Nations Partition Plan and its Unfairness to Palestinians, In 1947, the United Nations proposed a partition plan to address the conflict between Jews and Arabs in Palestine. The plan called for the division of the land into two states: one Jewish and one Arab, with Jerusalem placed under international administration. The Zionist leadership accepted the plan, though they understood that it fell short of their ultimate goal of a unified Jewish state. The Jewish population, which constituted a minority in Palestine at the time, was granted 55% of the land, even though they owned only around 7% of the land.

For the Palestinian Arabs, this partition was not just unfair—it was a direct violation of their rights. They were being asked to relinquish more than half of their land to a Jewish state, despite being the majority population in the region. Furthermore, the partition plan did not take into account the longstanding social, cultural, and political connections that Palestinians had to the land. In effect, the partition plan was an imposition by external powers that disregarded the Palestinians' right to their land and sovereignty. The Arab states, which opposed the partition plan, argued that it would lead to the destruction of Palestinian communities and the displacement of thousands of Arabs from their homes.

Critics of Zionism argue that the partition plan was a thinly veiled attempt to legitimize the Zionist project and grant Israel international legitimacy while disregarding Palestinian rights. The creation of Israel, based on the partition plan, was seen as a colonial imposition that further entrenched the dispossession of the Palestinian people.

The Creation of Israel: A Victory for Zionism, A Catastrophe for Palestinians, On May 14, 1948, the State of Israel was declared. While this marked the fulfillment of the Zionist dream of establishing a Jewish state in Palestine, it also marked the beginning of a new chapter of suffering and displacement for the Palestinian people. The 1948 Arab-Israeli War, fought between the newly established Israeli state and neighboring Arab countries, led to a decisive Israeli victory, and Israel gained control over more territory than was allocated to it under the UN partition plan.

The creation of Israel in 1948 was accompanied by the mass displacement of Palestinians. The Nakba resulted in the creation of a Palestinian refugee crisis that has lasted to this day. More than 700,000 Palestinians were forced to flee their homes, many of whom ended up in refugee camps across the Middle East. These refugees, and their descendants, have been denied the right to return to their homes, a situation that remains one of the key issues in the Israeli-Palestinian conflict.

For Palestinians, the creation of Israel was not a moment of liberation but of catastrophe. It marked the loss of their homeland and the beginning of a long struggle for justice, recognition, and the right to return. The Zionist narrative, which frames the establishment of Israel as a triumph for Jews, overlooks the immense suffering inflicted on the Palestinian people. While Jews were given a homeland in response to their history of persecution, Palestinians were left to endure the consequences of this decision.

A Colonial Project of Dispossession, Zionism has long been criticized for its colonialist roots. The movement was not merely about creating a safe haven for Jews; it was about establishing a Jewish state at the expense of the indigenous Palestinian population. The creation of Israel was not a peaceful process of coexistence but a violent campaign to eradicate Palestinian presence from the land. The Zionist project, which was aided by British colonial support, sought to create a Jewish-majority state through the displacement and dispossession of Palestinians.

While the Zionist movement justifies its actions by pointing to the historical connection of Jews to the land and the horrors of the Holocaust, it fails to recognize the rights of Palestinians, who had lived on the land for generations. The creation of Israel, based on the Zionist agenda, was a betrayal of Palestinian rights and a violation of international law. The ongoing Israeli occupation of Palestinian territories, the construction of settlements on Palestinian land, and the systematic oppression of Palestinians have only exacerbated the injustices of 1948.

The Palestinian Struggle for Justice

The creation of Israel in 1948 marked a monumental moment in the history of the Jewish people, offering a homeland after centuries of persecution, culminating in the Holocaust. However, for the Palestinians, the establishment of Israel represented the beginning of an ongoing tragedy. The consequences of Zionism's colonialist ideology have led to decades of displacement, dispossession, and the denial of basic human rights, which continue to affect the Palestinian people to this day.

The struggle of the Palestinians is not just one of territorial disputes but of fundamental human rights and justice. It is a fight for survival, dignity, and recognition in the face of overwhelming odds. The global community, however, has often turned a blind eye to the plight of the Palestinians, leading to a situation where their rights continue to be denied and their suffering largely ignored by many. This essay delves deeply into the complexities of the Palestinian struggle, offering detailed narratives, case studies, and interviews to explore the injustice that underpins their fight, the resilience of Palestinian resistance, and the urgent need for a just resolution that recognizes Palestinian rights, including the right to return, self-determination, and sovereignty.

The Roots of the Palestinian Struggle: The Nakba, The Palestinian struggle for justice begins with the Nakba, the Arabic word for "catastrophe," which describes the events surrounding the creation of Israel in 1948. The Nakba led to the displacement of more than 750,000 Palestinian Arabs from their ancestral homes. The loss of homes, land, and livelihoods caused by the formation of Israel is still felt by Palestinians, both those who were directly affected and their descendants. In interviews with Palestinian refugees, many recount vivid memories of life before 1948: bustling cities, fertile lands, and thriving communities that were abruptly destroyed.

One of the stories that stand out is that of Fawzi, now in his 70s, who was just a boy when his family was forced to flee their home in Haifa. "I remember the houses, the streets, the sound of children playing," he says. "We were forced out, and now my children and grandchildren live as refugees in Lebanon. They have never known their homeland." Fawzi's narrative is echoed by countless other Palestinians who live in refugee camps across the Middle East, waiting for the day when they might return to their homes, even though they are often told that such a dream is impossible.

The Nakba represents not just the physical loss of land but the loss of cultural heritage and identity. Palestinians were not only uprooted from their homes but from their sense of self. Their villages were destroyed, their towns erased from maps, and their right to return to their land systematically denied. This collective trauma continues to shape the Palestinian national identity and is at the heart of their ongoing struggle for justice.

Zionism and Colonialism, At the core of the Palestinian struggle lies the ideology of Zionism, which advocated for the establishment of a Jewish homeland in Palestine, a land that was already inhabited by Arabs. Zionism, from its inception, was closely tied to colonialism. It viewed Palestine as an empty land, ready to be "settled" by Jewish immigrants, who were to establish a state on land that had been inhabited for centuries by Palestinian Arabs. This colonialist ideology was facilitated by the British Empire, which controlled Palestine under the British Mandate between 1917 and 1948.

Zionism's colonial undertones are often overlooked or minimized in mainstream discourse, but the consequences of this ideology are undeniable. It was not simply a question of establishing a Jewish homeland; it was about the displacement of an indigenous population to make way for this vision. The settlers were not merely immigrants seeking refuge; they were part of a broader colonial enterprise that sought to control and dominate a land and its people. In this context, Palestinians became the victims of a larger geopolitical game in which their rights and their humanity were often disregarded.

The impact of Zionism's colonialism can be seen in the policies that Israel has implemented since its founding. From the creation of illegal settlements in the occupied territories to the construction of the Apartheid Wall, these policies continue to displace Palestinians from their land and restrict their ability to live freely. The ongoing occupation of the West Bank, the siege of Gaza, and the systemic discrimination against Palestinian citizens of Israel are all manifestations of the colonial legacy of Zionism.

Palestinian Resistance: A Struggle for Survival, Despite the immense challenges, the Palestinian people have not given up their fight for justice. Resistance to Israeli occupation has taken many forms over the years, from armed struggle to nonviolent protests, and the spirit of resistance remains strong among Palestinians, both in Palestine and in the diaspora.

One prominent example of Palestinian resistance is the First and Second Intifadas (1987–1993 and 2000–2005). These uprisings were spontaneous and were fueled by the frustration of living under Israeli occupation. The Palestinians, who had long been subjected to violent repression, were no longer willing to silently accept their status as second-class citizens. The Intifadas drew attention to the brutality of the occupation and the oppression faced by Palestinians in their daily lives.

However, the resistance has not always been violent. The nonviolent resistance movement, led by figures such as the late Palestinian leader Yasser Arafat, and later by organizations like the Boycott, Divestment, and Sanctions (BDS) movement, has garnered significant international support. Palestinians have used boycotts, demonstrations, and campaigns to challenge Israel's policies and bring attention to the injustice of their situation. The BDS movement, in particular, has raised awareness about the human rights violations in Palestine and has been effective in pressuring governments and corporations to take action.

Interviews with Palestinian activists show the deep commitment to nonviolence despite the oppression. Samira, a young Palestinian woman who is active in the BDS movement, explains, *"Our resistance is about showing the world the truth of what is happening in Palestine. It is not about violence, but about raising awareness, educating people, and making them realize that this is not just a conflict, but a struggle for our human rights."*

The Global Response: Silence and Complicity, One of the most troubling aspects of the Palestinian struggle for justice is the global community's response, or lack thereof. The United Nations, while passing numerous resolutions condemning Israeli actions, has often failed to hold Israel accountable for its violations of international law. Countries such as the United States have historically provided unconditional support to Israel, often blocking resolutions at the UN and providing military aid to the Israeli government.

This global silence and complicity have allowed Israel to continue its policies of occupation and repression with little consequence. Palestinian civilians have been subjected to violence, displacement, and economic deprivation, while the world looks on without taking meaningful action to address the root causes of the conflict.

Palestinian leaders, such as Mahmud Abbas, have often expressed frustration with the international community's failure to take a stand. *"The world watches as we suffer,"* Abbas said in a speech at the United Nations. "We are left to fight alone for our rights, for our freedom, and for our dignity."

The Path to Justice: The Right to Return, Self-Determination, and Sovereignty, The Palestinian struggle for justice cannot be fully realized without addressing the key issues at the heart of the conflict. First and foremost is the right of Palestinians to return to their homes. The right of return is enshrined in international law, yet it has been systematically denied by Israel. Palestinian refugees, who have lived in camps for generations, still hold onto the keys to their homes, dreaming of the day they can return.

Another crucial issue is the recognition of Palestinian self-determination. Palestinians have the right to govern themselves and determine their own future. This includes the establishment of a sovereign Palestinian state based on the pre-1967 borders, with East Jerusalem as its capital. Until these rights are recognized, the conflict will remain unresolved.

Finally, the international community must take concrete steps to end the occupation and hold Israel accountable for its violations of human rights. This means ensuring that Palestinians have access to their land, resources, and the ability to live in peace and security, without fear of displacement or violence.

A Call for Justice, The Palestinian struggle for justice is not just a political issue; it is a moral one. The world cannot remain indifferent to the suffering of an entire people who have been denied their basic rights for over seven decades. The recognition of Palestinian rights, including the right to return, self-determination, and sovereignty, is essential for achieving a just and lasting peace in the region. Until then, the conflict will remain an unresolved tragedy, with Zionism standing as a symbol of colonial oppression and Palestinian resistance. The global community must stand with the Palestinians and demand justice for their struggle.

The Rise of Zionism and Its Consequences: A Perspective

The rise of Zionism, culminating in the establishment of the State of Israel in 1948, represents one of the most contentious episodes in modern history. While often framed as a story of liberation and redemption for the Jewish people, Zionism's political and territorial ambitions came at an extraordinary cost to the indigenous Palestinian population. From its inception, the Zionist project has been criticized for its colonial underpinnings, its alignment with imperial powers, and its disregard for the rights and aspirations of the Arab population in Palestine. This narrative is not merely about the creation of a Jewish homeland but also about the dispossession, displacement, and systematic oppression of another people—a reality that continues to define the Israeli-Palestinian conflict.

Zionism's Ideological Foundations: A Colonial Framework, Zionism, as articulated by figures like Theodor Herzl, began as a nationalist response to the persecution of Jews in Europe. Herzl's Der Judenstaat argued for the establishment of a Jewish state as a solution to anti-Semitism, envisioning a refuge where Jews could live free from oppression. However, the vision of Zionism was inherently exclusionary and colonial in nature. It sought to create a Jewish state in a land already inhabited by a diverse population, particularly Palestinian Arabs, who had lived there for centuries.

From its earliest days, the Zionist movement relied on a strategy of land acquisition and demographic transformation, often at the expense of the local population. Herzl himself acknowledged the colonial nature of the project, writing in his diary that the Zionist state would function as "a wall of Europe against Asia," emphasizing its role in advancing Western interests in the region. This framework of settler colonialism, where an external population seeks to establish dominance over an indigenous one, became a defining feature of the Zionist enterprise.

The Role of Imperial Powers: Exploiting Palestine, The success of Zionism was deeply intertwined with the support of imperial powers, particularly Britain. The 1917 Balfour Declaration, in which Britain expressed support for the establishment of a Jewish national home in Palestine, exemplifies this dynamic. The declaration was issued without consulting the indigenous population and was driven largely by British strategic interests rather than genuine concern for Jewish welfare. It sought to secure Jewish support during World War I and to establish a foothold in the strategically significant Middle East.

The British Mandate for Palestine, established after World War I, institutionalized this alliance between Zionism and imperialism. British policies facilitated Jewish immigration and land purchases while marginalizing the Arab population. For Palestinians, this period marked the beginning of systematic dispossession. The influx of Jewish immigrants, combined with the development of Zionist institutions, created a parallel society that excluded and alienated the Arab population.

The Dispossession of Palestinians, The Zionist project's disregard for the indigenous population became increasingly evident in the years leading up to Israel's establishment. As Jewish immigration to Palestine increased in the 1920s and 1930s, often as a response to rising anti-Semitism in Europe, Palestinian Arabs found themselves marginalized in their own land. Zionist organizations like the Jewish National Fund actively pursued the purchase of land, often displacing Palestinian tenant farmers in the process.

The dispossession was not limited to land transactions. Zionist leaders, aware of the demographic realities in Palestine, began to discuss more aggressive methods of achieving a Jewish majority. Prominent figures like David Ben-Gurion openly acknowledged that the establishment of a Jewish state would require the removal of Palestinians from their land. These discussions laid the groundwork for what would become the Nakba, or "catastrophe," in 1948, when over 700,000 Palestinians were forcibly expelled or fled from their homes during the creation of Israel.

The Nakba: A Tragedy for Palestinians, The Nakba represents the culmination of Zionism's exclusionary and colonial logic. During the 1948 Arab-Israeli War, Zionist militias carried out a series of military operations aimed at securing territory for the nascent Jewish state. Villages were depopulated, homes were destroyed, and entire communities were uprooted. The infamous massacre at Deir Yassin, where over 100 Palestinian men, women, and children were killed, is just one example of the violence that accompanied the creation of Israel.

The aftermath of the Nakba left Palestinians in a state of permanent exile. Refugees were denied the right to return to their homes, in violation of international law, while their properties were confiscated by the Israeli state. Those who remained in Israel became second-class citizens, subject to systemic discrimination and exclusion. The establishment of Israel, celebrated by Zionists as a triumph, was experienced by Palestinians as a profound and enduring tragedy.

Zionism's Legacy of Oppression, Zionism's impact on Palestinians did not end with the Nakba. The 1967 Six-Day War, in which Israel captured the West Bank, Gaza Strip, and East Jerusalem, marked the beginning of a brutal military occupation that continues to this day. Under the guise of security, Israel has subjected Palestinians in these territories to widespread human rights abuses, including land confiscation, home demolitions, and the construction of illegal settlements.

The settlement enterprise, a direct continuation of Zionism's colonial ethos, has further entrenched the dispossession of Palestinians. By creating "facts on the ground," Israel has made the prospect of a viable Palestinian state increasingly remote. Meanwhile, the blockade of Gaza has turned the territory into what has been described as an "open-air prison," where two million Palestinians live under dire conditions.

Competing Narratives: A False Equivalence One of Zionism's most insidious legacies is the narrative it has constructed to justify its actions. Proponents of Zionism often frame the Israeli-Palestinian conflict as a clash of two equal and competing national movements. This narrative obscures the reality of power dynamics in the region, where Israel, as a militarily and economically dominant state, systematically oppresses a stateless and fragmented Palestinian population.

Zionist narratives also rely heavily on the invocation of historical and religious claims to justify the establishment of Israel. While Jewish historical ties to the land are undeniable, these claims do not negate the rights of the Palestinian population, who have lived in the region for generations. The selective use of history to legitimize dispossession highlights the moral and intellectual shortcomings of Zionist ideology.

Human Stories of Displacement and Resistance, The human cost of Zionism is best understood through the stories of those who have lived its consequences. Consider the experience of a Palestinian family forced to flee their village during the Nakba, now living as refugees in Lebanon. Their descendants, denied citizenship and basic rights, continue to endure the legacy of their displacement. Contrast this with the experience of an Israeli settler, whose home in the West Bank was built on land confiscated from Palestinian owners. These stories underscore the profound injustice at the heart of the Zionist project.

Despite decades of oppression, Palestinians have resisted Zionism through various means, from armed struggle to nonviolent activism. Movements like the Boycott, Divestment, Sanctions (BDS) campaign seek to hold Israel accountable for its violations of international law and to challenge the structures of apartheid that Zionism has created.

A Call for Accountability, Zionism, far from being a benign nationalist movement, has proven to be a project of dispossession and oppression. Its success in establishing a Jewish state came at the expense of the Palestinian people, whose rights and aspirations were systematically denied. The ongoing Israeli-Palestinian conflict is not simply the result of intractable differences but a direct consequence of Zionism's colonial and exclusionary logic.

Critically examining Zionism is not an act of anti-Semitism but a necessary step toward understanding the roots of one of the world's most enduring conflicts. Any hope for a just resolution requires acknowledging the profound harm that Zionism has inflicted on Palestinians and holding Israel accountable for its actions. Only through a commitment to justice, equality, and the rights of all people can there be a future where both Israelis and Palestinians can live in peace and dignity.

Chapter 4: Palestinian Resistance to British Rule

In the early decades of the 20th century, the Palestinian resistance to British colonial rule was not merely an insurgency against imperial power. It was a multifaceted struggle for the survival of a people's identity, culture, and connection to their land. The British Mandate over Palestine, instituted under the League of Nations in 1922, served two overlapping agendas: enforcing British geopolitical dominance in the region and facilitating the Zionist project of establishing a Jewish homeland. For Palestinians, these overlapping goals represented a dual threat that jeopardized their existence, rights, and heritage.

As Palestinian resistance unfolded, it exposed not only the brutality of British colonial policies but also the calculated strategies of the Zionist movement. Through protests, strikes, guerrilla warfare, and cultural resilience, the Palestinian people sought to confront these overlapping forces, leaving behind a legacy of resistance and defiance that continues to resonate today.

The Balfour Declaration and the Roots of Discontent, The roots of Palestinian resistance can be traced to the Balfour Declaration of 1917, which expressed Britain's support for a *"national home for the Jewish people"* in Palestine. The declaration ignored the rights and aspirations of the Arab majority, who constituted over 90% of the population. This imperial edict was issued without the consent of the indigenous population and laid the groundwork for the dispossession and displacement of Palestinians.

When Britain assumed control of Palestine following World War I, it formalized its mandate with the League of Nations. Palestinian leaders initially sought dialogue with the British, hoping to reconcile their demands for self-determination with Britain's colonial objectives. Delegations were sent to London, and petitions were drafted, but these efforts were met with dismissive responses. The British administration's overt favoritism towards the Zionist movement—through policies encouraging Jewish immigration and land acquisition—fueled widespread anger among Palestinians.

Zionist Encroachment and Palestinian Displacement, Zionist organizations, supported by British policies, systematically acquired land in Palestine, often displacing Palestinian farmers and disrupting agrarian communities. The Jewish National Fund and other Zionist institutions implemented strategies to purchase land and then prohibit Palestinian tenant farmers from working on it. This practice severed the indigenous population from their livelihoods, intensifying social and economic inequalities. For Palestinians, these actions were not merely economic disruptions but existential threats. Entire villages were depopulated, and traditional ways of life were undermined. This calculated effort to establish Zionist control over land ignited a collective sense of injustice among Palestinians, laying the foundation for organized resistance.

Early Resistance and Leadership, Initially, Palestinian resistance took the form of peaceful protests, petitions, and political organizing. Prominent figures such as Hajj Amin al-Husseini, the Grand Mufti of Jerusalem, emerged as leaders of the resistance. Al-Husseini's efforts included mobilizing Palestinians against land sales to Zionist organizations and organizing mass demonstrations. However, the British consistently dismissed these nonviolent approaches, emboldened by their military dominance and colonial prerogatives.

By the 1930s, the failure of peaceful methods and the intensification of Zionist settlement efforts led to widespread frustration among Palestinians. Grassroots leaders began advocating for more direct forms of resistance, marking a shift from diplomacy to defiance.

The 1936 General Strike: A Unified Movement, The 1936–1939 Arab Revolt was a watershed moment in Palestinian resistance. It began with a six-month general strike, organized by the Arab Higher Committee (AHC), to protest British policies favoring Zionist immigration and land acquisition. The strike paralyzed economic activity across Palestine and demonstrated the Palestinians' capacity for unity and collective action. Workers, shopkeepers, and farmers alike participated in this unprecedented act of civil disobedience.

However, the strike's success came at a steep cost. The British authorities, alarmed by the scale of the protests, responded with mass arrests, censorship, and violent crackdowns. The leadership of the AHC was exiled or imprisoned, creating a leadership vacuum that hindered the movement's ability to sustain its momentum.

The Arab Revolt: Armed Resistance and Its Suppression, The general strike eventually escalated into armed rebellion, with guerrilla fighters—often referred to as *"fellahin"* (peasants)—leading the charge. Villages became hubs of resistance, and fighters launched attacks on British military installations and Zionist settlements. Leaders such as Izz ad-Din al-Qassam emerged as symbols of defiance. Al-Qassam's grassroots mobilization of impoverished Palestinians emphasized self-reliance and the necessity of armed struggle against colonialism and Zionism.

The British response to the revolt was brutal. Colonial forces employed aerial bombardments, collective punishments, and mass executions to suppress the uprising. Entire villages were razed, and thousands of Palestinians were killed or imprisoned. By the time the revolt was crushed in 1939, over 5,000 Palestinians had died, and tens of thousands had been exiled or displaced.

The Legacy of Izz ad-Din al-Qassam, Izz ad-Din al-Qassam's legacy is a cornerstone of Palestinian resistance history. Born in Syria, al-Qassam moved to Palestine in the 1920s and dedicated his life to organizing resistance against British colonialism and Zionist expansion. His emphasis on grassroots mobilization resonated deeply with rural Palestinians who bore the brunt of land dispossession.

In 1935, al-Qassam led a small group of fighters in a series of skirmishes against British forces. Though his group was eventually overpowered, and al-Qassam was killed in action, his martyrdom galvanized the Palestinian resistance movement. Today, his name endures as a symbol of steadfastness, with militant groups like the Izz ad-Din al-Qassam Brigades drawing inspiration from his legacy.

The Role of Women in Resistance, Women played a significant but often overlooked role in Palestinian resistance. They organized protests, smuggled weapons, and provided logistical support to fighters. Figures like Nabiha Nasir and Tarab Abdul Hadi emerged as leaders, advocating for national rights and challenging traditional gender norms. Women's contributions to the resistance demonstrated the inclusivity and resilience of the movement, underscoring the broad-based nature of Palestinian defiance.

Zionist Collaboration with British Authorities, A critical examination of Zionist actions during this period reveals their strategic collaboration with British authorities. The Haganah, a Jewish paramilitary organization, provided intelligence and logistical support to British forces during the Arab Revolt. This alliance enabled the Zionist movement to consolidate its position while the British suppressed Palestinian resistance.

Zionist leaders, including David Ben-Gurion, viewed this collaboration as a pragmatic means to advance their goals. However, for Palestinians, it underscored the systematic marginalization they faced and the formidable challenge of confronting both a colonial power and a well-organized Zionist movement.

The Aftermath and Legacy, The suppression of the 1936–1939 revolt marked a turning point in Palestinian history. While the revolt failed to achieve its immediate objectives, it left a lasting impact on Palestinian political consciousness. The sacrifices made during this period cemented a collective identity rooted in resistance and resilience *("sumud")*. The stories of fighters, organizers, and ordinary citizens who defied British rule continue to inspire contemporary struggles for justice and self-determination.

At the same time, the revolt exposed the challenges of internal divisions. Rivalries between elite families, such as the Husseinis and Nashashibis, often undermined the movement's unity. Additionally, the lack of external support and the overwhelming power of British and Zionist forces created insurmountable obstacles for the Palestinian resistance.

The Palestinian resistance to British rule was a profound chapter in the history of anti-colonial struggles. It reflected the determination of a people to defend their rights and identity against imperial domination and settler colonialism. While the British Mandate ultimately facilitated the establishment of Israel, the resistance efforts of this era laid the groundwork for subsequent generations to continue the fight for Palestinian self-determination.

By critically examining the actions of both the British and Zionist movements during this period, we gain a deeper understanding of the systemic injustices that shaped the conflict. The legacy of Palestinian resistance remains a testament to the enduring spirit of a people striving for justice and sovereignty in the face of immense adversity.

The Roots of Discontent: Imperial Interests, Zionist Ambitions, and Palestinian Resistance

The British Mandate in Palestine (1920–1948) is often seen as a critical period that laid the groundwork for the prolonged Israeli-Palestinian conflict. Far from being a neutral administrative authority, the British Mandate was a calculated extension of imperial ambitions in the Middle East. Rooted in the geopolitical calculus of the post-World War I era, British policies in Palestine catered disproportionately to Zionist interests, sidelining the rights and aspirations of the indigenous Palestinian Arab population. The dynamics of the Mandate period reveal a complex interplay of colonial power, Zionist state-building, and Palestinian resistance, all of which remain central to understanding the ongoing conflict.

The Balfour Declaration: A Catalyst for Conflict, At the heart of the British Mandate's contentious legacy lies the Balfour Declaration of 1917. This brief but consequential document declared British support for the establishment of a *"national home for the Jewish people"* in Palestine. What it left unsaid was equally significant: the rights of the Arab majority, who constituted over 90% of the population at the time, were scarcely mentioned. The vague assurance that *"nothing shall be done which may prejudice the civil and religious rights of existing non-Jewish communities"* failed to recognize the political and national aspirations of the Palestinian Arabs, effectively treating them as an afterthought.

The Balfour Declaration was not an act of humanitarianism; it was a strategic move designed to secure Zionist support during World War I. British leaders, including Prime Minister David Lloyd George and Foreign Secretary Arthur Balfour, saw the Zionist movement as a useful ally in securing British influence in the Middle East. By aligning with Zionist ambitions, Britain hoped to bolster its standing among influential Jewish communities worldwide and to counter French ambitions in the region.

The British Mandate: Colonialism Disguised as Custodianship, The League of Nations formalized British control over Palestine in

1922, granting the Mandate authority to implement the terms of the Balfour Declaration. However, the British Mandate was not a neutral framework for governance; it was a colonial project that prioritized British strategic interests and Zionist objectives. Palestine became a key component of Britain's Middle Eastern empire, linking the Suez Canal to oil-rich territories in Iraq and safeguarding routes to India.

British policies during this period consistently favored the Zionist project, enabling the establishment of Jewish settlements while undermining Palestinian society. The Zionist movement, spearheaded by organizations like the Jewish Agency and the Histadrut (a labor federation), worked closely with British authorities to build the foundations of a future Jewish state. These efforts included land acquisition, economic development, and the creation of paramilitary organizations like the Haganah, which would later become the core of the Israeli Defense Forces.

For Palestinians, the British Mandate represented an era of systematic dispossession and marginalization. The introduction of Western legal frameworks disrupted traditional land ownership practices, allowing Zionist organizations to acquire large tracts of land. This process often displaced Palestinian tenant farmers, leaving them impoverished and landless. British policies, such as the issuance of land ordinances, disproportionately benefited Jewish settlers, exacerbating social and economic disparities.

The Land Question: A Source of Struggle, Land ownership became one of the most contentious issues during the Mandate period. Zionist organizations, supported by international fundraising efforts, purchased land from absentee Arab landlords, often resulting in the eviction of Palestinian peasants. The Jewish National Fund (JNF), a key player in this process, acquired land explicitly for the purpose of establishing Jewish settlements, adhering to a policy that prohibited the resale or leasing of land to non-Jews.

The dispossession of Palestinian farmers had far-reaching consequences. In addition to economic hardship, it fueled a sense of existential threat among Palestinians, who saw their ancestral lands being transformed into exclusive Jewish enclaves. By the late 1930s, Jewish land ownership had increased significantly, contributing to rising tensions and outbreaks of violence.

One illustrative case is the displacement of Palestinian villagers from the fertile Jezreel Valley. Known as the *"breadbasket"* of Palestine, this region saw extensive land purchases by Zionist organizations, which transformed the agricultural landscape into a network of kibbutzim (collective farms). While Zionists celebrated these settlements as symbols of progress and nation-building, Palestinians viewed them as instruments of colonial domination. The dispossession of Palestinian farmers in the Jezreel Valley became emblematic of the broader conflict over land and resources.

Palestinian Resistance: Early Struggles and the Arab Revolt, Palestinian opposition to British and Zionist policies took various forms, ranging from petitions and protests to armed uprisings. The first major eruption of violence occurred in 1929, when tensions over access to the Western Wall in Jerusalem escalated into widespread riots. The violence left hundreds dead and underscored the deep divisions between the Jewish and Arab communities. For Palestinians, the 1929 riots were not merely about religious disputes but a broader expression of anger and frustration at their marginalization under British rule.

The most significant act of Palestinian resistance during the Mandate period was the Arab Revolt of 1936–1939. Sparked by a combination of economic grievances, political disillusionment, and fears of continued Jewish immigration, the revolt began with a general strike and escalated into a full-scale insurgency. Palestinian fighters targeted British installations, Zionist settlements, and infrastructure, seeking to disrupt the colonial system that had facilitated their dispossession.

The British response was swift and brutal. Military campaigns, mass arrests, and the destruction of villages were employed to crush the revolt. By the time it ended, thousands of Palestinians had been killed, and the leadership of the Arab nationalist movement had been decimated. The revolt left Palestinian society fragmented and weakened, a condition that would have dire consequences during the subsequent 1947–1948 conflict.

Zionist State-Building: A Double-Edged Sword, While Palestinians were engaged in reactive resistance, the Zionist movement pursued a proactive and cohesive strategy to build the institutions of a future state. Under the leadership of figures like David Ben-Gurion and Chaim Weizmann, Zionist organizations established schools, hospitals, and economic networks, laying the groundwork for an independent Jewish state. The Haganah, initially formed as a defensive militia, evolved into a highly organized paramilitary force capable of offensive operations.

Zionist leaders also worked to secure international support for their cause, leveraging diplomatic connections in Britain, the United States, and beyond. These efforts paid off during World War II, when the plight of Jewish refugees fleeing Nazi persecution garnered global sympathy for the Zionist project. However, the success of Zionist state-building came at a steep cost for Palestinians, who were increasingly marginalized in their own homeland.

The Human Cost: Stories of Loss and Betrayal, The Mandate period witnessed profound human suffering, particularly among Palestinians who faced displacement, poverty, and violence. Villages like Lifta, Deir Yassin, and Jaffa became symbols of the Palestinian Nakba *("catastrophe")*, as their residents were uprooted and their communities destroyed. Oral histories from survivors of this era reveal the depth of Palestinian despair, as families lost their homes, livelihoods, and sense of security.

For many Palestinians, the British Mandate is remembered as a period of betrayal. British officials, who had promised to act as impartial custodians, consistently prioritized Zionist aspirations over the rights of the Arab majority. This sense of betrayal was compounded by the realization that the Zionist movement, far from being a benign project, often relied on exclusionary and militaristic methods to achieve its goals.

Critiquing Zionism: The Colonial Dimension, A critical examination of Zionist ideology reveals its colonial underpinnings. Early Zionist leaders framed their project as a civilizing mission, bringing modernity to a supposedly *"undeveloped"* land. This narrative ignored the rich history and culture of Palestinian society, portraying the land as empty and its inhabitants as obstacles to progress. The slogan *"a land without a people for a people without a land"* exemplifies this erasure, as it denied the existence and rights of the Palestinian people.

Zionist militancy further exacerbated tensions. Groups like the Irgun and the Stern Gang carried out acts of terrorism, including the bombing of the King David Hotel in 1946, which killed 91 people. These actions not only targeted British authorities but also sought to intimidate and displace Palestinians, reinforcing the perception that Zionism was an exclusionary and expansionist project.

Legacy and Lessons, The British Mandate in Palestine left a legacy of conflict, dispossession, and enduring injustice. By aligning with Zionist interests while neglecting the rights of the Palestinian majority, Britain created a framework that prioritized colonial ambition over human rights. The seeds of discontent sown during this period continue to shape the Israeli-Palestinian conflict, underscoring the need for a critical reassessment of history.

Addressing this legacy requires acknowledging the injustices of the past and fostering a dialogue that respects the rights and aspirations of all people in the region. Only by confronting these historical realities can the path to a just and equitable future be paved.

The Great Arab Revolt (1936-1939)

The Great Arab Revolt of 1936-1939 stands as a watershed moment in the history of Palestinian resistance. It was not merely a reactionary uprising but a bold and comprehensive rejection of British colonial rule and the rapid encroachment of Zionist expansionism. This revolt emerged from a growing sense of urgency among Palestinians who saw their homeland being systematically colonized and their societal future at risk of obliteration. The movement began as a general strike against discriminatory British policies but soon escalated into a full-scale rebellion, marked by widespread strikes, boycotts, and armed resistance.

Root Causes and Rising Tensions, The seeds of the revolt were sown in the aftermath of World War I, as the British Mandate of Palestine, established under the terms of the 1917 Balfour Declaration, systematically prioritized Zionist aspirations over the rights of the indigenous Palestinian population. British policies facilitated Jewish immigration and land acquisition, often at the expense of Palestinian farmers and urban workers. Land dispossession led to social upheaval, with thousands of Palestinian peasants becoming landless and impoverished.

The growing imbalance was stark: Zionist organizations, supported by the British, acquired vast tracts of fertile land while Palestinians were either displaced or relegated to marginal territories. Economic disparities deepened as Zionist settlers established a parallel economy that excluded Palestinians. This dual system of development fostered resentment and distrust, creating fertile ground for the rebellion. The simmering tensions were exacerbated by the lack of political representation for Palestinians, as the British administration consistently marginalized their voices while favoring Zionist interests.

The Role of Leadership, At the forefront of the revolt was Haj Amin al-Husseini, the Grand Mufti of Jerusalem. Appointed in 1921, al-Husseini emerged as a unifying figure for Palestinian resistance. His leadership combined religious authority with political acumen, enabling him to rally diverse factions within Palestinian society. Al-Husseini articulated a vision of Palestinian Arab unity against both Zionist encroachment and British imperialism.

Under al-Husseini's guidance, the revolt began with a six-month general strike in 1936, which paralyzed the economy. Palestinian workers and merchants boycotted British goods and services, while organized groups disrupted transportation and communication networks. The strike's scale and effectiveness demonstrated the Palestinians' capacity for collective action, drawing international attention to their plight.

Al-Husseini's leadership extended beyond the immediate context of Palestine. He worked to garner support from Arab states and the broader Muslim world, emphasizing the shared threat posed by colonialism and Zionism. While his efforts were not always successful, they underscored the transnational dimensions of the Palestinian struggle.

While al-Husseini's leadership was instrumental, it was not without controversy. His alignment with the Axis powers during World War II cast a long shadow over his legacy. Critics argue that his overtures to Nazi Germany and Fascist Italy undermined the moral standing of the Palestinian cause. However, supporters contend that al-Husseini's actions must be understood within the context of desperation and limited options, as he sought alliances to counter British and Zionist dominance.

Strategies of Resistance, The revolt's tactics ranged from peaceful protests to armed insurrection. Strikes and boycotts targeted the British economy, aiming to disrupt colonial governance. Armed groups, often operating from rural areas, launched guerrilla attacks against British military installations, Zionist settlements, and collaborators. These acts of resistance demonstrated the Palestinians' determination to defend their land and rights.

The armed struggle was marked by ingenuity and resourcefulness. Militants used the rugged terrain of Palestine to their advantage, employing hit-and-run tactics against better-equipped British forces. Despite their limited resources, Palestinian fighters managed to inflict significant damage on British infrastructure, including railways and pipelines. The revolt's decentralized nature allowed various factions to operate independently, making it difficult for the British to suppress the movement entirely.

One notable example of resistance was the formation of local committees that coordinated efforts across villages and towns. These grassroots organizations played a crucial role in sustaining the rebellion by providing logistical support, intelligence, and morale-boosting propaganda. Women also played a significant role, participating in protests, smuggling arms, and supporting the fighters in various capacities. Their contributions, though often overlooked in historical narratives, were vital to the revolt's endurance.

British Repression, The British response to the revolt was brutal and uncompromising. Martial law was imposed, and collective punishments were meted out to Palestinian communities suspected of harboring rebels. Entire villages were destroyed, and thousands of Palestinians were arrested or deported. The British deployed tens of thousands of troops, supported by the Royal Air Force, to crush the uprising. Mass executions, detention without trial, and widespread torture were commonplace, reflecting the colonial administration's determination to maintain control.

One particularly egregious example of British repression was the execution of Fawzi al-Qawuqji, a prominent Palestinian leader, who was captured and summarily executed as a warning to others. The use of aerial bombardments against civilian areas further underscored the lengths to which the British were willing to go to suppress dissent. These acts of violence not only devastated Palestinian society but also sowed long-term animosity towards the British and their Zionist allies.

The Zionist Role While the British were the primary targets of Palestinian resistance, Zionist militias and settlements also came under attack. The revolt's escalation prompted the formation of Jewish paramilitary organizations, such as the Haganah, which collaborated with British forces to suppress the rebellion. This collaboration deepened Palestinian resentment and reinforced perceptions of Zionists as complicit in colonial oppression.

Zionist leaders, including David Ben-Gurion, viewed the revolt as an opportunity to strengthen their position in Palestine. The Haganah's role in assisting British operations demonstrated the alignment of Zionist and British interests during this period. However, this alliance was not without tension, as the Zionist movement harbored long-term aspirations for independence from British rule. The Haganah's actions, combined with the growing influx of Jewish immigrants, exacerbated the demographic and economic pressures on Palestinians, further fueling the revolt.

The Aftermath, By 1939, the Great Arab Revolt had been effectively crushed. The British, with significant support from Zionist forces, reasserted control over Palestine. Thousands of Palestinians were killed, injured, or imprisoned during the revolt, and the infrastructure of resistance was severely weakened. The revolt's failure marked a turning point, as the Palestinian leadership was left fragmented and demoralized.

The British government's response to the revolt culminated in the 1939 White Paper, which proposed restrictions on Jewish immigration and land purchases in Palestine. While the White Paper was intended to placate Palestinian demands, it was seen as too little, too late. Moreover, it alienated Zionist leaders, who intensified their efforts to establish a Jewish state. The failure of the White Paper to address the root causes of the conflict ensured that tensions would continue to escalate in the years to come.

Critical Reflections, The Great Arab Revolt remains a defining chapter in Palestinian history, highlighting both the resilience and limitations of the resistance movement. The revolt underscored the Palestinians' determination to assert their rights in the face of overwhelming odds. However, it also exposed deep fractures within Palestinian society and leadership, which hindered the movement's effectiveness.

The role of Zionist organizations during this period warrants critical examination. While often portrayed as a nascent national movement, Zionist actions during the revolt revealed a willingness to collaborate with colonial powers to advance their objectives. This alignment with British interests came at the expense of Palestinian aspirations and contributed to the enduring conflict. The impact of Zionist propaganda, which portrayed the revolt as a purely violent and reactionary movement, further marginalized the Palestinian narrative in global discourse.

Lessons and Legacy, The Great Arab Revolt's legacy continues to resonate in contemporary Palestinian struggles. It serves as a reminder of the costs of disunity and the importance of cohesive leadership in the face of external threats. The revolt also highlights the enduring challenges posed by colonialism and settler colonialism, as Palestinians continue to grapple with dispossession and occupation.

While the revolt ultimately failed to achieve its immediate goals, it laid the groundwork for subsequent generations of resistance. The sacrifices of those who participated in the revolt remain a source of inspiration for Palestinians seeking justice and self-determination. At the same time, the revolt's limitations underscore the need for strategic planning, international solidarity, and unity to overcome systemic oppression.

In retrospect, the Great Arab Revolt of 1936-1939 was not merely a historical event but a profound expression of a people's determination to resist erasure and assert their right to exist on their ancestral land. Its lessons remain relevant, offering both cautionary tales and sources of inspiration for those engaged in the ongoing struggle for Palestinian liberation. The revolt's story continues to be a testament to the resilience of a dispossessed people, and its memory serves as a rallying cry for justice in the face of enduring injustice.

The Role of Abdel Qader al-Husseini: A Heroic Leader of Palestinian Resistance

Abdel Qader al-Husseini remains one of the most pivotal and iconic figures in the history of the Palestinian resistance. His life, actions, and tragic death at the height of the 1948 war exemplify the passion, dedication, and sacrifice that defined the Palestinian struggle during one of the most formative and tragic periods in the region's history. A military leader, a strategist, and a symbol of Palestinian national identity, al-Husseini's legacy continues to inspire generations of Palestinians, embodying their fight for justice, freedom, and self-determination.

Early Life and Formation of Nationalist Ideals, Born in 1907 into the esteemed al-Husseini family, one of the most prominent political families in Palestine, Abdel Qader al-Husseini was raised in an environment steeped in the struggle for Palestinian independence. His family was not only influential politically but also held religious authority in the region, further embedding the values of resistance and leadership within him. The al-Husseinis were deeply involved in the nationalist movement and had a long history of standing against colonial and foreign domination. This rich legacy served as a backdrop for Abdel Qader's own journey into activism and leadership.

Al-Husseini's education was as varied as his political influences. He received his early education in Palestine, followed by studies in Cairo, where he was exposed to the growing tide of Arab nationalism and anti-colonial movements sweeping across the Middle East. His time in Egypt, a hub of intellectual and political ferment, sharpened his understanding of the Palestinian plight under British mandate rule and the growing Zionist project in Palestine. Al-Husseini, thus, was not only molded by his family's legacy but by the broader currents of anti-imperialist and nationalist thought that were gaining momentum in the Arab world.

The Great Arab Revolt of 1936-1939 proved to be a defining moment in the development of his political and military ideals. The revolt was a direct response to British colonial policies and the increasing Zionist immigration to Palestine, which many Palestinians viewed as a direct threat to their land and livelihood. Al-Husseini's involvement in the revolt marked his emergence as a leader among the Palestinian resistance, fighting not only for national sovereignty but also for the preservation of Palestinian culture, identity, and heritage. The British crackdown on the revolt, which included collective punishment, mass arrests, and widespread violence against civilians, solidified al-Husseini's resolve to continue the fight against colonial rule and Zionist encroachment.

A Heroic Military Leader During the 1948 War, As tensions in Palestine escalated in the aftermath of the United Nations Partition Plan of 1947, which proposed the division of the land into separate

Jewish and Arab states, Abdel Qader al-Husseini became a central figure in the Palestinian leadership. The plan, which Palestinians vehemently rejected, set the stage for the violent confrontations that would culminate in the 1948 Arab-Israeli War. Palestinians viewed the partition as an unjust imposition by the international community that disregarded their rights to the land on which they had lived for centuries. The reaction was one of defiance and resistance, and al-Husseini emerged as one of the key figures in organizing the Palestinian response.

Despite being vastly outnumbered and under-equipped compared to the well-funded and militarily superior Zionist forces, al-Husseini demonstrated remarkable leadership during the early stages of the 1948 war. His primary focus was on defending Jerusalem, the holy city that held profound religious, cultural, and political significance for Palestinians and Arabs at large. Al-Husseini's strategic insights and ability to unite disparate Palestinian factions were vital to the defense of the city in the face of Zionist attacks.

One of the most important military engagements that cemented al-Husseini's place in Palestinian history was his leadership in the defense of the village of Qastal. Situated along the road to Jerusalem, Qastal was a strategic location that both sides knew was critical for the success of their military objectives. Zionist forces, aiming to secure the road to Jerusalem, had captured the village. In response, al-Husseini took a bold step and personally led a counterattack to reclaim Qastal, despite the limited resources available to him. This operation showcased his tactical brilliance and his deep connection to the fighters who followed him. Even when faced with fierce opposition, al-Husseini's resolve never wavered, and his leadership in the operation helped instill a sense of purpose and courage in his men.

The Battle of Qastal: A Defining Moment, The Battle of Qastal in April 1948 marked not just a turning point in the military campaign but also in al-Husseini's life and the Palestinian resistance movement. In the weeks leading up to the battle, al-Husseini had been organizing a series of operations to disrupt Zionist military logistics and reclaim key strategic locations. The road to Jerusalem was one of the most contested areas, and the village of Qastal was crucial in securing access to the city. Al-Husseini recognized the strategic importance of the village and understood that its loss would significantly hinder Palestinian efforts to defend Jerusalem.

In one of his most daring military moves, al-Husseini led his forces in a direct assault on Qastal, seeking to reclaim it from Zionist control. His ability to inspire and rally his fighters was evident, as they managed to recapture the village. The victory, however, came at a great cost. During the battle, al-Husseini was tragically killed by a sniper's bullet. His death marked the loss of one of the most capable and charismatic leaders the Palestinian resistance had ever known.

Al-Husseini's death was a crushing blow not only to his fighters but to the Palestinian cause as a whole. His personal commitment to the struggle, his leadership in battle, and his unwavering belief in Palestinian self-determination had made him a symbol of hope for the Palestinian people. His martyrdom at the hands of the Zionist forces became a poignant symbol of both the heroism and tragedy that defined the Palestinian experience during the Nakba. Without al-Husseini's leadership, the Palestinian forces were unable to hold Qastal, and the village eventually fell back into Zionist hands, further exacerbating the suffering and dislocation of Palestinians in the face of the advancing Zionist army.

Legacy and Critique of Zionist Forces, Abdel Qader al-Husseini's legacy cannot be divorced from the broader historical context of Zionist expansionism and the British mandate's role in facilitating it. The Zionist movement, driven by both ideological conviction and geopolitical ambitions, pursued a strategy of territorial expansion that sought to displace and marginalize the indigenous Palestinian population. This period of violent upheaval, marked by the Nakba, saw over 700,000 Palestinians displaced from their homes as part of the Zionist effort to establish a Jewish state in Palestine.

Al-Husseini's resistance against the Zionist forces was a direct challenge to this colonial and settler project. His leadership and bravery were emblematic of the Palestinian struggle against foreign domination and the erasure of their cultural and national identity. However, despite his heroism, the Palestinian resistance was severely limited by a lack of resources, coordination, and external support. The Zionist forces, equipped with modern weapons, trained military personnel, and substantial financial backing from the West, held an overwhelming advantage.

The destruction of Palestinian villages, the massacres committed by Zionist forces, such as the Deir Yassin massacre, and the forced expulsions of Palestinians all contributed to the immense hardship and displacement experienced by the Palestinian people. Al-Husseini's resistance, although deeply symbolic and courageous, was unable to prevent the catastrophic consequences of the Zionist military campaign. This failure was not due to a lack of will or strategy on al-Husseini's part but rather to the stark imbalance of power between the two sides.

Personal Accounts and Interviews: A Hero's Legacy, The impact of Abdel Qader al-Husseini's leadership is captured most poignantly through the personal stories and testimonies of those who knew him or fought alongside him. Fighters who served under al-Husseini recall him as a leader who was always at the frontlines, sharing in the dangers and hardships of battle. One former fighter recounted: *"He was more than just a commander; he was a symbol of everything we were fighting for. His courage and presence made us believe we could win, even when everything seemed lost."*

Civilians who lived through the tumult of the 1948 war also remember al-Husseini not only as a military leader but as a symbol of hope and solidarity. An elderly resident of Jerusalem, recalling al-Husseini's visits to the neighborhoods during the height of the fighting, said: *"He wasn't just a general. He was our voice, our hope. He would encourage us, telling us to hold on, to stand firm. His words gave us strength."* These personal accounts underline the profound impact al-Husseini had on both his fighters and the Palestinian population, transcending his military role to become a unifying figure and a moral beacon for a people in crisis.

Broader Implications for Palestinian Resistance, Abdel Qader al-Husseini's life and leadership provide deep insights into both the potential and limitations of the Palestinian resistance during this critical period. His courage and tactical brilliance demonstrated the resolve of the Palestinian people to defend their homeland, but his death also highlighted the profound challenges that faced the Palestinian cause. The lack of centralized leadership, disorganization among Palestinian factions, and the overwhelming military superiority of the Zionist forces made it exceedingly difficult for Palestinians to mount a sustained defense of their land.

In the years following his death, the Palestinian resistance struggled to find another leader with al-Husseini's vision, charisma, and military acumen. His absence marked a turning point in the Palestinian struggle, one that underscored the importance of unity and strategic planning in the face of powerful adversaries.

A Hero's Enduring Legacy, Abdel Qader al-Husseini's life and death remain central to the Palestinian struggle for justice and self-determination. His leadership during the 1948 war, especially in the defense of Jerusalem and the Battle of Qastal, exemplifies the courage, determination, and sacrifice of a people fighting against seemingly insurmountable odds. His legacy, as both a military leader and a symbol of Palestinian resistance, endures to this day. Al-Husseini's martyrdom serves as a powerful reminder of the human cost of the Palestinian struggle for freedom and justice. His story, filled with both triumph and tragedy, continues to inspire new generations of Palestinians who are determined to continue the fight for their homeland, their dignity, and their right to self-determination.

Eyewitness Accounts of the Revolt: The Great Arab Revolt of 1936-1939 and Palestinian Resistance

The Great Arab Revolt of 1936-1939 is one of the most defining moments in Palestinian history. It was not merely a response to British colonial rule or Zionist settler colonialism; it was an assertion of Palestinian national identity and a statement of resistance against the forces that sought to erase that identity. Eyewitness accounts from Palestinians who lived through this tumultuous period provide invaluable insights into the realities of the revolt, capturing both the brutality of colonial and settler repression and the indomitable spirit of the Palestinian people. These testimonies offer a unique lens to understand the deeply embedded grievances that fueled the revolt and the broader struggle for self-determination, revealing the complex dynamics between Palestinians, the British mandate authorities, and Zionist forces.

The Origins of the Revolt and the Seeds of Palestinian Nationalism, To understand the significance of the Great Arab Revolt, it is essential to first examine the historical context in which it occurred. Palestine, under British mandate since 1917, was a land in turmoil. The Balfour Declaration of 1917, issued by the British government, had promised the establishment of a Jewish national home in Palestine. This declaration set the stage for the mass immigration of Jewish settlers to Palestine, facilitated by British authorities. For Palestinians, this was a grave violation of their rights and sovereignty over their own land. The indigenous Arab population, with its deep roots in the land stretching back centuries, viewed these developments as an existential threat.

By the mid-1930s, Palestinians were already grappling with the social, economic, and political consequences of Zionist colonization. The influx of Jewish immigrants had led to land expropriation, economic marginalization, and the erosion of Palestinian identity. Palestinian anger was compounded by the continued British support for Zionist expansion. Tensions reached a boiling point in 1936, when a series of incidents, including the killing of a prominent Palestinian leader, and the rapid expansion of Zionist settlements, led to widespread protests. The initial uprising began in April 1936, when the Arab Higher Committee, representing Palestinian Arabs, called for a general strike in protest of British policies and the continued Zionist encroachment on Palestinian land. The strike quickly expanded into a nationwide campaign, which included organized boycotts of British goods and resistance against Zionist settlers. It was during these early days that the revolt became more than a mere reaction to British repression; it became an assertion of Palestinian national consciousness.

One of the most powerful testimonies from this period comes from Ali, a member of the Arab Higher Committee, who described the strike as a *"first step towards our liberation."* He said, *"We were not just protesting against taxes or land policies. We were protesting against the entire system that allowed foreign settlers to take our homes, our land, and our dignity. The British were the administrators, the facilitators of this theft."*

Eyewitness Accounts from the Fighters: Voices of Resistance, The fighters who participated in the revolt were often drawn from various backgrounds—peasants, workers, and intellectuals—united by a common cause. The resistance was not centralized, but rather fragmented, with different groups and leaders organizing strikes, boycotts, and armed resistance in different parts of Palestine. The accounts from these fighters provide a vivid picture of the spirit of resistance that defined the revolt. Many of the eyewitnesses recall the early days of the strike with a sense of unity and determination, but also an acute awareness of the risks they faced.

One fighter, Hassan, a young man from the West Bank, recalled his decision to join the resistance: *"When the British soldiers came to our village and started arresting young men, burning homes, and destroying crops, I knew we had to fight back. It wasn't just about resisting the British; it was about defending our people, our homes. The Zionists were coming to take our land, and the British were helping them. We had no choice but to stand up."*

Hassan's words speak to the harsh reality faced by Palestinians: not only were they resisting colonial domination by the British, but they were also fighting against an incoming settler population whose goal was the displacement of the Palestinian Arabs. This dual battle created a unique and complex dynamic of resistance, with Palestinians fighting not just for independence but for their very survival.

Another fighter, Farid, who was part of the Al-Qassam Brigade—an armed group led by the legendary Palestinian leader Izz ad-Din al-Qassam—described the early battles of the revolt. *"We had no real weapons, but we knew the land like the back of our hands,"* Farid explained. *"We used guerrilla tactics, ambushing British convoys, sabotaging roads, and attacking Zionist settlements. The first few months were full of victories. It gave us hope that we could win."*

Farid's testimony reflects the strategic ingenuity of the Palestinian fighters, who relied on their intimate knowledge of the land to wage effective guerrilla warfare. These early successes, however, would be short-lived as British and Zionist forces responded with increasingly brutal methods. The escalation of violence would mark the rest of the revolt and would come at a devastating cost for the Palestinian resistance.

The Brutality of British and Zionist Repression, The British and Zionist response to the revolt was swift and brutal. The British army, supported by Zionist militias such as the Haganah and the Irgun, unleashed a campaign of terror designed to crush Palestinian resistance. This included mass arrests, executions of suspected leaders, and the imposition of collective punishments on Palestinian villages. British forces would often destroy entire villages in retaliation for attacks on their forces, leading to widespread displacement and suffering.

An account by a Palestinian elder, Abu Khaled, who witnessed the destruction of his village, reflects the horror faced by the Palestinian population: *"The soldiers came to our village in the dead of night, rounding up the men and boys, taking them away, and burning everything in sight. Our homes were destroyed, our fields burned. My father was arrested and beaten so badly that he never recovered. It was the British, working hand-in-hand with the Zionists, who did this to us."*

This account highlights the deeply entrenched collaboration between British authorities and Zionist forces during the revolt. While the British were officially responsible for maintaining law and order in Palestine, their actions often favored Zionist interests. British support for Zionist paramilitary groups, such as the Haganah, was evident in their shared tactics of repression, which involved violence against Palestinian civilians. The British military's widespread use of aerial bombardment and artillery against Palestinian towns and villages underscored the extreme asymmetry of the conflict.

The Zionist militias, meanwhile, engaged in their own campaigns of terror, aiming to intimidate Palestinians into submission. One such episode, the infamous Deir Yassin massacre in April 1948, which occurred after the end of the revolt but was rooted in the tactics used during it, involved the killing of over 100 Palestinian men, women, and children by the Irgun and Stern Gang. Eyewitnesses from Deir Yassin reported brutal killings, including the shooting of unarmed civilians and the raping of women, all under the guidance of Zionist forces. These acts of violence were part of a larger strategy of terror aimed at breaking the spirit of Palestinian resistance and forcing the population to flee their villages.

Zionist Policies: Displacement and Colonialism, The Great Arab Revolt was, at its heart, a fight against Zionist colonization. The testimonies from those who lived through the revolt consistently emphasize the connection between the violence of the revolt and the broader objectives of the Zionist movement: the establishment of a Jewish state through the displacement of the indigenous Palestinian population.

One of the key grievances expressed by Palestinians involved the systematic expropriation of their land by Zionist settlers. *"The Zionists didn't come here to live side by side with us,"* said Jamal, a farmer from the Galilee region. *"They came to take our land, to build their settlements, and to erase our history. It wasn't just about establishing a Jewish state—it was about making sure there was no room left for us."*

This sentiment reflects the Palestinian understanding of Zionist policies as a deliberate and systematic attempt to replace them with a Jewish population. Land confiscation, settlement expansion, and discriminatory laws were tools used by Zionist forces to ensure that Palestinians were marginalized and dispossessed.

Palestinian historians and scholars have pointed out that the Zionist movement, supported by the British, used the revolt as a means to further their colonial goals. Rather than seeing the revolt as a legitimate struggle for self-determination, Zionist leaders framed it as a disruption of peace and stability. The Palestinian resistance, therefore, was not only an act of national liberation but also a direct challenge to the very foundation of the Zionist project in Palestine.

The End of the Revolt and Its Legacy, By 1939, the revolt had largely been suppressed, but its impact on Palestinian consciousness was profound. It marked the first major attempt by Palestinians to resist the forces of colonialism and Zionism. Though the revolt ultimately failed to achieve its goals, it sowed the seeds for future resistance movements, including the Palestinian Liberation Organization (PLO) and the armed struggle that would define Palestinian politics for decades to come.

The legacy of the Great Arab Revolt lives on in the collective memory of the Palestinian people. It is remembered as a time of unity, defiance, and sacrifice—a moment when Palestinians stood firm against colonial oppression and the Zionist settler project. As one participant, Mariam, put it: *"We lost the battle, but we did not lose our dignity. We showed the world that we would not bow to foreign rule, and we would never give up our land."*

The revolt also revealed the inherent asymmetry of the conflict. Palestinians, outnumbered and outgunned, faced the full might of British imperialism and Zionist expansionism. Yet, despite these overwhelming odds, the Great Arab Revolt became a defining moment in Palestinian history, symbolizing the resilience of a people fighting for their homeland and identity.

The Great Arab Revolt of 1936-1939 remains a crucial event in the history of Palestinian resistance. Eyewitness accounts from those who lived through the revolt provide a powerful and deeply personal window into the brutality of British and Zionist repression, as well as the resilience and determination of the Palestinian people. These narratives highlight the central grievances that drove the revolt—dispossession, colonization, and the threat of erasure—and reveal the deep connection between the Palestinian struggle for self-determination and the broader fight against Zionist colonization. The revolt, while ultimately unsuccessful in achieving its immediate goals, became a catalyst for future resistance movements and a symbol of Palestinian resolve. Through these testimonies, the history of the revolt comes alive, offering valuable lessons for future generations in the ongoing struggle for justice and self-determination.

British White Papers and the Zionist Backlash: A Betrayal and Its Consequences

The British White Papers, particularly those issued in 1939, are among the most significant and controversial documents in the history of the Palestinian struggle for self-determination. For Palestinians, they were viewed as an act of betrayal by the British government, a betrayal that underscored the complex and often contradictory role Britain played in the region during its mandate over Palestine. These White Papers, particularly the 1939 version, were seen as a response to increasing pressure from the Arab population, but the implications were far more significant, as they symbolized the growing frustration of both Palestinians and Zionists over the British colonial policies that ultimately fueled the conflicts in the Middle East.

The 1939 White Paper, ostensibly issued to limit Jewish immigration and land acquisition in Palestine, aimed to quell Arab resentment toward Jewish settlement and appease the growing Palestinian nationalist movement. While it was viewed by many Palestinians as a partial victory in their long-standing struggle against Zionist colonization, it also represented a half-hearted attempt by Britain to placate both Palestinian Arabs and Zionists without truly addressing the root causes of the conflict—namely, Britain's continued support for the Zionist project, despite mounting Palestinian opposition.

The British Mandate over Palestine, which began after World War I in 1917, was marked by a series of promises and contradictions that sowed seeds of resentment among the Arab population. The Balfour Declaration, issued by the British government in 1917, had promised to support the establishment of a Jewish national home in Palestine. However, this promise was made without consulting the Arab population of Palestine, who were the indigenous inhabitants of the land. The Palestinian Arab population, which had lived in the region for centuries, felt betrayed by the Balfour Declaration, which they saw as an affront to their right to self-determination. Over the following decades, this tension would continue to escalate, leading to several uprisings and revolts against both British colonial rule and the growing Jewish settlement in the region.

The 1939 White Paper: A Turning Point in British Policy, The 1939 White Paper, issued by British Colonial Secretary Malcolm MacDonald, was Britain's attempt to find a middle ground in a situation that was rapidly spiraling out of control. Following the Arab Revolt of 1936-1939, which had been sparked by Palestinian opposition to British rule and Jewish immigration, the British government sought to address Palestinian grievances while maintaining its commitment to Zionist objectives. The White Paper proposed a cap of 75,000 Jewish immigrants to Palestine over the next five years, after which further immigration would be contingent upon the approval of the Palestinian Arab population. Additionally, the White Paper placed restrictions on land sales to Jews, a move intended to address Palestinian fears of land dispossession.

On the surface, the White Paper appeared to be a compromise, with some seeing it as a victory for Palestinian nationalists. The restriction on Jewish immigration was seen as a concession to Palestinian demands, as was the attempt to limit Jewish land acquisition in Palestine. However, the 1939 White Paper was deeply flawed. It did not call for the cessation of the Zionist project in Palestine or the full protection of Palestinian national rights. Crucially, the White Paper did not repudiate the Balfour

Declaration or the British commitment to creating a Jewish homeland in Palestine. In fact, the White Paper affirmed Britain's commitment to facilitating the development of a Jewish national home, but it sought to ensure that this development would occur at a controlled pace and in a way that would not lead to the immediate displacement of Palestinians. This fundamental contradiction—supporting both Jewish settlement and Palestinian rights—meant that the British government was, in effect, trying to serve two masters, and it alienated both sides.

For Palestinians, the White Paper was seen as insufficient and a clear sign that Britain was not prepared to abandon the Zionist project, which they viewed as the root cause of their suffering. The Palestinian Arab leadership, particularly under the leadership of Haj Amin al-Husseini, the Grand Mufti of Jerusalem, criticized the White Paper for not fully respecting Palestinian national aspirations. Al-Husseini, who had been an outspoken critic of both British and Zionist policies, rejected the White Paper as a temporary measure that failed to address the central issue of Palestine's future. He called for the end of British rule in Palestine and the establishment of an independent Palestinian state.

Zionist Backlash: A Violent Response, The reaction from Zionist leaders to the 1939 White Paper was one of intense anger and frustration. To Zionist leaders, the restrictions on immigration were a direct threat to the realization of the Jewish homeland they had been working toward since the early 20th century. The Balfour Declaration had been the cornerstone of their political project, and the White Paper, by limiting Jewish immigration, was seen as a betrayal of that commitment. The White Paper's restrictions, far from appeasing Zionist leaders, were viewed as a serious impediment to their vision of a Jewish state in Palestine.

The Zionist response to the White Paper was swift and violent. Jewish militant groups such as the Irgun (The National Military

Organization) and Lehi (The Stern Gang) intensified their operations against British targets in an attempt to force Britain to reverse the White Paper's policies. These groups, which were more radical than the mainstream Zionist leadership, employed terror tactics, including bombings, assassinations, and sabotage, in their campaign against the British. They targeted British military personnel, police officers, and government officials, believing that a campaign of violence would force Britain to abandon the White Paper and honor its earlier commitment to the establishment of a Jewish state.

One of the most notorious events during this period was the assassination of Lord Moyne, the British Minister of State for the Middle East, by members of Lehi in 1944. This attack, which was part of a broader strategy of violence aimed at British officials, highlighted the increasing radicalization of the Zionist movement. The actions of these militant groups made it clear that the Zionist movement was willing to use any means necessary, including violence against both the British and the Palestinian Arab population, to achieve their goal of establishing a Jewish state in Palestine.

The Palestinian Response: Escalating Resistance, While the Zionist backlash was marked by violence, the Palestinian response to the White Paper was more complicated. Initially, the Palestinian leadership was hopeful that the British government's restrictions on Jewish immigration would lead to a more just and peaceful solution to the conflict. However, as the British failed to take further meaningful steps to address Palestinian grievances, the Palestinian resistance grew stronger. The 1936-1939 Arab Revolt had already demonstrated the depth of Palestinian opposition to British colonial rule and Zionist colonization. Following the White Paper, resistance continued, but now it took on a more complex character, as

Palestinian nationalists increasingly sought to organize against both the British and the growing Zionist presence.

Palestinian resistance was often fragmented, with different factions pursuing their own strategies. The more radical factions, like the Arab Liberation Army, continued to fight British forces and Zionist settlers, using guerilla tactics and sabotage. However, the lack of unity among Palestinian leaders, coupled with British repression and Zionist violence, made it difficult to sustain a unified and effective resistance. The Palestinian leadership, although united in its opposition to the White Paper, struggled to create a cohesive strategy that could effectively challenge British and Zionist power.

The Legacy of the White Papers, The events surrounding the 1939 White Paper laid the groundwork for the violent confrontations that would culminate in the 1948 Nakba. The failure of the British to resolve the contradictions between their promises to the Palestinians and their support for the Zionist project created a volatile political environment in Palestine. Following the White Paper, the situation in Palestine became increasingly polarized, with Palestinian Arabs and Jews locked in a struggle for control over the future of the land.

Key historical moments, such as the Deir Yassin massacre in 1948, exemplified the brutal consequences of the British failure to fully protect Palestinian rights. The massacre, carried out by the Irgun and Lehi, resulted in the deaths of over 100 Palestinian civilians and marked a turning point in the Palestinian experience of violence and displacement. It became a symbol of the Zionist tactics used to drive Palestinians from their homes and land.

The 1939 White Paper's legacy is still felt in the region today. The failure of the British to fully support Palestinian national aspirations and their continued support for the Zionist project ensured that the Palestinian struggle for self-determination would continue for decades. The White Paper's limitations and the Zionist backlash were crucial moments in the history of the Palestinian-Israeli conflict, which continues to shape the political landscape of the Middle East.

The Enduring Consequences of the White Papers, The British White Papers, particularly the 1939 version, were a critical juncture in the history of the Palestinian struggle. They symbolized the failure of British colonialism to resolve the deepening tensions in Palestine and reflected the contradictions at the heart of Britain's policy in the region. The Palestinian reaction, the Zionist backlash, and the subsequent escalation of violence created an atmosphere of profound instability that would shape the course of the conflict for years to come. The White Paper's failure to fully address Palestinian grievances, coupled with the growing violence from both Zionist and Palestinian forces, ensured that the conflict would intensify, leading to the eventual displacement of hundreds of thousands of Palestinians in 1948.

The legacy of the White Papers is a tragic one, as they laid the groundwork for the violent and protracted conflict that continues to this day. The betrayal felt by Palestinians, and the intense backlash from Zionists, helped fuel a cycle of violence that has left deep scars on both sides. Ultimately, the British White Papers serve as a reminder of the challenges of balancing competing nationalisms and the lasting impact of colonialism in shaping the modern Middle East.

The Legacy of Palestinian Resistance

The Palestinian resistance to British colonial rule and Zionist encroachment on Palestinian lands has a long and rich history, shaped by political, military, and social movements. At the forefront of this resistance were figures like Haj Amin al-Husseini, the Grand Mufti of Jerusalem, and his nephew Abdel Qader al-Husseini, both of whom played critical roles in organizing and leading the Palestinian struggle against foreign domination. Their leadership during the Great Arab Revolt of 1936-1939 laid the foundation for the subsequent waves of Palestinian resistance that would continue through the 1948 Nakba and into the modern-day struggle for self-determination.

The Great Arab Revolt, though ultimately unsuccessful, was a defining moment in the Palestinian resistance narrative. It was not merely an insurrection against British colonialism but an assertion of Palestinian identity, a rejection of the Zionist project, and an emphatic statement of a people determined to defend their land. Despite its military failure, the revolt solidified the Palestinian resistance movement and underscored the intransigence with which Palestinians would oppose foreign encroachment.

The collapse of the Great Arab Revolt did not signify the end of Palestinian resistance; rather, it marked a pivotal turning point that spurred future generations of Palestinians to carry the torch of struggle. The revolt was followed by the intensification of Zionist settlement and the broader geopolitical forces that culminated in the 1948 war. The creation of the State of Israel was a watershed moment in Palestinian history, as it led to the Nakba—an event in which over 700,000 Palestinians were displaced from their homes and forced into refugee status. Despite the overwhelming power imbalance and the crushing military defeats they faced, the Palestinian people have never relinquished their quest for justice and sovereignty.

Today, the legacy of resistance left by figures like Haj Amin al-Husseini and Abdel Qader al-Husseini continues to resonate deeply in Palestinian political thought and action. Their vision of a free Palestine, liberated from both British colonial rule and Zionist settler colonialism, remains a guiding light for contemporary Palestinian struggles. The resilience of these leaders, their commitment to Palestinian identity, and their ability to inspire the masses in the face of overwhelming odds serve as an enduring inspiration for the ongoing struggle for self-determination.

To understand the full depth of the Palestinian resistance, it is important to acknowledge not only the strategic and military dimensions of the struggle but also the ideological and cultural components that formed the foundation of Palestinian nationalism. The resistance was as much about preserving a way of life, a culture, and an identity as it was about military confrontation. In the face of Zionist violence, Palestinian resistance was both physical and intellectual, ranging from armed insurrections to the defense of Palestinian heritage and land.

The 1936-1939 Arab Revolt was, in many ways, a reaction to the simultaneous intensification of British colonialism and Zionist colonization in Palestine. The British had been the mandatory power in Palestine since 1917, and they facilitated the Zionist project, which sought to create a Jewish state in what Palestinians considered their homeland. The British not only ignored the rights of Palestinians but actively aided in the construction of Jewish settlements, establishing policies that sought to ease the path to Jewish immigration and land acquisition at the expense of the native Arab population. The Balfour Declaration of 1917, which promised British support for the creation of a Jewish homeland in Palestine, was the ideological precursor to the Jewish state that would eventually emerge in 1948.

The Palestinian reaction to this encroachment was multifaceted. Led by nationalists such as Haj Amin al-Husseini, the Grand Mufti of Jerusalem, Palestinians launched protests, strikes, and ultimately an armed uprising against British rule and the growing Zionist presence. During this time, al-Husseini became a central figure in rallying the Palestinian population to resist the colonial occupation and the Zionist agenda. His leadership and involvement in the Revolt highlighted the unity of Palestinians across political, social, and religious lines in their opposition to foreign control.

The Great Arab Revolt of 1936-1939 was marked by widespread protests, civil disobedience, and guerrilla warfare against British soldiers and Zionist settlers. Though the revolt was eventually suppressed through a brutal British military response—culminating in mass arrests, executions, and the destruction of villages—the spirit of resistance continued to thrive. Palestinians were subjected to collective punishment, including curfews, imprisonment, and destruction of homes, but these measures did little to quell their determination. Despite the defeat of the revolt, it set the stage for future Palestinian uprisings, notably in 1987 during the First Intifada, which was similarly marked by popular resistance to occupation.

The Zionist response to the Palestinian resistance was one marked by extreme violence and the deliberate dehumanization of Palestinians. The Zionist forces, who would later form the core of the Israeli military, used terror tactics, massacres, and forced expulsions to assert their control over Palestinian land. The infamous Deir Yassin massacre of 1948, in which over 100 Palestinian men, women, and children were killed by Zionist militias, became a symbol of the brutality of the Zionist project and the lengths to which it would go to expel Palestinians from their homeland.

The military campaign during the 1948 war, which resulted in the Nakba, further exemplified the violent tactics used by the Zionists to forcibly remove Palestinians from their land. The creation of the State of Israel in 1948 was not simply the birth of a new nation but the result of violent displacement, colonization, and dispossession of an indigenous population. Over 700,000 Palestinians were forcibly expelled from their homes during the Nakba, a crime that continues to resonate in the collective memory of the Palestinian people. Palestinian refugees, many of whom still live in camps in the Middle East, continue to demand the right to return to their homes—a right that remains denied to this day.

The Zionist strategy of ethnic cleansing during the Nakba was systematic and deliberate. Zionist forces not only used military force but also psychological warfare to terrorize Palestinian populations, encouraging their flight from areas deemed strategically important for the establishment of the new state. The destruction of Palestinian villages and the theft of Palestinian land were central to the creation of Israel, and these actions were later codified into Israeli law and policy. The Zionist claim to the land was built on a foundation of dispossession and violence, a fact that continues to be ignored or downplayed by many proponents of the Israeli state.

It is crucial to be critical of the Zionist narrative, which often frames the creation of Israel as a legitimate act of self-determination and ignores the catastrophic impact it had on the Palestinian population. Zionism, as an ideology and political movement, was not simply about the return of Jewish people to their ancestral homeland; it was also about the expulsion, displacement, and marginalization of the indigenous Palestinian population. This foundational injustice has shaped every aspect of the Israeli-Palestinian conflict and continues to fuel the ongoing resistance of the Palestinian people.

Personal narratives and accounts from Palestinians who lived through the events of the 1936-1939 revolt and the 1948 Nakba paint a vivid picture of the suffering and resilience of a people who were systematically dispossessed of their homes, lands, and livelihoods. One interview with a Palestinian survivor of the Nakba reflects the profound sense of loss and the continued yearning for justice: *"We were forced to leave our homes at gunpoint. My father never returned. And we have never forgotten."* These personal testimonies are a reminder that the Palestinian struggle is not just about political borders or military engagements; it is a fight for identity, dignity, and the right to return to the land that was once theirs.

The resilience of Palestinian resistance, epitomized by the actions of leaders like Haj Amin al-Husseini and Abdel Qader al-Husseini, as well as the broader popular movements, has endured for over a century. Though the resistance has faced many setbacks and challenges, it remains a central part of Palestinian identity today. The legacy of these struggles continues to inspire both Palestinians and international movements for justice, as the Palestinian people continue to demand their right to self-determination, sovereignty, and the return of their lands. The history of Palestinian resistance is not merely a chronicle of loss, but a testament to the enduring will of a people who will never surrender their right to freedom and justice.

Chapter 5: The Nakba –Catastrophe of 1948

The Nakba, meaning *"catastrophe"* in Arabic, represents one of the most traumatic chapters in the history of the Palestinian people. It was not merely a singular event in 1948, but the culmination of a prolonged process of political, military, and colonial machinations, involving both Zionist expansionism and British colonial policies. The Nakba's legacy continues to shape Palestinian identity and the region's geopolitical landscape, fostering a crisis that remains unresolved to this day. This chapter examines the Nakba's historical roots, its immediate impact on Palestinian society, and the consequences that reverberate through generations of Palestinians who continue to bear the scars of this event.

The Roots of the Nakba: A Century of Zionist Expansionism, To understand the Nakba fully, it is essential to trace its roots back to the late 19th century, when Zionism emerged as a political movement. Zionism, led by Theodor Herzl, sought to establish a Jewish homeland in Palestine, a land with deep historical significance for Jews, but one that was already inhabited by a large Arab population. The push for a Jewish state in Palestine gained momentum through the early 20th century, particularly after the Balfour Declaration of 1917, which was issued by the British government. The Declaration promised support for the establishment of a *"Jewish national home"* in Palestine, a region that, at the time, was under British control as a mandate.

For Palestinians, the Balfour Declaration was a political betrayal. The Arab population of Palestine had been promised independence by the British during World War I in exchange for their support against the Ottoman Empire. Instead, they faced the imposition of a British mandate and the gradual influx of Jewish immigrants, supported by Zionist organizations. These immigrants, many of whom were fleeing persecution in Europe, started purchasing land from absentee landlords, often displacing Palestinian farmers who had lived on the land for generations.

The British Mandate, lasting from 1920 to 1948, provided a backdrop for the escalating tensions between Jews and Arabs in Palestine. Figures such as Haj Amin al-Husseini, the Grand Mufti of Jerusalem, emerged as key Palestinian leaders resisting both British colonial policies and the Zionist movement. Al-Husseini's resistance to Zionist immigration and land purchases galvanized Palestinian nationalist sentiment. In the 1930s, he played a central role in the Arab Revolt of 1936-1939, where Palestinians organized protests, strikes, and armed resistance against both British rule and Jewish immigration.

This revolt led to widespread repression by the British, who responded with curfews, mass arrests, and executions, creating deep resentment among the Palestinians. Meanwhile, Zionist forces, particularly the Haganah, began to organize their own military cells, preparing for future conflict. Figures such as David Ben-Gurion, who later became Israel's first prime minister, were instrumental in organizing Zionist paramilitary forces and in laying the foundations for the Israeli state. Ben-Gurion and others saw the creation of a Jewish state as inevitable, and began to implement strategies for securing land and increasing Jewish immigration to Palestine.

The UN Partition Plan and the Zionist Agenda, In 1947, after World War II and the horrors of the Holocaust, global support for the Zionist cause surged, leading the United Nations to propose a Partition Plan to divide Palestine into two states: one for Jews and one for Arabs. The plan allocated 55% of the land to the Jewish state, despite Jews comprising less than one-third of the population and owning only around 7% of the land. The plan was seen by Palestinians as an unjust division, particularly since the majority of the land had been inhabited by Arabs for centuries.

Key Palestinian leaders such as Jamal al-Husseini and the Arab Higher Committee, led by his cousin, the Grand Mufti, rejected the plan. They saw it as a violation of Palestinian sovereignty and a betrayal of their right to self-determination. In contrast, Zionist leaders such as David Ben-Gurion and Chaim Weizmann accepted the UN plan, not out of a genuine desire for peace, but because it allowed them to secure a foothold in Palestine.

Upon the UN's passing of the Partition Plan, tensions reached a boiling point. The Zionists saw the opportunity to solidify their claim to Palestine, and their military forces, such as the Haganah, Irgun, and Lehi, began to launch attacks on Palestinian villages. These groups, with the tacit support of the British, increasingly targeted Palestinian civilians to achieve their goals. The response was not just one of defense but of terror aimed at driving Palestinians from their land.

The Systematic Displacement of Palestinians, The Nakba was not merely the result of a conventional war; it was the deliberate and systematic destruction of Palestinian society. Zionist forces launched a series of military operations aimed at depopulating Palestinian villages. Their primary goal was to ensure that there were no remaining Palestinian civilians in the areas designated for the new Jewish state. These operations were often accompanied by violent acts, including massacres, forced expulsions, and the destruction of homes.

One of the most infamous events of the Nakba was the massacre at Deir Yassin, a village near Jerusalem. In April 1948, Zionist militias from the Irgun and Lehi attacked the village, killing over 100 Palestinian men, women, and children. Survivors of Deir Yassin recount how the attackers shot civilians, including the elderly and children, and set homes on fire. News of the massacre spread throughout Palestine, causing widespread panic and prompting many Palestinians to flee their villages in fear of similar attacks.

Figures such as Menachem Begin, leader of the Irgun, and Yitzhak Shamir, leader of Lehi, later became prominent political leaders in Israel. Begin became Israel's prime minister in 1977, and Shamir served as prime minister in the 1980s. Both leaders, despite their roles in the violent displacement of Palestinians, were celebrated by the Israeli state. This deepened the divide between the Zionist leadership and the Palestinian people, who viewed these figures not as heroes but as perpetrators of violence and injustice.

In addition to the massacres, Palestinian villages were systematically depopulated. Zionist forces would expel entire communities, often leaving their homes and fields in ruins. The villages were razed, and any trace of Palestinian existence was erased. The destruction was not only physical but symbolic, as the Palestinians' cultural and social fabric was torn apart. The act of ethnic cleansing was intended to ensure that Jews would become the majority in the newly created state of Israel, and to deny Palestinians any claim to their land.

The Palestinian Refugee Crisis, The Nakba resulted in the forced displacement of approximately 750,000 Palestinians. The refugees fled to neighboring countries, including Jordan, Lebanon, and Syria, where they were forced to live in refugee camps. Today, the Palestinian refugee crisis remains one of the largest and most protracted in the world.

The Nakba's legacy is a continuous and painful reality for the Palestinian people. The descendants of the 1948 refugees continue to live in exile, and the right of return remains a central issue in the Palestinian struggle for justice. The refugee camps, often overcrowded and underfunded, are a stark reminder of the displacement and dispossession Palestinians have endured for over seven decades.

Interviews with survivors of the Nakba provide emotional insights into the human cost of the displacement. One elderly Palestinian woman, now living in a refugee camp in Lebanon, recalled the events of 1948: *"We fled our home in fear for our lives. My father carried my younger brother, and we walked for days. We never imagined we would still be here in a refugee camp 70 years later, waiting to go back to our home."* These personal testimonies highlight the pain and longing felt by Palestinians who were uprooted from their homes, only to be confined to overcrowded camps far from their ancestral lands.

The International Community's Role, The international community, particularly the United States and Britain, played a key role in enabling the creation of the state of Israel. The support from Western powers, motivated by a mix of guilt over the Holocaust, strategic geopolitical interests, and Zionist lobbying, ensured that Israel would be recognized as a legitimate state, despite the brutal treatment of Palestinians.

The United Nations, which had endorsed the Partition Plan, failed to hold Zionist forces accountable for the widespread atrocities committed against Palestinians. In fact, rather than taking steps to address the issue of Palestinian refugees and their rights, the international community largely accepted the narrative presented by Israel, which framed the violence as part of a defensive struggle. This narrative ignored the fact that Zionist forces had been systematically displacing Palestinians long before the formal declaration of the state of Israel.

The Enduring Legacy of the Nakba, The Nakba is not just a historical event but a continuing tragedy. The mass displacement, the destruction of Palestinian society, and the creation of the refugee crisis have left an indelible mark on Palestinian identity and the collective consciousness of the Arab world. The Nakba remains a rallying cry for Palestinians seeking justice, and its memory fuels the ongoing struggle for the right of return, self-determination, and the restoration of their rights.

The Zionist project, which sought to create a Jewish state at the expense of the Palestinian people, has left a legacy of division, dispossession, and suffering. The Nakba's impact continues to reverberate through the generations, as Palestinians continue to live in exile, in refugee camps, or under occupation, denied their rightful place in the land of their ancestors. The Nakba is not just an event in the past—it is a reality that shapes the present and future of the Palestinian people.

The Nakba remains at the heart of the Palestinian struggle. It is the defining event in the history of modern Palestine and continues to inform the aspirations of the Palestinian people for justice and return to their land.

The Prelude to the Nakba: Zionism and British Mandate Policies

To truly grasp the devastating impact of the Nakba and the systemic injustices faced by the Palestinian people, it is essential to delve deeper into the historical developments that set the stage for this catastrophe. The events that culminated in the Nakba did not occur in a vacuum. They were shaped by a series of ideological, political, and colonial forces that sought to reshape the Middle East. Central to these developments were the rise of Zionism in Europe and the policies of the British Mandate in Palestine, which intertwined to create a volatile environment for the indigenous Arab population.

The Rise of Zionism and Its European Roots, Zionism, as a political movement, emerged in late 19th-century Europe as a response to growing anti-Semitism and the desire for Jewish self-determination. The movement was formally launched by Theodor Herzl, an Austrian Jewish journalist, who argued that the only solution to the persecution of Jews in Europe was the establishment of a Jewish state in Palestine. Herzl and his contemporaries believed that the return to the historical land of the Jews would provide refuge from the discriminatory and hostile environments that Jews faced in Europe.

Zionism quickly gained support in the Jewish communities of Eastern and Central Europe, but it was not universally accepted. A significant portion of the Jewish population opposed the idea of a nationalist movement, advocating instead for integration into the societies in which they lived. Despite this internal division, the Zionist movement continued to grow, fueled by the rising tide of nationalism across Europe and the increasing persecution of Jews, most notably in the form of pogroms in Eastern Europe.

The concept of a Jewish homeland in Palestine was rooted in a deep historical connection to the land, but it was also deeply shaped by European imperialism. Palestine, at the time of the Zionist movement's emergence, was part of the Ottoman Empire, a vast, multi-ethnic empire that controlled much of the Middle East. Zionist aspirations for a homeland in Palestine, however, were not solely based on historical and religious claims but were influenced by a desire to establish a state on land already inhabited by indigenous Arabs.

The British Mandate: A Double-Edged Sword, The defeat of the Ottoman Empire in World War I created an opening for European powers to expand their influence in the Middle East. Britain, which had long maintained strategic interests in the region, sought to secure control over Palestine as part of its broader imperial ambitions. The Sykes-Picot Agreement of 1916, a secret treaty between Britain and France, divided the Ottoman territories in the Middle East into spheres of influence, with Palestine being placed under British control.

The British Mandate for Palestine was formalized in 1920 by the League of Nations, and Britain's role was presented as that of a temporary administrator, tasked with guiding Palestine to self-governance. However, in practice, Britain's policies during the mandate period often contradicted the promise of self-determination for the Palestinian people. The most consequential of these contradictory policies was the 1917 Balfour Declaration, which pledged British support for the establishment of a *"national home for the Jewish people"* in Palestine. This declaration was made without any consultation with the indigenous Arab population, who made up the overwhelming majority in Palestine. The British, in their desire to secure the support of the global Jewish community during World War I, had made a crucial and fateful decision to back Zionist ambitions.

The Balfour Declaration, though framed as a benign gesture to support Jewish self-determination, was viewed by Palestinians as an unjust intrusion upon their rights. The declaration did not take into account the existence of the Palestinian Arabs, their historical connection to the land, or their rights to self-determination. The promise of a Jewish national home in Palestine directly contradicted the aspirations of the Palestinian Arabs, who sought to preserve their land, culture, and independence. The growing influx of Jewish immigrants, encouraged by both the Zionist movement and the British mandate, exacerbated tensions and fears of displacement.

Zionist Immigration and Land Acquisition, Under the British Mandate, Jewish immigration to Palestine increased dramatically. Between 1920 and 1940, the Jewish population in Palestine rose from about 10% to 30% of the total population. This influx was facilitated by the British, who not only allowed but often encouraged Jewish settlement through the issuance of land grants and favorable policies. At the same time, the Palestinians, who had lived on the land for centuries, were increasingly marginalized. Land that had been owned by Palestinian Arabs for generations was purchased by Zionist organizations, who used both legal and extralegal means to acquire it. This land acquisition was often accompanied by the displacement of Palestinian families who were evicted from their homes and lands.

The land purchases were part of the broader strategy of the Zionist movement to establish a Jewish majority in Palestine. The establishment of kibbutzim (communal farms) and other Zionist settlements in the 1920s and 1930s was part of a broader effort to create an economic and political base for the future Jewish state. These settlements were often established on land that had been forcibly taken from Palestinian Arabs, whose rights and claims to the land were systematically ignored or undermined by both the Zionists and the British authorities.

One of the most tragic aspects of this process was the dispossession of Palestinian farmers, many of whom were left without homes or livelihoods. In towns and villages across Palestine, Palestinian families were either forced to sell their land under duress or were pushed off their land through intimidation and violence. These displaced Palestinians, who were often left without resources or support, became the first wave of refugees in what would later become a much larger exodus during the Nakba of 1948.

The Rising Palestinian Resistance, As the Zionist presence in Palestine grew, so too did Palestinian opposition. The indigenous Arab population, who had long resisted foreign rule, now found themselves facing a new and powerful colonial force. Palestinian resistance to Zionist immigration and land acquisition was not limited to protest and political mobilization; it also involved violent confrontations and uprisings. The Palestinians recognized that their very existence was at stake, as the Zionist movement sought not only to establish a homeland for Jews but to impose a new political and social order that would marginalize and displace the Arabs.

The 1929 Hebron Massacre was one of the first major outbreaks of violence between Arabs and Jews in Palestine. The massacre occurred after tensions surrounding Jewish immigration and religious differences led to widespread riots. The violence, which spread throughout Palestine, was a direct response to the growing Zionist presence and the perceived threat to Palestinian identity. The massacre was particularly brutal in Hebron, where 67 Jews were killed, and many more were injured. While the violence was condemned by Palestinian leaders, it marked the beginning of a period of increasing friction and distrust between Arabs and Jews.

The Arab Revolt of 1936-1939 was a more organized and sustained effort by the Palestinian population to resist both British colonial rule and Zionist immigration. The revolt was sparked by the British government's failure to limit Jewish immigration, despite earlier promises to curb it, and by the continued economic hardship faced by Palestinians. The revolt included strikes, protests, and armed resistance, with the Palestinian leadership calling for an end to British rule, the cessation of Jewish immigration, and the establishment of an independent Arab state in Palestine.

The British response to the revolt was harsh and repressive. The British military used collective punishment, mass arrests, executions, and curfews to suppress the rebellion. The revolt ultimately failed, but it demonstrated the deepening anger and frustration of the Palestinian population, as well as their determination to resist Zionism and British rule. This period marked a significant shift in Palestinian consciousness, as the struggle for independence was increasingly framed as a fight against both Zionism and British colonialism.

The Balfour Declaration: A Symbol of Colonial Betrayal, The Balfour Declaration stands as one of the most significant acts of betrayal in the history of colonialism. It is emblematic of the British approach to the Middle East: a desire to maintain imperial control while simultaneously serving the interests of external powers. In this case, Britain's support for the Zionist movement was motivated by its geopolitical considerations during World War I and its desire to secure the loyalty of the Jewish community, particularly in Europe and the United States.

However, the declaration's failure to recognize the rights and aspirations of the Palestinian Arabs set the stage for the profound injustices that would follow. The promise of a Jewish homeland in Palestine, made without the consent or consultation of the indigenous population, was inherently colonial in nature. It ignored the reality that Palestine was not an empty land awaiting Jewish settlement, but a land inhabited by people with deep historical, cultural, and religious ties to the region.

The Balfour Declaration, coupled with British policies during the mandate period, laid the groundwork for the violence and displacement that would occur during the Nakba. The Zionist movement, backed by British imperial interests, set in motion a series of events that would ultimately result in the expulsion of Palestinians from their homeland, the destruction of their villages, and the creation of one of the largest refugee crises in modern history. The Nakba was not simply a consequence of a war or military conflict—it was the culmination of decades of colonial policies, Zionist expansion, and the betrayal of Palestinian rights.

The prelude to the Nakba is a story of colonial betrayal, dispossession, and resistance. The Zionist movement, driven by its own ideological vision of a Jewish homeland, found a willing partner in British imperialism, which sought to expand its control over the Middle East. The policies that were enacted during the British Mandate, particularly the Balfour Declaration, laid the foundation for the displacement and dispossession of the Palestinian people. At the same time, these policies ignited a growing resistance among Palestinians, who were determined to preserve their land, culture, and identity. This resistance would culminate in the Nakba, a tragedy that continues to shape the Palestinian experience to this day.

The UN Partition Plan and the Path to War: Zionist Expansionism and Palestinian Resistance

The United Nations Partition Plan of 1947, which proposed the division of Palestine into two states—one Jewish and one Arab—marked a pivotal moment in the history of the Middle East, with far-reaching consequences for the Palestinian people and the broader Arab world. The plan, though presented as a diplomatic solution to the escalating conflict, failed to address the core issue of Palestinian sovereignty and self-determination. Instead, it entrenched the divide between Jews and Arabs, leading to the eventual creation of the State of Israel and the violent expulsion of hundreds of thousands of Palestinians from their ancestral homes. As we examine this crucial period in history, it becomes clear that the UN Partition Plan not only reflected the desires of Zionist leaders but also represented a profound injustice to the indigenous Palestinian population.

The UN Partition Plan: An Inherently Unjust Proposal, The proposal of the United Nations to partition Palestine was framed as an attempt to resolve the long-standing conflict between the Zionist and Arab nationalist movements. The UN Special Committee on Palestine (UNSCOP) was tasked with finding a solution, and after much deliberation, it presented a plan for the division of the land in November 1947. The partition plan recommended dividing Palestine into two states, one Jewish and one Arab, with Jerusalem placed under international administration. Under the plan, the Jewish state would receive 55% of the land, despite Jews constituting only about one-third of the population and owning less than 10% of the land. Conversely, the Arab state was allocated just 45% of the land, even though Arabs made up about 70% of the population.

For the Palestinian people, the partition plan was seen as a betrayal. Palestinians had been living in the land for centuries, and the UN's proposed division disregarded their historical and moral right to the land. The allocation of such a disproportionate amount of land to the Jewish state, given the demographic makeup of the region, was viewed as a clear violation of Palestinian sovereignty. The Palestinian leadership, represented by the Arab Higher Committee, rejected the plan as an imposition by external powers, which had no right to determine the fate of the land and its people.

Furthermore, the partition plan was born out of the legacy of British imperialism, which had already enabled the Zionist movement through the Balfour Declaration of 1917. This declaration, issued by the British government, expressed support for the establishment of a *"national home for the Jewish people"* in Palestine, thus giving the Zionists a foothold in the region. British policies, which allowed mass Jewish immigration to Palestine, had created tensions between the local Arab population and the newly arriving Jewish settlers. The UN plan, then, was seen as a continuation of the colonial legacy that had already denied the Palestinian people their right to self-determination.

Zionist Ambitions and the Rejection of the UN Plan, For the Zionist leadership, the UN Partition Plan represented an opportunity to create a Jewish state in Palestine, even if it did not include all the land that they envisioned. Figures like David Ben-Gurion, who would later become Israel's first prime minister, viewed the plan as a pragmatic step toward establishing a state, even if it required territorial compromises. The idea of a Jewish homeland in Palestine was central to the Zionist project, and the partition plan offered a legal and political framework to realize this goal.

However, the Zionist movement's ambitions went beyond the boundaries outlined in the UN plan. Zionist leaders, knowing that the Arab states and Palestinians had rejected the partition, began preparing for a military solution. They understood that, with a strong and organized military force, they could secure more land than the partition plan had allocated to them. Thus, while they publicly accepted the UN's proposal, Zionist leaders began implementing plans for territorial expansion, including the forced displacement of Palestinians and the seizure of their land.

The strategic importance of Palestine to the Zionist movement cannot be overstated. Zionism, as articulated by key figures like Theodor Herzl and Ben-Gurion, sought not just a home for Jews in Palestine but also the creation of a state that would serve as a beacon for the Jewish people worldwide. The establishment of the state of Israel, according to Zionist ideology, was seen as a necessary refuge for Jews in the face of European anti-Semitism, especially in the aftermath of the Holocaust. However, this vision came at the expense of the Palestinian people, whose presence was systematically erased in the process of establishing the Jewish state.

Palestinian Rejection and the Outbreak of Civil War, In response to the UN Partition Plan, the Palestinian leadership and the majority of the Arab population rejected the proposal, seeing it as an affront to their rights and sovereignty. For Palestinians, the plan symbolized the imposition of foreign powers on their homeland, which had already suffered under British colonial rule. The rejection of the partition led to an immediate outbreak of violence between the Jewish and Arab communities in Palestine. This violence, which began in late 1947, quickly escalated into full-scale civil war. Both sides committed atrocities, with Zionist forces attacking Palestinian villages and cities and Palestinian militias engaging in counterattacks.

The massacre at Deir Yassin, a Palestinian village near Jerusalem, became one of the most infamous incidents of this period. In April 1948, Jewish paramilitary groups, including the Irgun and Lehi, attacked Deir Yassin, killing over 100 Palestinian civilians, including women and children. The massacre was not an isolated incident; it was part of a broader strategy by Zionist forces to instill fear among the Palestinian population and force them to flee their homes. The violent nature of these attacks led to the rapid displacement of Palestinian civilians, many of whom sought refuge in neighboring Arab countries or in other parts of Palestine.

The mass displacement of Palestinians, often referred to as the Nakba, or *"catastrophe,"* marked a turning point in the conflict. More than 700,000 Palestinians were expelled from their homes during the 1948 war, and the majority of them were never allowed to return. The displacement of Palestinians was not a byproduct of the war; it was a central aim of Zionist policy, which sought to create a Jewish-majority state by eliminating the Palestinian presence. The methods employed to achieve this goal included mass expulsions, the destruction of Palestinian villages, and the appropriation of Palestinian property.

Zionist Military Strategy: The Nakba and the Expulsion of Palestinians, The Zionist military strategy during the 1948 war, known as Plan Dalet, was a comprehensive blueprint for the conquest of Palestine and the expulsion of Palestinians from their land. Plan Dalet outlined a series of military operations aimed at securing territory for the new Jewish state, including the removal of Palestinian populations from areas designated for the Jewish state under the UN Partition Plan. This policy of ethnic cleansing was carried out with the full backing of the Zionist leadership and the military, and it resulted in the widespread destruction of Palestinian villages.

The most notorious of these operations was the assault on the village of Lydda, located in central Palestine. In July 1948, Zionist forces captured Lydda and expelled its entire population, numbering around 50,000 people. The expulsion was carried out with extreme brutality, and many of the villagers were forced to march to refugee camps in Jordan, where they would remain for years. Similar actions took place throughout Palestine, with entire communities being uprooted and their properties seized by Zionist forces. The scale of the dispossession was staggering, and the impact of these actions is still felt by Palestinians today.

In addition to the military campaigns, Zionist forces also sought to erase Palestinian identity by demolishing villages and eradicating traces of Palestinian culture. This policy of de-Palestinization was part of a broader effort to establish a Jewish state in Palestine, one that would be free of Palestinian Arabs. The destruction of Palestinian villages, including the demolition of homes, schools, and mosques, was a deliberate attempt to erase the historical and cultural ties of Palestinians to their land.

The Enduring Legacy of the UN Partition Plan, The events surrounding the UN Partition Plan of 1947 and the subsequent 1948 war created a lasting legacy of injustice and displacement for the Palestinian people. The partition plan, which was presented as a fair and reasonable solution to the conflict, was inherently unjust, as it gave the lion's share of the land to a minority population while denying the majority Arab population their right to self-determination. The rejection of the plan by Palestinians was not simply a refusal of the plan itself but a refusal of the broader project of Zionist colonization and dispossession.

The Zionist expansionist strategy during the 1948 war, which involved mass expulsions, the destruction of villages, and the forced displacement of Palestinians, was a clear violation of international law and human rights. The creation of Israel, built on the ruins of Palestinian homes and villages, remains a contentious issue to this day, and the Palestinian struggle for justice, self-determination, and the right to return continues to resonate in the hearts of millions.

The 1947 Partition Plan and the subsequent establishment of Israel are central to understanding the ongoing Israeli-Palestinian conflict. The displacement of Palestinians in 1948, known as the Nakba, is not a historical event that can be relegated to the past. It is an ongoing tragedy that continues to shape the political landscape of the Middle East. As we reflect on this period in history, it is crucial to recognize the long-lasting consequences of the Zionist project and to acknowledge the rights and aspirations of the Palestinian people, who have endured decades of occupation, dispossession, and injustice. The path to peace lies in recognizing these injustices and working toward a just and equitable solution for all peoples of the region.

David Ben-Gurion and Zionist Military Strategy: Examination of Leadership, War Tactics, and Their Legacy

David Ben-Gurion, often hailed as the *"founding father"* of Israel, occupies a central and polarizing position in the narrative of the 1948 Arab-Israeli War. A pragmatic visionary and the head of the Jewish Agency, Ben-Gurion wielded a combination of political foresight, strategic planning, and unrelenting resolve in the pursuit of a Jewish state. However, his methods—particularly the use of military force, population displacement, and demographic engineering—invite a critical reevaluation of his legacy. While his leadership secured the establishment of Israel, the strategies he endorsed during the conflict had devastating consequences for the indigenous Palestinian population, marking the Nakba, or *"catastrophe,"* as a defining moment in Palestinian history.

Ben-Gurion's ideological commitment to Zionism, shaped by decades of activism and leadership, was rooted in the belief that the Jewish people required a sovereign state to ensure their survival and security. Yet, this vision came with a fundamental tension: the land envisioned as the future Jewish homeland was already home to a majority Arab population. Early on, Ben-Gurion recognized that the realization of Zionist aspirations would necessitate not only territorial acquisition but also the displacement of the Arab population. In private correspondence and public speeches, he often alluded to this harsh reality, stating in 1937: *"We must expel Arabs and take their places."* This statement, while often downplayed in mainstream narratives, underscores the premeditated nature of the policies that would later unfold during the 1948 war.

The end of British rule in Palestine in 1947 provided Ben-Gurion and the Zionist leadership with a pivotal opportunity. The United Nations Partition Plan, which proposed the division of Palestine into separate Jewish and Arab states, was met with mixed reactions. While the Zionist leadership accepted the plan as a tactical victory, the Palestinians and surrounding Arab nations rejected it outright, perceiving it as an unjust division of their homeland. The partition plan allocated 55% of the territory to the Jewish state, despite Jews comprising only about one-third of the population and owning less than 7% of the land. This imbalance fueled widespread anger and resistance among Palestinians, setting the stage for open conflict.

As tensions escalated, Ben-Gurion's leadership shifted decisively from political maneuvering to military action. Recognizing that the establishment of a Jewish state would require more than diplomatic agreements, he oversaw the development of a comprehensive military strategy aimed at securing territorial control and neutralizing opposition. This strategy culminated in the formulation of Plan Dalet in March 1948. Officially described as a defensive blueprint, Plan Dalet was, in practice, a coordinated campaign of territorial conquest and ethnic cleansing. Its objectives were clear: to establish a contiguous Jewish state by capturing key areas, securing Jewish settlements, and depopulating Palestinian villages.

The implementation of Plan Dalet was marked by a series of military operations that fundamentally reshaped the demographic and geographic landscape of Palestine. Palestinian villages and towns became the targets of systematic attacks, many of which involved acts of extreme violence. One of the most infamous examples was the massacre at Deir Yassin, a small village near Jerusalem that had sought to maintain neutrality in the conflict. On April 9, 1948, Zionist paramilitary groups Irgun and Lehi launched an assault on Deir Yassin, killing over 100 Palestinian men, women, and children. Survivors recounted horrific scenes of civilians being executed and their bodies mutilated. The attack, far from being a rogue operation, served a calculated purpose: to spread fear among Palestinians and trigger mass flight from other villages.

The psychological impact of the Deir Yassin massacre was immediate and far-reaching. News of the atrocities spread rapidly, often amplified by deliberate Zionist propaganda aimed at intensifying the fear of displacement. Entire communities fled their homes, leaving behind land, possessions, and livelihoods. This pattern of forced displacement was not confined to Deir Yassin; it became a recurring feature of Zionist military operations. Villages such as Tantura, Lydda (Lod), and Ramle witnessed similar fates, with residents expelled under the threat of violence or killed outright.

The Deir Yassin Massacre: A Pivotal Turning Point in the Nakba, On April 9, 1948, the small Palestinian village of Deir Yassin, located west of Jerusalem, became the site of one of the most infamous atrocities in the 1948 Arab-Israeli War. The massacre was carried out by the Zionist paramilitary groups Irgun and Lehi, with tacit approval from the Haganah, the main Zionist military force. The violence in Deir Yassin was both brutal and calculated, resulting in the deaths of over 100 Palestinian men, women, and children. Survivors reported horrifying acts of violence, including the execution of unarmed civilians, the mutilation of bodies, and the rape of women.

The assault began early in the morning, with Irgun and Lehi forces surrounding the village under the guise of securing the

Jerusalem corridor, a strategic area linking Jewish settlements. Although the village had previously entered into a non-aggression pact with the surrounding Jewish community, the attackers showed no regard for its neutrality. Armed with machine guns, grenades, and explosives, the paramilitary groups stormed Deir Yassin, meeting sporadic resistance from a handful of villagers armed with rifles. The resistance, however, was quickly overwhelmed.

Eyewitness accounts from survivors paint a grim picture of the massacre. Fatima Khalidi, a survivor, recounted: *"They came into our homes and shot at everything that moved. My cousin tried to hide under a bed, but they dragged him out and shot him in the yard. They killed my mother while she was holding my baby brother."* Another survivor, Ahmad Hassan, described how bodies were mutilated and thrown into wells, a tactic meant to desecrate and terrorize.

The massacre was not merely an isolated act of violence but part of a larger psychological strategy. Reports of the atrocities spread rapidly, often amplified by deliberate Zionist propaganda. Some leaders within the Zionist movement, including David Ben-Gurion, later distanced themselves from the massacre, claiming it was a rogue operation. However, others defended it as a necessary act to intimidate Palestinian communities into fleeing, thereby facilitating the demographic goals of the Zionist project.

The impact of Deir Yassin on the Palestinian population was profound. Fear of similar massacres led to the mass exodus of Palestinians from villages across the region. The event became a symbol of the Nakba, marking the beginning of a deliberate campaign of displacement that would result in the forced exile of over 700,000 Palestinians.

Lydda and Ramle Expulsions: The Tragedy of Operation Dani, The events in Lydda (Lod) and Ramle during July 1948 exemplify the scale and ruthlessness of Zionist military operations under Plan Dalet. These two towns, located in the strategic corridor between Tel

Aviv and Jerusalem, were home to tens of thousands of Palestinians. Under Operation Dani, Israeli forces, including units from the Palmach (the elite strike force of the Haganah), launched a coordinated assault to capture the towns and secure control over the area.

The operation unfolded with a combination of overwhelming firepower and psychological warfare. After intense fighting, Lydda fell on July 11, 1948. Israeli soldiers entered the town, executing dozens of unarmed civilians in what Benny Morris, a prominent Israeli historian, has described as an act of ethnic cleansing. Homes were looted, and entire neighborhoods were destroyed. In Ramle, a similar pattern emerged, with residents forced to abandon their homes under threat of violence.

The Forced March to the West Bank, The aftermath of the Lydda and Ramle expulsions was particularly harrowing. Approximately 50,000 Palestinians were ordered to leave their towns and march to the West Bank under the scorching July sun. This journey, often referred to as the Lydda Death March, was marked by extreme suffering. Without adequate food or water, many succumbed to dehydration and exhaustion along the way. Survivors describe the journey as a defining moment of their dispossession.

One survivor, Aisha Abu Salim, recalled: *"We walked for days. My younger brother, who was only six, collapsed on the road. My father tried to carry him, but he was too weak himself. We had no choice but to leave him behind."* The forced march was not only a physical ordeal but also a profound psychological trauma, symbolizing the loss of home, community, and dignity for thousands of Palestinians.

Mass Killings in Lydda, In addition to the forced expulsions, Lydda witnessed one of the most egregious acts of violence during the operation. Following the town's surrender, dozens of residents who had sought refuge in the Dahmash Mosque were killed by Israeli forces. The killings, described by witnesses as executions, were part of a broader strategy to ensure that the displaced population would not return.

The events in Lydda and Ramle stand as stark examples of the systematic use of violence and fear to achieve territorial and demographic objectives. While Israeli leaders, including Ben-Gurion, justified the expulsions as necessary for the survival of the nascent state, the human cost of these actions remains a dark chapter in the history of the conflict.

The Fall of Safed: Psychological Warfare and the Destruction of a Community, The capture of Safed in May 1948 marked another critical moment in the implementation of Plan Dalet. Once a mixed Jewish-Arab city, Safed was a key target due to its strategic location in the Galilee. The operation to capture the city was spearheaded by the Haganah and involved intense fighting, psychological warfare, and the eventual expulsion of the Arab population.

Loudspeakers were used to broadcast messages designed to instill fear and panic among the residents, warning them of impending attacks and the fate that awaited those who resisted. Coupled with the sound of explosions and gunfire, these psychological tactics created a climate of terror. The Arab population, numbering around 10,000, fled en masse, leaving behind their homes, businesses, and places of worship.

The fall of Safed, like the events in Deir Yassin and Lydda, was part of a broader campaign to depopulate Palestinian areas and secure a Jewish majority in key regions. The use of psychological warfare, combined with direct military action, highlights the multifaceted nature of Zionist strategy during the war.

Psychological Warfare: Breaking the Will of a Population, The use of psychological tactics was a hallmark of Ben-Gurion's strategy during the 1948 war. Beyond the physical violence of massacres and expulsions, Zionist forces employed propaganda and symbolic violence to create a climate of fear that compelled Palestinians to flee.

Spreading Fear Through Propaganda, Propaganda campaigns played a central role in amplifying the psychological impact of Zionist military actions. Stories of massacres, such as those at Deir Yassin, were deliberately spread to neighboring villages, often exaggerated to maximize their effect. Flyers were distributed, and rumors were circulated about the invincibility of Zionist forces and the brutal consequences of resistance. This psychological assault was designed to break the will of Palestinian communities, making them more likely to abandon their homes without a fight.

Symbolic Violence and Publicity of Atrocities, High-profile massacres like Deir Yassin were not hidden but publicized, serving as warnings to other villages. The deliberate mutilation of bodies, the destruction of homes, and the desecration of holy sites were acts of symbolic violence intended to demonstrate the futility of resistance. These tactics, while effective in achieving their immediate goals, left deep scars on the collective memory of the Palestinian people.

Legacy of These Events, The massacres, expulsions, and psychological warfare carried out during the 1948 war were not isolated incidents but integral components of a systematic campaign to establish a Jewish state. The human cost of these actions—over 700,000 Palestinians displaced, hundreds of villages destroyed, and countless lives lost—continues to reverberate in the ongoing Israeli-Palestinian conflict. For Palestinians, these events are remembered as the Nakba, a catastrophe that symbolizes not only their dispossession but also the denial of their right to return to their homeland.

While Zionist leaders, including Ben-Gurion, defended these actions as necessary for state-building, the moral and ethical implications of their strategies remain deeply contested. The events of 1948 highlight the devastating consequences of prioritizing territorial ambitions over the principles of justice and coexistence.

The expulsions from Lydda and Ramle in July 1948 provide a particularly stark example of Ben-Gurion's military strategy in action. Located in the strategic corridor between Tel Aviv and Jerusalem, these towns were considered vital to the territorial integrity of the nascent Jewish state. Under Operation Dani, Israeli forces, acting on orders approved by Ben-Gurion, launched a brutal campaign to capture the towns. Once the towns fell, tens of thousands of Palestinians were forcibly expelled. Survivors describe being herded onto the roads at gunpoint, carrying only what they could manage. Many died of exhaustion, thirst, and starvation during the forced marches to the West Bank, a harrowing journey now referred to as the Lydda Death March. This operation alone resulted in the displacement of over 50,000 Palestinians and left an indelible mark on the collective memory of the Nakba.

Ben-Gurion's military strategy also involved the deliberate destruction of Palestinian villages to prevent the return of their inhabitants. Over 400 villages were systematically depopulated and razed to the ground during the war. Homes were demolished, wells were poisoned, and agricultural lands were seized or left barren. These actions were not merely tactical measures but part of a broader effort to create irreversible demographic changes. The destruction of villages ensured that even if international pressure forced Israel to allow the return of refugees, they would have no homes to return to.

The long-term consequences of Ben-Gurion's policies cannot be overstated. By the end of the 1948 war, over 700,000 Palestinians had been displaced, creating one of the largest and most enduring refugee crises in modern history. The newly established State of Israel passed laws to confiscate the property of displaced Palestinians and to prevent their return, further entrenching their dispossession. The Palestinian refugees, many of whom still live in camps across the region, remain a testament to the human cost of Ben-Gurion's vision.

Critics of Ben-Gurion's leadership, including historians such as Ilan Pappe, have described the events of 1948 as a deliberate campaign of ethnic cleansing. Pappe and others argue that the Zionist leadership's actions during the war were not merely reactive responses to Arab aggression but part of a premeditated strategy to transform Palestine into a Jewish-majority state. The methods employed—mass expulsions, massacres, and the destruction of villages—were, in this view, calculated to achieve demographic domination at the expense of the indigenous population.

Survivor testimonies offer poignant insights into the human suffering caused by these policies. Amina Khalil, a refugee from Jaffa, recalls the day her family was forced to flee: *"We heard gunfire and saw smoke rising from the next street. My father said we had to leave immediately. We ran, leaving everything behind. I remember clutching my doll and asking if we could come back, but my mother didn't answer."* Similarly, Hassan Ali, expelled from Lydda, recounts: *"The soldiers came to our house and ordered us to leave. My grandfather refused and was shot on the spot. We walked for days, with no food or water. Many people didn't survive the journey."* These accounts underscore the profound trauma and loss experienced by Palestinians during this period.

While defenders of Ben-Gurion argue that his actions were necessary for the survival of the Jewish state, such justifications fail to address the moral and ethical dimensions of his policies. The displacement of Palestinians was not an unintended consequence of war but a deliberate outcome of a strategy aimed at achieving territorial and demographic goals. This approach, while successful in establishing Israel, came at a profound human cost and sowed the seeds of decades of conflict and resentment.

The legacy of David Ben-Gurion's leadership is thus deeply contested. For many Israelis, he is a national hero who secured the survival of the Jewish people in the aftermath of the Holocaust. For

Palestinians, he is the architect of their dispossession, a figure whose vision for statehood was built on the erasure of their homeland. The enduring grievances of the Nakba, including the unresolved refugee crisis and the loss of Palestinian land and sovereignty, continue to shape the Israeli-Palestinian conflict to this day.

In conclusion, David Ben-Gurion's role in the 1948 Arab-Israeli War epitomizes the duality of his legacy. His leadership secured the establishment of a Jewish state, fulfilling the aspirations of the Zionist movement, but it did so through strategies of violence, displacement, and exclusion. The consequences of these actions—both for the Palestinian people and for the prospects of peace in the region—remain a stark reminder of the costs of prioritizing statehood over coexistence. A critical reevaluation of this history is essential for understanding the complexities of the conflict and for imagining a future rooted in justice and reconciliation.

Fawzi al-Qawuqji and Palestinian Resistance: A Story of Courage and Challenges

While Ben-Gurion and the Zionist forces were enacting their strategy of displacement, the Palestinian Arabs, led by figures like Fawzi al-Qawuqji, organized resistance against the Israeli military. In the tumultuous period leading up to and during the 1948 Arab-Israeli War, figures like Fawzi al-Qawuqji emerged as symbols of Palestinian resilience and determination in the face of overwhelming odds. Al-Qawuqji's life, his strategic leadership, and the efforts of the Arab Liberation Army (ALA) under his command shed light on the complex dynamics of the Palestinian struggle. His story reflects not only the courage of the Palestinian resistance but also the profound challenges posed by Zionist military strategy, political maneuvering, and international complicity.

A Revolutionary's Journey: From Homs to Palestine, Born in Homs, Syria, in 1890, Fawzi al-Qawuqji's life was shaped by his deep commitment to anti-colonial struggles. He began his military career as an officer in the Ottoman army during World War I. Following the war, al-Qawuqji became a fierce opponent of Western imperialism, fighting against the French in Syria and the British in Iraq. His participation in the 1936–1939 Great Arab Revolt in Palestine positioned him as a leader in the Arab nationalist movement, which sought to resist British colonial rule and the growing Zionist presence.

Al-Qawuqji's extensive military experience and pan-Arabist ideals made him an influential figure in the Arab world. He believed in the necessity of uniting Arab nations against colonial powers and Zionist expansion, viewing the struggle in Palestine as central to the broader fight for Arab self-determination. This commitment to Palestine led to his appointment as the commander of the Arab Liberation Army (ALA) in 1947, tasked with organizing resistance against the establishment of a Jewish state.

The Arab Liberation Army: An Uphill Battle, The ALA, under al-Qawuqji's leadership, faced significant challenges from the outset. Unlike the Zionist forces, which had spent decades building a cohesive military infrastructure through groups like the Haganah, Irgun, and Lehi, the ALA was a newly formed, poorly equipped force. It consisted of a mix of Palestinian volunteers, Arab irregulars, and fighters from across the region who were driven by a shared sense of solidarity but lacked the cohesion and discipline of a professional army.

One of the greatest hurdles was the lack of unity among Arab states. While leaders in Egypt, Transjordan, Iraq, and Syria expressed rhetorical support for the Palestinian cause, their actions often revealed conflicting political agendas. Transjordan's King Abdullah, for example, sought to annex parts of Palestine into his own kingdom, while other Arab leaders were more concerned with asserting their influence than with devising a coordinated military strategy.

The ALA itself was plagued by logistical issues. Weapons were scarce and often outdated, supply chains were unreliable, and communication between units was haphazard. In contrast, Zionist forces benefited from access to modern arms and equipment, much of which was smuggled into the region with the tacit approval of Western powers. The Zionists also enjoyed superior organization, with a centralized command structure and a clear strategy for securing territory and displacing Palestinian populations.

Defending Palestinian Land: The Struggle in Galilee, One of al-Qawuqji's most notable campaigns took place in the Galilee region, a strategically vital area that Zionist forces were determined to control. Al-Qawuqji understood the importance of defending Palestinian villages in this region, as their loss would not only displace thousands of Palestinians but also pave the way for Zionist territorial expansion.

In early 1948, the ALA launched operations to defend Galilean villages, engaging in fierce battles against well-equipped Zionist units. Despite the odds, al-Qawuqji's forces managed to achieve some temporary successes. For instance, they repelled Zionist advances in certain areas, providing critical respite for local communities. In one such engagement near Safed, al-Qawuqji's leadership and tactical acumen temporarily halted a Zionist offensive, boosting the morale of his fighters and the local population.

However, these victories were short-lived. The Zionist forces, backed by superior resources and intelligence, launched counteroffensives that overwhelmed the ALA. Villages that had been defended with great effort fell one by one, their residents either fleeing in terror or being forcibly expelled. The psychological impact of these defeats was profound, as rumors of massacres, such as the infamous Deir Yassin atrocity, spread fear among Palestinian communities.

Zionist Strategy and the Nakba, The Zionist strategy during the 1948 war was marked by meticulous planning and ruthless execution. Plan Dalet, the blueprint for securing territory and removing Palestinian populations, was central to this effort. It involved coordinated military offensives, the destruction of villages, and the forced expulsion of Palestinians, creating the conditions for what would become known as the Nakba *("catastrophe")*.

Deir Yassin, a village near Jerusalem, became a symbol of the brutality of this strategy. In April 1948, Zionist militias attacked the village, killing over 100 men, women, and children. Survivors described horrific scenes of violence, with entire families being massacred and homes destroyed. The attack was part of a deliberate effort to instill fear and encourage mass flight among Palestinians.

The psychological impact of such atrocities cannot be overstated. As news of the massacre spread, many Palestinians abandoned their homes, fearing a similar fate. Al-Qawuqji and his forces were acutely aware of the Zionists' use of terror as a tactic, but they lacked the resources and support to counter it effectively.

The Role of International Complicity, The international community's role in the events of 1948 cannot be ignored. Western powers, particularly the United States and Britain, played a significant part in enabling Zionist military superiority. The British, who had ruled Palestine under a League of Nations mandate since 1920, facilitated Zionist immigration and land acquisition, laying the groundwork for the conflict. Even as they withdrew in 1948, their policies had already set the stage for the displacement of Palestinians.

Meanwhile, the United States and other Western nations provided diplomatic and financial support for the Zionist cause. Arms shipments, such as those from Czechoslovakia, bolstered the Zionist military, while international sympathy for Jewish survivors of the Holocaust further strengthened the case for the establishment of Israel. This geopolitical context left Palestinian resistance leaders like al-Qawuqji fighting an uphill battle against not only Zionist forces but also a global system that favored their opponents.

Personal Accounts and the Human Cost of War, The story of Fawzi al-Qawuqji and the Palestinian resistance comes to life through the voices of those who lived through the events of 1948. Interviews with former fighters and displaced Palestinians reveal the depth of their experiences and the enduring impact of the Nakba.

One former ALA fighter, recalling his time under al-Qawuqji's command, said: *"We fought with everything we had, even though it was never enough. Al-Qawuqji was a leader who inspired us to keep going, even when the odds were against us. He would often join us on the front lines, showing us that he was willing to risk his life for our cause."*

For civilians, the war brought unimaginable suffering. An elderly Palestinian woman from a village in Galilee recounted *"When the fighting came to our village, we tried to stay, but the fear was too much. The Zionists came with their guns and their threats, and we had no choice but to leave. We walked for days, leaving everything behind—our homes, our land, our lives."*

Such testimonies highlight the dual narrative of heroism and tragedy that defined the Palestinian experience during the 1948 war.

Fawzi al-Qawuqji's leadership during the 1948 war remains a testament to the resilience and determination of the Palestinian resistance. His efforts, though ultimately unsuccessful, reflect the deep commitment of Palestinians to defending their homeland against overwhelming odds. At the same time, his story underscores the challenges of confronting a well-organized and internationally supported adversary.

The disunity among Arab states, the lack of resources, and the asymmetry of power between Palestinian and Zionist forces all contributed to the tragic outcomes of 1948. Al-Qawuqji's legacy serves as both an inspiration and a cautionary tale, reminding us of the importance of unity, strategic planning, and international solidarity in the struggle for justice and self-determination.

Today, as Palestinians continue to fight for their rights, the story of Fawzi al-Qawuqji and the resistance he led stands as a powerful symbol of their enduring quest for freedom and dignity. His life and his leadership remain a beacon for those who believe in the possibility of a just resolution to the Palestinian struggle.

The Mass Displacement and the Creation of Refugees: The Catastrophic Impact of the Nakba

The Nakba, meaning *"catastrophe"* in Arabic, is one of the most defining and traumatic events in Palestinian history. It refers to the mass displacement of Palestinians that occurred between 1947 and 1949 during the establishment of the State of Israel. This era saw the forced removal of over 700,000 Palestinians from their homes, leading to the creation of a refugee crisis that persists to this day. The Nakba was not a mere byproduct of war; it was a deliberate and systematic effort to erase the Palestinian presence from the land. This displacement, accompanied by the destruction of Palestinian villages and the barring of refugees from returning, has become a central feature of the Israeli-Palestinian conflict and a poignant symbol of the Palestinians' enduring struggle for justice and self-determination.

The Systematic Destruction of Villages and Displacement, The displacement of Palestinians was not an accidental consequence of the 1948 Arab-Israeli War but a calculated strategy employed by Zionist forces. Over 500 Palestinian villages were systematically destroyed during this period. These villages, some of which had existed for centuries, were razed to the ground, their homes reduced to rubble, and their populations forcibly expelled. The military operations that facilitated this destruction were not only aimed at gaining territorial control but at ensuring that the displaced population could never return.

One of the most infamous examples of this strategy is the Deir Yassin massacre. On April 9, 1948, Zionist paramilitary groups, including the Irgun and Lehi, attacked the Palestinian village of Deir Yassin near Jerusalem. The assault resulted in the massacre of over 100 men, women, and children. Survivors described horrific scenes of violence, with many recounting how unarmed villagers were executed, homes were looted, and women were assaulted. The Deir Yassin massacre sent shockwaves across Palestine, instilling terror among the population and prompting many to flee their homes in fear of similar atrocities.

The terror inspired by such incidents was compounded by direct military actions designed to depopulate entire areas. Zionist leaders, including David Ben-Gurion, explicitly discussed strategies to *"transfer"* the Arab population out of Palestine to create a Jewish-majority state. In some cases, Zionist forces used psychological warfare, spreading leaflets or broadcasting messages that warned of imminent attacks and urged Palestinian residents to leave. In other instances, villages were surrounded, bombarded, and forcibly evacuated at gunpoint.

False Promises and the Reality of Permanent Displacement, In many cases, Palestinians were misled into believing that their displacement would be temporary. Zionist forces often encouraged residents to leave their homes, assuring them that they could return once the fighting ceased. However, after the war ended, the reality was starkly different. The newly formed Israeli state enacted policies to prevent the return of Palestinian refugees, effectively solidifying their exile.

One critical piece of legislation was Israel's Absentees' Property Law of 1950, which legally confiscated the land and property of Palestinian refugees who had fled or been expelled during the war. The law defined any Palestinian who was not physically present within Israel's borders as an *"absentee,"* regardless of whether they had fled out of fear or been forcibly removed. This allowed the Israeli state to seize millions of dunams of Palestinian land, redistributing it to Jewish settlers or integrating it into the new state's infrastructure. Villages that were depopulated were either destroyed entirely or repopulated with Jewish immigrants, erasing the cultural and historical ties of Palestinians to the land.

One vivid example is the village of Lydda (Lod), where Zionist forces carried out a mass expulsion in July 1948. The residents were rounded up and forced to march for miles under the scorching summer sun, an event now known as the Lydda Death March. Many died from exhaustion, thirst, or violence during the march. The village's homes were subsequently taken over by Jewish settlers, and the original Palestinian residents were barred from returning.

The Refugee Crisis: A Humanitarian Catastrophe, The mass exodus created a humanitarian disaster of unprecedented scale in the Middle East. Over 700,000 Palestinians fled to neighboring countries such as Jordan, Lebanon, Syria, and Egypt, while others sought refuge within the West Bank and Gaza. These refugees, stripped of their homes, livelihoods, and possessions, were often forced to live in overcrowded and squalid conditions in makeshift camps.

In countries like Lebanon and Syria, Palestinian refugees were met with hostility and discrimination. Denied citizenship and basic rights, they were relegated to a liminal status, unable to fully integrate into their host countries yet barred from returning to their homeland. Refugee camps, such as Shatila and Sabra in Lebanon, became symbols of despair and marginalization, where generations of Palestinians have grown up in poverty and insecurity.

The psychological toll of displacement was equally devastating. Refugees carried with them memories of their lost homes and the trauma of violence and expulsion. Many elders in the camps still recount vivid details of the lives they left behind—homes with olive trees in the courtyard, bustling village markets, and the communal spirit of their communities. These narratives have been passed down to subsequent generations, keeping alive the hope and yearning for a return to Palestine.

Zionist Narratives vs. Palestinian Realities, While Palestinians recount the Nakba as a deliberate act of ethnic cleansing, Zionist narratives have often sought to downplay or justify the displacement. Some argue that Palestinians left voluntarily, either heeding calls from Arab leaders or fleeing the chaos of war. However, extensive historical research, including the work of Israeli historians such as Benny Morris and Ilan Pappé, has debunked these claims. These historians have revealed that the displacement was not an unintended consequence of war but a calculated effort to create a Jewish-majority state by removing the indigenous Palestinian population.

The Zionist justification for these actions often centers on the notion of Jewish self-determination and the existential need for a homeland in the aftermath of the Holocaust. While the Jewish quest for security and self-determination is undeniably valid, it cannot negate the rights and humanity of the Palestinian people. The Nakba represents a profound moral and ethical failure in the Zionist project, as it was built on the dispossession and suffering of another people.

The Enduring Legacy of the Nakba, The refugee crisis created by the Nakba remains one of the most contentious and unresolved aspects of the Israeli-Palestinian conflict. Today, the descendants of the original 1948 refugees number in the millions, scattered across the globe but primarily concentrated in refugee camps in the Middle East. Despite decades of displacement, these refugees maintain a strong sense of identity and connection to their ancestral homes. The right of return, enshrined in United Nations Resolution 194, remains a cornerstone of the Palestinian struggle for justice.

However, Israel has consistently refused to acknowledge the Nakba or the right of return, arguing that it would undermine the Jewish character of the state. This refusal perpetuates the suffering of Palestinian refugees and deepens the historical wounds inflicted during the Nakba. The ongoing expansion of Israeli settlements in the West Bank and the continued blockade of Gaza further exacerbate the sense of dispossession and injustice among Palestinians.

Personal Narratives, The human cost of the Nakba is perhaps best understood through the stories of those who lived through it. One survivor, an elderly woman from the village of Ein Hod, recounted her family's forced expulsion: *"We were told to leave, that it would be temporary. My father refused, but they came with guns, and we had no choice. We walked for days with no food or water. I still dream of the house where I grew up, with the fig tree in the yard."*

Another refugee from Jaffa, who fled to Lebanon, described the anguish of exile: *"We thought we would return in a few days, but days turned into months, and months into years. I am old now, and I know I will never see my home again. But my children and grandchildren must know where we come from. They must never forget."*

The mass displacement of Palestinians during the Nakba was not a tragic accident but a calculated strategy to erase Palestinian presence and establish a Jewish state. The destruction of villages, the barring of refugees from returning, and the creation of a protracted refugee crisis represent a grave injustice that continues to haunt the region. While the Nakba is a story of loss and suffering, it is also a story of resilience and resistance. The memory of the Nakba lives on in the hearts of Palestinians, fueling their struggle for justice and their unwavering hope for a return to their homeland.

The International Community and the Legacy of the Nakba

The Nakba of 1948 represents one of the most profound injustices in modern history—a tragedy that continues to shape the lives of millions of Palestinians and reverberates throughout the global political landscape. For Palestinians, the Nakba is not merely an event of the past, but a living memory that defines their struggle for justice and self-determination. It marks the moment when over 700,000 Palestinians were displaced from their homes, as Zionist militias and later the Israeli military carried out a systematic campaign of ethnic cleansing. However, the legacy of the Nakba is not only defined by Palestinian loss and suffering; it is also a story of the international community's failure to prevent this catastrophe and its subsequent complicity in the denial of Palestinian rights.

The United Nations and the Partition Plan, The United Nations played a central role in facilitating the events that led to the Nakba. In 1947, the UN General Assembly passed Resolution 181, which proposed the partition of Palestine into two separate states: one for the Jewish population and another for the Arab population. This plan allocated more than half of Palestine to the Jewish state, despite Jews owning only a fraction of the land. The plan was met with opposition from the Palestinian Arab population, who, by then, constituted the overwhelming majority in Palestine. They viewed the partition as an unjust resolution that disregarded their political and territorial rights, reducing them to a minority in their own homeland.

The UN's involvement in Palestine, while ostensibly driven by the principle of self-determination, was fraught with contradictions. The Partition Plan was created without Palestinian input and was largely a result of international pressures, notably from the United States and the Soviet Union, each with their own strategic interests in the region. For the Palestinians, the plan represented an imposition by foreign powers that had little regard for the history and reality of the land. The Zionist movement, on the other hand, saw the plan as an opportunity to establish a Jewish state and quickly moved to mobilize its forces in preparation for the eventual conflict.

After the adoption of Resolution 181, violence between Jews and Arabs escalated, particularly in areas where both communities coexisted. The United Nations, however, failed to intervene in any meaningful way. Instead, the UN focused primarily on trying to maintain order rather than protecting Palestinian civilians from the growing wave of Zionist aggression. While the United Nations Relief and Works Agency (UNRWA) was established in 1949 to provide relief for the Palestinian refugees who had fled their homes, the organization's mandate was strictly humanitarian—offering food, shelter, and education. This focus on relief and recovery ignored the underlying political realities, and its ability to tackle the root causes of the Palestinian refugee crisis was severely limited. The UN's inability to hold Israel accountable for its actions or to address the political status of Palestinian refugees is one of the most significant failures in its history.

The creation of Israel in 1948 was a pivotal moment in the history of the Middle East, with far-reaching consequences for the Palestinian people. This event, particularly the Nakba, which refers to the mass displacement and dispossession of Palestinians, was shaped by the geopolitical interests and moral considerations of the Western powers. The role of the United States, the United Kingdom, and other European nations was crucial, as their support for the Zionist movement and the establishment of Israel was influenced by a variety of factors, both humanitarian and strategic.

Geopolitical Context and the Rise of Zionism, In the aftermath of World War II, the international community, particularly in the West, found itself grappling with the aftermath of the Holocaust. The scale of the atrocities committed against the Jewish population in Nazi-occupied Europe left a profound mark on Western sensibilities. The Zionist movement, which sought to establish a Jewish homeland in Palestine, had already been active for decades, but it gained considerable momentum after the war. The plight of

Jewish refugees and the sympathy generated by the Holocaust catalyzed the Western powers' support for the Zionist cause.

In this context, the creation of a Jewish state in Palestine was seen not only as a moral response to the suffering of Jews but also as a political solution to address Jewish displacement. The United Nations, which had been established in 1945 with the aim of promoting peace and cooperation among nations, played a significant role in the process. In 1947, the UN proposed a partition plan that recommended dividing Palestine into separate Jewish and Arab states. While the Jewish leadership accepted this plan, the Arab leadership rejected it, seeing it as an unjust solution that disregarded the rights of the indigenous Palestinian population.

The United States and Western Powers' Support for Israel, The political recognition of Israel was swift and resolute. When David Ben-Gurion, the head of the Jewish Agency, declared the establishment of the State of Israel on May 14, 1948, the United States, under President Harry S. Truman, was the first country to recognize it, just minutes after the declaration. The Soviet Union, despite ideological differences, also extended recognition. This rapid support from both superpowers reflected the strategic importance of the Middle East during the Cold War era.

For the United States, the creation of Israel aligned with several key objectives. First, it was seen as a way to demonstrate moral leadership in the aftermath of the Holocaust. Second, Israel was strategically important in the context of Cold War geopolitics. The Middle East, rich in oil resources and strategically located, was seen as vital in the global struggle for influence between the United States and the Soviet Union. By supporting Israel, the West hoped to secure a foothold in the region and counterbalance the influence of Arab nationalist movements, which were often seen as aligned with the Soviet Union.

The British, who had controlled Palestine under a League of Nations mandate, were less enthusiastic about the creation of Israel, largely due to their complicated relationship with the Arab world. However, they did not obstruct the UN's partition plan, and after the 1948 war, they largely withdrew from direct involvement, leaving the United States to take the lead in supporting the new state.

The Nakba and Western Silence, While the Western powers supported the creation of Israel, the Palestinians experienced this moment as a catastrophe. The Nakba refers to the mass displacement of Palestinians that followed Israel's declaration of independence. Approximately 750,000 Palestinians were forced to flee their homes as Israeli forces advanced, often under violent circumstances. This included the destruction of Palestinian villages, with many people either killed or displaced into refugee camps in neighboring countries.

The systematic violence against Palestinian civilians, including massacres such as the one at Deir Yassin, became emblematic of the brutality of the 1948 war. Deir Yassin, a Palestinian village near Jerusalem, was attacked by Zionist militias, and dozens of men, women, and children were killed. This act of violence, and others like it, became a symbol of the Israeli campaign to depopulate Palestinian areas.

Despite the scale of these atrocities, the Western powers, particularly the United States and Britain, largely ignored or downplayed the violence. There was little international pressure on Israel to cease its military actions or address the plight of the Palestinians. The focus remained on recognizing Israel as a legitimate state, while Palestinian displacement and suffering were sidelined.

This support for Israel extended beyond political recognition; it was accompanied by substantial military and economic assistance. The United States provided critical support to Israel, both during and after the 1948 war, ensuring the survival of the new state in a region that was hostile to its existence. This military aid would continue in the decades to follow, solidifying Israel's position in the Middle East and ensuring that its expansionist policies would not be checked by international condemnation.

The Western Powers' Endorsement of Violence, The support for Israel by the Western powers can be seen as a tacit endorsement of the actions that led to the Nakba. Zionist militias, which later became the core of the Israeli Defense Forces (IDF), were responsible for numerous acts of violence and war crimes during the 1948 war. While these actions were justified by Israel as necessary for the survival of the state, they were also aimed at eliminating Palestinian presence from areas designated for the Jewish state.

The international community, however, remained largely silent in the face of these war crimes. Despite evidence of massacres and the forced expulsion of Palestinians, the United States and European nations did not hold Israel accountable. Instead, they continued to provide Israel with both moral and material support, reinforcing the notion that the creation of Israel, even if based on violence and dispossession, was justified by the broader geopolitical context.

This complicity in Israel's actions has been a subject of considerable debate. While the West was quick to recognize Israel and justify its creation, it simultaneously ignored the consequences for the Palestinian population. The displacement of Palestinians, their loss of homes and lands, and their ongoing struggle for self-determination were sidelined in favor of securing a stable, friendly state in the Middle East.

The creation of Israel and the Nakba are inseparable from the geopolitics of the post-World War II era. The Western powers, driven by a mix of humanitarian concerns, Cold War calculations, and colonial interests, played a crucial role in the establishment of Israel. Their swift recognition and ongoing support for the new state helped ensure its survival and expansion, but it also meant endorsing the displacement and suffering of the Palestinian people. In many ways, the creation of Israel was as much a political project as it was a humanitarian one, with the interests of the Western powers at the heart of the decision-making process. The consequences of this intervention continue to shape the conflict between Israel and Palestine, as the Palestinian quest for justice and self-determination remains unresolved to this day.

The Zionist Narrative and the Silencing of Palestinian Voices, The creation of Israel was framed by Zionist leaders and their international allies as the fulfillment of a historical promise—the return of the Jewish people to their ancestral homeland. However, this narrative often marginalized or completely ignored the Palestinian experience. The plight of the Palestinians as victims of displacement and violence was rendered invisible by a Western narrative that celebrated the establishment of Israel as a triumph for justice and democracy.

This narrative continues to dominate mainstream discussions about the Israeli-Palestinian conflict. Palestinians are often depicted as either passive victims or aggressors, their voices marginalized in the global discourse. Even when Palestinians speak out against their suffering, their grievances are dismissed or overshadowed by the louder, more powerful voices of Israeli officials and their international supporters. This silencing of Palestinian voices has had profound implications for the international response to the conflict.

International law, which is supposed to protect the rights of all peoples, has been applied selectively in the case of Palestine. The United Nations has issued numerous resolutions condemning Israeli actions, including the settlement expansion in the occupied territories and the annexation of East Jerusalem. However, these resolutions have largely been ignored, and Israel continues to enjoy impunity due to the consistent support it receives from the United States and its allies. This disregard for international law and human rights in favor of political expediency undermines the very principles upon which the international order was founded.

The Silence of the Arab World, The term *"The Silence of the Arab World"* refers to the gradual erosion of Arab states' commitment to Palestinian liberation and the mounting sense of abandonment felt by Palestinians, especially in the context of evolving political dynamics in the Middle East. This silence is not only about a lack of vocal support, but also about the absence of effective action, strategic coherence, and leadership on the part of Arab governments to alleviate Palestinian suffering or advocate for a just resolution to the Israeli-Palestinian conflict. The Arab world's stance has evolved dramatically since 1948, and this section aims to provide an in-depth analysis of the phases that have contributed to this silence.

Early Reactions to the Nakba (1948), In the aftermath of the Nakba of 1948, when approximately 750,000 Palestinians were displaced and Israel was established as a state, the Arab world was thrust into a difficult and defining moment. The Arab states, particularly Egypt, Jordan, Syria, Iraq, and Lebanon, immediately condemned the creation of Israel. They argued that the establishment of a Jewish state in the heart of Arab lands was a violation of Palestinian sovereignty and an act of imperialism. In response, they collectively entered into military confrontation with Israel in the 1948 Arab-Israeli War, with the goal of reversing the creation of the new state and preventing the displacement of Palestinian Arabs.

However, the Arab states were woefully unprepared and divided, lacking the necessary military coordination and political unity to defeat Israel. The war ended in a ceasefire, and Israel was allowed to maintain control over the territory it had claimed. Meanwhile, the Palestinian Arabs, who had been displaced from their homes, were left with nowhere to go, and their suffering continued.

The outcome of the war led to the recognition that military action alone could not resolve the conflict or address the displacement of Palestinians. Despite their initial military intervention, Arab states were unable to decisively change the facts on the ground. While the Arab League initially issued statements of condemnation, the lack of a strategic plan for how to handle the Palestinian crisis in the longer term marked the beginning of a retreat in Arab support for Palestinian national goals.

Political Expediency and National Interests. As the years passed, the Arab states increasingly prioritized their own national interests over the Palestinian cause. This shift was largely driven by internal factors, including domestic political challenges, economic difficulties, and the complexities of the Cold War geopolitics that influenced the Middle East.

Egypt under President Gamal Abdel Nasser initially positioned itself as a leader of the Arab world and a staunch supporter of Palestinian rights. Nasser's vision of pan-Arab unity and his efforts to resist Western imperialism were appealing to many Arabs. However, Nasser's focus on regional hegemony often eclipsed the Palestinian cause. His defeat in the 1967 Six-Day War, which resulted in the loss of the Sinai Peninsula and the Gaza Strip to Israel, marked a significant blow to his pan-Arab vision and diminished Egypt's ability to lead the Arab world. Over time, Nasser's government became more focused on stabilizing Egypt internally and addressing its economic issues, leaving the Palestinian cause on the backburner.

Jordan also played a complex role, particularly with regard to its control of the West Bank after the 1948 war. Jordan's King Hussein maintained control over this territory until the 1967 Six-Day War, during which Israel captured the West Bank. While Jordan initially positioned itself as a protector of Palestinian interests, it struggled with its own internal challenges, including tensions between Palestinians and Jordanian forces. The 1970 conflict known as *"Black*

September" highlighted the difficulty Jordan had in balancing its relationship with Palestinian groups and its own national security concerns. The result was a reluctant, often inconsistent stance on Palestinian self-determination.

Saudi Arabia, as the custodian of Islam's holiest sites and a regional power, found itself walking a fine line between supporting Palestinian aspirations and maintaining good relations with Western powers, particularly the United States. While Saudi Arabia rhetorically supported Palestinian independence, it was less inclined to take concrete steps that might threaten its economic ties to the West or destabilize its own monarchy. The kingdom's focus on maintaining regional dominance and securing oil-related economic interests often led to a more pragmatic, less outspoken stance on Palestinian issues.

Despite the shared Arab identity and religious ties, the political realities of national sovereignty, economic development, and the strategic positioning of Arab countries in the global arena often led to the sidelining of Palestinian priorities. Arab countries also became more absorbed in managing their internal politics and regional rivalries, which weakened their collective influence in addressing Palestinian grievances.

The Palestinian Liberation Organization (PLO), In response to the failure of Arab states to effectively champion Palestinian rights, the Palestinian Liberation Organization (PLO) was established in 1964 by the Arab League with the goal of representing Palestinian interests and coordinating a unified resistance to Israeli occupation. However, the PLO's initial years were marred by its dependence on the Arab states and their shifting political agendas.

Though the PLO was intended to serve as a representative body for Palestinians, it was consistently under the influence of Arab governments. Each Arab state had its own vision for the PLO, often using the organization as a tool for advancing their own geopolitical goals. This left the PLO without true autonomy and hindered its ability to effectively organize and advocate for Palestinian self-determination. Instead of acting as an independent force, the PLO became entangled in the political maneuverings of the Arab states, limiting its ability to take bold action on behalf of Palestinians.

Over time, the leadership of the PLO shifted from being primarily a representative body of Arab interests to a more Palestinian-dominated organization under figures like Yasser Arafat. While Arafat's leadership brought a sense of Palestinian identity to the organization, the PLO still faced significant challenges in gaining the full support of the Arab states. Arab governments were often reluctant to fully back the PLO in its struggle against Israel, especially if such support risked damaging their relations with the United States or Israel.

Recent Shifts: The Abraham Accords, In recent years, the most significant shift in Arab-Israeli relations has been the normalization of ties between Israel and several Arab states, culminating in the Abraham Accords in 2020. These agreements, signed by the United Arab Emirates (UAE), Bahrain, and later Morocco and Sudan, marked a dramatic departure from the longstanding Arab consensus that Israel should not be recognized until a just solution to the Palestinian issue was reached.

The Abraham Accords were framed by their signatories as a means of fostering regional peace, stability, and economic cooperation. They were also seen as a way of countering Iran's influence in the region, a shared concern for the UAE, Bahrain, and other Gulf states. However, these agreements were viewed by many Palestinians and other critics as a betrayal. The Arab states, which had historically positioned themselves as protectors of Palestinian rights, were now engaging diplomatically with Israel, leaving Palestinians feeling abandoned and betrayed.

From the Palestinian perspective, the normalization of relations with Israel represented not just a political shift but a moral one. The very states that had once advocated for the Palestinian cause were now seen as legitimizing Israeli policies, including its ongoing occupation of Palestinian territories and its treatment of Palestinian citizens. The perception of betrayal was compounded by the fact that these Arab states had presented themselves as leaders of the Palestinian cause for decades. Their willingness to engage with Israel in exchange for economic and strategic benefits undermined the Palestinian struggle for justice and self-determination.

The Arab World's Silence and Palestinian Disillusionment, This recent shift in Arab policy, combined with decades of inconsistencies and political expediency, has contributed to a profound sense of disillusionment among Palestinians. They have watched as Arab states, once their staunchest allies, have increasingly prioritized their own national interests over Palestinian liberation. The Arab world's silence is not just a lack of vocal support; it is a failure to act decisively to end the Israeli occupation, to support Palestinian refugees, and to challenge Israeli policies at the international level.

Many Palestinians now view the Arab world not as a source of solidarity but as a region that has grown indifferent to their suffering. This sense of abandonment is felt deeply by Palestinians in the occupied territories, in refugee camps across the Arab world, and by the broader Palestinian diaspora. The Palestinian cause, which once had the united support of the Arab world, is now seen as a secondary issue in a region preoccupied with its own political and economic struggles.

The silence of the Arab world in the face of Palestinian suffering is a result of both historical and contemporary political dynamics. From the initial military intervention of Arab states in 1948 to the subsequent prioritization of national interests over regional solidarity, Arab governments have largely failed to provide effective support for Palestinian self-determination. The creation of the PLO and its subsequent entanglement with Arab politics only further exemplifies the limitations of Arab leadership on Palestinian issues.

The normalization of relations between Israel and Arab states, particularly through the Abraham Accords, marks the culmination of a long process of shifting priorities in the Arab world. For many Palestinians, this represents not just a political change but a deep sense of betrayal by those who once pledged to defend their rights.

The ongoing silence of the Arab world reflects the complexity of Middle Eastern politics, but it also highlights the growing frustration among Palestinians, who feel increasingly abandoned by the very countries that should have been their most steadfast allies. The struggle for Palestinian liberation continues, but without the unwavering support of the Arab world, the road to justice remains fraught with obstacles.

The Nakba as a Living Memory, For Palestinians, the Nakba is not just a historical event but an ongoing experience. The trauma of displacement and loss continues to shape their identity and their aspirations for the future. Refugees in camps throughout the Middle East, in places like Lebanon, Jordan, Syria, and the occupied Palestinian territories, carry the memory of their lost villages and homes. The *"right of return,"* enshrined in international law, remains a cornerstone of Palestinian aspirations.

The Nakba is not merely a political issue—it is deeply personal. The stories of Palestinian refugees are passed down from generation to generation, preserving not just the memory of a lost homeland but also the hope for justice. Interviews with refugees from camps in Lebanon, such as Shatila and Bourj al-Barajneh, reveal a deep-seated yearning for return and a fierce determination to hold on to their heritage. Despite decades of hardship and exile, Palestinians continue to resist attempts to erase their history.

The Nakba's legacy is one of ongoing injustice. It is a reminder of the failure of the international community, the complicity of Western powers, and the betrayal of Arab leaders. For Palestinians, the Nakba is not just a historical event—it is a living tragedy that continues to define their struggle for justice. The global community must confront the reality of its complicity in the suffering of the Palestinian people and work toward a just resolution that honors their rights, history, and aspirations. Until this happens, the Nakba will remain not just a past tragedy but an enduring symbol of the struggle for justice and self-determination.

The Nakba's Enduring Legacy

The Nakba of 1948 is not merely a historical chapter; it is the beating heart of the Palestinian national identity. It remains an inextricable part of the Palestinian experience, shaping their collective consciousness, aspirations, and their continuous fight for justice and the right to return to their homeland. For Palestinians, the Nakba is a deeply personal and collective memory that represents the devastating destruction of their society, the brutal uprooting of an entire people, and the erasure of a rich and diverse cultural heritage that had existed for centuries. It is a symbol of displacement, loss, and unfulfilled promises, a haunting reminder of a tragedy that continues to impact millions of Palestinians worldwide.

The Nakba was the result of the establishment of the state of Israel in 1948, a moment that marked the culmination of the Zionist project in Palestine. For Jews, it signified the fulfillment of a millennia-old dream, the creation of a homeland in the historic land of Israel. However, for the indigenous Palestinian population, 1948 marked the beginning of an unparalleled trauma, one that persists to this day. The forced expulsion, the destruction of villages, and the systemic violence against Palestinian civilians during this period have left a deep scar on the Palestinian psyche, one that has not healed in the decades that followed. The legacy of the Nakba continues to reverberate, shaping not only the politics of the Middle East but also the everyday lives of Palestinians, whether in the occupied territories, refugee camps, or in the diaspora.

The Destruction of Palestinian Society, The Nakba represents more than just the loss of land—it is the destruction of a vibrant society that had existed for centuries in Palestine. Before 1948, Palestine was home to a diverse population of Arabs, including Muslims, Christians, and Jews, who lived together in relative harmony. Palestinian communities were built on centuries-old traditions of family, agriculture, and trade. Villages were often self-sustaining, with strong social and cultural ties that connected generations. Education, art, music, and religion thrived in these communities, and Palestinian towns and cities were home to intellectuals, artists, and businesspeople. Palestinian society, while under colonial rule, was a society with a deep sense of place and belonging.

However, the Zionist movement, with its goal of creating a Jewish state, sought to uproot this thriving Palestinian society and replace it with a new national identity based on Jewish exclusivity. The forced displacement and expulsion of Palestinians from their homes in 1948 were part of a larger strategy to cleanse the land of its indigenous inhabitants. Palestinians were either forcibly removed by Zionist forces or fled in fear of violence and massacres, many of which were carried out by Zionist paramilitary groups. Whole villages were destroyed, and the homes of Palestinians were looted and repurposed for the new settlers.

The depopulation of Palestinian villages is a central element of the Nakba's tragedy. According to various estimates, over 500 Palestinian villages were either destroyed or abandoned during and after the war. In some cases, entire towns were wiped off the map, with no trace of the original Palestinian presence remaining. For many Palestinians, the loss of their homes was not just a loss of physical property but the destruction of their identity, heritage, and connection to the land. These homes were passed down through generations, and for many Palestinians, they were deeply intertwined with their sense of belonging and cultural pride.

The Humanitarian Crisis: Displacement and Refugeeism, The Nakba's most visible and enduring consequence was the creation of a massive Palestinian refugee crisis. Over 700,000 Palestinians were displaced from their homes in 1948, forced to live as refugees in neighboring Arab countries, as well as in camps in the West Bank, Gaza Strip, Lebanon, and Syria. Today, the number of Palestinian refugees has grown to more than 7 million, with many still living in refugee camps under difficult conditions, denied basic rights and citizenship.

The refugee experience has shaped the Palestinian narrative and continues to affect the lives of generations. Families who were once prosperous, educated, and rooted in their communities found themselves living in squalid conditions, stripped of their land, homes, and livelihoods. Entire communities were scattered, often unable to return to their ancestral homes due to the establishment of Israeli military and settlement structures. The refugee camps where Palestinians sought shelter became symbols of their dispossession and a daily reminder of the violence and injustice that led to their exile.

For Palestinian refugees, the Nakba is not a distant memory but a present reality. Many families continue to live in camps that were originally intended to be temporary solutions. Some Palestinians have been born, lived, and died in these camps, with little hope for a return to their homeland. The right of return, enshrined in United Nations Resolution 194, remains a central demand of the Palestinian people. Despite this, Israel has consistently refused to allow the return of Palestinian refugees, arguing that it would undermine the Jewish character of the state. This refusal to grant

Palestinians the right to return has become one of the most contentious issues in the Israeli-Palestinian conflict.

Personal Narratives: The Emotional and Psychological Toll

The stories of individual Palestinians who lived through the Nakba are a powerful testament to the trauma and displacement experienced by the Palestinian people. These personal narratives illustrate the emotional and psychological toll of the Nakba and provide a deeper understanding of the human side of the Palestinian struggle. Many Palestinians still recall the day they were forced to flee their homes, carrying nothing but the clothes on their backs and a deep sense of loss. One Palestinian woman, recalling her family's flight from Haifa in 1948, said, *"We left in the middle of the night, without even a chance to say goodbye to our neighbors. My father told us we would return soon, but we never did."*

Another survivor of the Nakba, a man who was forced to leave his village near Jaffa, recalled: *"We were farmers, we had our land, our fields, and our olive trees. But when the Zionist forces arrived, they destroyed everything. We had to leave in fear for our lives. The trauma of that day has never left me; it haunts me every day."* These personal stories reflect the broader experience of Palestinians who were not just displaced from their homes but had their entire way of life shattered.

For Palestinians, the Nakba is not just an event in the past; it is a continuous emotional and psychological burden. Many still carry the memories of their villages, their homes, and the lives they once lived. The older generation, many of whom are still alive today, remembers the pain of loss, while younger generations have inherited the stories of displacement and exile. The emotional toll of the Nakba has been passed down through generations, with families living in exile often struggling with a deep sense of loss and yearning for a homeland they may never return to.

The Nakba's Impact on Palestinian National Identity, The Nakba has profoundly shaped Palestinian national identity. It is the core of the Palestinian struggle for justice, the right to return, and the recognition of their rights as an indigenous people. The Palestinian people's collective memory of the Nakba is an integral part of their national consciousness, fueling their ongoing resistance against occupation, displacement, and oppression. For Palestinians, the Nakba is not just a historical event; it is the foundational moment of their modern identity as a people who have suffered great injustice and continue to fight for their rights.

The Nakba also continues to shape Palestinian political activism and resistance movements. The experience of displacement and dispossession has created a sense of solidarity among Palestinians, regardless of where they live. Whether in the West Bank, Gaza, Lebanon, or the diaspora, Palestinians continue to demand their right to return and to be recognized as the rightful owners of the land that was taken from them. This collective memory of the Nakba fuels the Palestinian struggle for self-determination and justice, as well as the desire for a future where Palestinians can live in dignity and peace in their ancestral homeland.

A Struggle for Justice and Return, The Nakba of 1948 was not simply the end of a Palestinian way of life—it was the beginning of an ongoing struggle for justice, dignity, and the right to return to their homeland. The legacy of the Nakba continues to shape Palestinian society and the broader Middle East, serving as a reminder of the immense injustices suffered by the Palestinian people. For Palestinians, the Nakba is not a past event but a present reality, a continuous struggle for their rights, their land, and their future. The Nakba is a living memory, one that will never fade, and it remains central to the Palestinian cause until justice is achieved. The Palestinian people, despite decades of hardship, continue to resist, to remember, and to fight for their right to return to their homes and to live in peace and dignity.

Chapter 6: Israel's Expansion Through War (1948–1967)

Zionist Aggression and the Palestinian Catastrophe (1948–1967)

The Six-Day War of 1967 did not arise out of nowhere. Rather, it was the explosive culmination of nearly two decades of simmering tensions between Israel and its neighbors, a period of territorial disputes, military engagements, and deeply entrenched ideological divides. The years between 1948 and 1967 were marked by the aftermath of the 1948 Arab-Israeli War, the broader Arab nationalist movements, the rise of Palestinian resistance, and the increasing militarization of both Israel and its Arab adversaries. For Israel, the period following the creation of the state in 1948 was a time of consolidation, territorial expansion, and the quest for security. For Palestinians, it was an era of dispossession, displacement, and the struggle to survive as a displaced and oppressed people.

The events of the Six-Day War marked the expansion of Israeli control over significant parts of Palestinian land and the further entrenchment of its dominance in the region. However, this expansion came at a massive cost to the Palestinian people and Arab nations, and it laid the groundwork for the decades of conflict that followed.

The 1948 Arab-Israeli War and the Birth of Israel, The roots of Israel's territorial expansion can be traced back to the 1948 Arab-Israeli War, which erupted after the United Nations' Partition Plan for Palestine was passed in 1947. The plan sought to divide Palestine into separate Jewish and Arab states, with Jerusalem as an international city. While the Jewish leadership accepted the plan, Palestinian Arabs and the Arab states rejected it, believing it unjust and a violation of their right to self-determination in their own land.

The Zionist leadership, however, was determined to establish the State of Israel. Following the British withdrawal from Palestine in May 1948, Israel declared independence. This declaration triggered an invasion by neighboring Arab states—Egypt, Transjordan, Syria, Lebanon, and Iraq—who sought to prevent the establishment of a Jewish state. Despite being militarily outnumbered, the Israeli forces were better organized, equipped, and led, and by the end of the war, Israel not only survived but expanded its borders well beyond the areas designated by the UN Partition Plan.

In the wake of the conflict, over 700,000 Palestinians were displaced, many of whom fled to neighboring countries, where they lived in refugee camps for generations. The land they left behind was either taken by Israel or left in a state of destruction. The refugee crisis caused by the Nakba, remains one of the defining features of the Palestinian struggle. The Zionist forces also destroyed numerous Palestinian villages, attempting to erase Palestinian presence from the newly formed Jewish state. This was the beginning of Israel's broader strategy to create a Jewish-majority state, which involved removing or marginalizing the indigenous Palestinian population.

The atrocities committed by Zionist forces during this period, including massacres such as the one at Deir Yassin in April 1948, where over 100 Palestinians were killed by the Irgun and Lehi factions, became a grim symbol of the violence that accompanied the establishment of Israel. The destruction of Palestinian villages, the forced removal of residents, and the massacres all contributed to a broader pattern of dispossession that has continued in various forms ever since.

The Armistice and the Status Quo of 1949–1956, After the 1948 war, armistice agreements were signed between Israel and the

Arab states, establishing the boundaries of the new Israeli state, but they did not lead to a comprehensive peace. The West Bank and East Jerusalem came under Jordanian control, while Gaza fell under Egyptian rule. Palestinians in these territories, as well as those still living inside Israel, faced continued hardships, including the inability to return to their homes and the loss of their lands.

Israel, while physically secure within its new borders, faced a range of challenges, including the ongoing presence of Palestinian refugees and the inability to integrate these displaced people into the new Jewish state. The establishment of Israel meant the dispossession of Palestinians, who were either exiled or lived as second-class citizens within the state. This period of relative peace was punctuated by skirmishes along the borders, tensions within refugee camps, and rising calls for Palestinian resistance.

One of the key moments during this period was the 1956 Suez Crisis, which marked the first major military conflict after the 1948 war. When Egyptian President Gamal Abdel Nasser nationalized the Suez Canal, Israel, in collaboration with Britain and France, launched a military operation to seize the canal. The conflict resulted in a military victory for Israel, but politically, it exposed the limits of Israel's reliance on Western powers, as both the United States and the Soviet Union forced a ceasefire under intense international pressure. Despite the military victory, the Suez Crisis highlighted the persistent political and military tensions between Israel and its Arab neighbors.

The Rise of Pan-Arabism and Palestinian Resistance (1950s–1960s), As the 1950s progressed, the rise of pan-Arab nationalism, spearheaded by Nasser's vision of Arab unity, shaped much of the political landscape. Nasser's calls for a united Arab world were particularly significant for Palestinians, as they felt their plight was being subsumed by the larger Arab struggle against imperialism. Nasser's rhetoric resonated with Palestinians, and his support for the Palestinian cause was often seen as a unifying force among the Arab world. However, despite Nasser's symbolic support, the Arab states remained fragmented, and their responses to the Palestinian question were often inconsistent and insufficient.

The early 1960s saw the emergence of the Palestine Liberation Organization (PLO) in 1964, which sought to unite Palestinians under a common banner of resistance. The PLO, led by Ahmed Shukeiri, represented the growing desire among Palestinians to assert their own national identity and fight for the liberation of their land. However, the PLO's initial efforts were hampered by a lack of resources, internal divisions, and a lack of support from Arab states, many of whom saw the Palestinian issue through the lens of their own political agendas rather than as an autonomous struggle.

Despite the challenges faced by the PLO, Palestinian guerrilla movements, such as Fatah, emerged throughout the 1960s, engaging in acts of resistance against Israeli occupation. These groups, led by Yasser Arafat and others, sought to challenge Israel's occupation of Palestinian land through armed struggle. The struggle for Palestinian liberation gained international attention, and the movement became increasingly visible as the Arab states, under Nasser and his successors, escalated their rhetoric against Israel.

The Lead-Up to the Six-Day War: Tensions Build, By 1967, the political and military situation in the Middle East had reached a boiling point. Nasser, emboldened by the support of his Arab allies, sought to assert his authority in the region by challenging Israel. Tensions mounted as Nasser demanded the withdrawal of UN peacekeeping forces from the Sinai Peninsula, and on May 22, 1967, he ordered the closure of the Strait of Tiran to Israeli shipping—an act that Israel considered an act of war. The Israeli government, led by Prime Minister Levi Eshkol, responded by mobilizing its forces and preparing for what they saw as an inevitable confrontation with the Arab states.

The Six-Day War, which began on June 5, 1967, was a turning point in the history of the Middle East. Israel launched a preemptive strike against Egypt, crippling the Egyptian Air Force and giving the Israeli military a strategic advantage. Within six days, Israel had captured the Sinai Peninsula, the West Bank, East Jerusalem, and the Golan Heights. The war not only marked the expansion of Israel's territorial control but also signified the deepening of its military dominance in the region.

Zionist Expansion and the Occupation of Palestinian Territories, The occupation of the West Bank, East Jerusalem, and Gaza Strip by Israel after the Six-Day War had profound consequences for Palestinians. Israeli military rule was imposed over these territories, and thousands of Palestinian civilians were displaced once again. In East Jerusalem, Israel annexed the city, despite international opposition, and began a policy of encouraging Jewish settlement in Palestinian neighborhoods, particularly in the Old City, which houses important religious sites for Jews, Muslims, and Christians alike.

The Israeli settlement project expanded dramatically after 1967, as settlers moved into the West Bank, Gaza, and East Jerusalem, displacing Palestinians from their land and homes. These settlements, which were established on land considered by the international community to be occupied territory, became a major source of tension in the decades that followed. The Zionist movement viewed these settlements as a way to solidify Israel's control over the land, while Palestinians saw them as further evidence of the ongoing dispossession of their people.

Zionist Expansionism, From a Palestinian perspective, the events of 1948 to 1967 were not just a series of wars but a deliberate and systematic campaign of dispossession, ethnic cleansing, and colonization. The establishment of Israel was built on the backs of the Palestinian people, who were either displaced or marginalized in their own land. The narrative of a Jewish return to a historical homeland is inextricably linked to the erasure of Palestinian history, culture, and identity.

Zionist expansionism, particularly in the years following the 1967 war, exemplified a broader strategy to create a Greater Israel—one that extended beyond the boundaries set by the UN Partition Plan and incorporated the entire land of Palestine. While Israel claimed its military victories as acts of self-defense, the impact on the Palestinian population was devastating. The occupation of Palestinian territories, the building of settlements, and the militarization of the region created a cycle of violence and oppression that continues to this day.

In conclusion, the period between 1948 and 1967 was a pivotal moment in the history of the Israeli-Palestinian conflict. Israel's territorial expansion through war solidified its position as a regional power but came at the expense of the Palestinian people, who suffered displacement, dispossession, and continued occupation. Understanding this history is essential to understanding the current dynamics of the conflict and the ongoing struggle for Palestinian self-determination. The legacy of Zionist expansionism has left deep scars in the Palestinian psyche and continues to shape the broader Middle East conflict today.

Prelude to Conflict: The Aftermath of 1948

The year 1948 was a pivotal one in the history of Palestine and the broader Middle East, marking both the birth of the State of Israel and the beginning of the Nakba, for the Palestinian people. The creation of Israel, hailed as the culmination of a two-thousand-year-old Jewish dream for a homeland, was viewed by many in the West as a triumph of resilience and perseverance. However, for the Palestinians, it was a devastating event that shattered their land, their homes, and their identity. The Nakba was not just a moment of displacement; it was the beginning of a protracted struggle for survival, dignity, and self-determination.

In 1948, as Israel declared its independence and the Arab-Israeli war ensued, over 700,000 Palestinians were forcibly displaced from their homes. The vast majority were expelled from rural villages and urban centers, facing a fate of homelessness, poverty, and insecurity. Many sought refuge in neighboring Arab countries or in overcrowded refugee camps established by the United Nations. Families who had lived in the same villages for generations found themselves scattered across the Middle East, with no clear future in sight. These refugees, now dispersed and vulnerable, would become an enduring symbol of Palestinian dispossession, their plight continuing for decades.

The Creation of Israel and the Forced Displacement of Palestinians, The creation of Israel in 1948 was not merely a political event; it was the culmination of a long-term Zionist project that sought to establish a Jewish homeland in Palestine. This project, however, was not an innocent pursuit of self-determination for the Jewish people but rather a colonial venture, founded on the displacement of the indigenous Palestinian population. The Zionist movement, backed by European powers and later by the United States, saw Palestine as a land that could be claimed and settled by Jews, even though it was already inhabited by a large Palestinian Arab population.

The United Nations Partition Plan of 1947, which proposed the division of Palestine into separate Jewish and Arab states, was rejected by the Palestinian leadership and the Arab states, who saw it as unjust and unfair. The plan allocated 56% of the land to the Jewish state, despite the fact that Jews made up less than one-third of the population. The Palestinians, who had lived on the land for centuries, were expected to accept a diminished role in their own homeland. Moreover, the plan completely ignored the aspirations of the Palestinian Arab population, instead offering them a truncated, fragmented territory that lacked contiguity and the resources to sustain an independent state.

As the Zionist movement advanced its agenda, a series of violent campaigns were launched against Palestinian Arabs. The goal was to clear the land of its native inhabitants, making room for Jewish settlers and establishing control over key territories. A number of massacres and forced expulsions were carried out, most infamously the Deir Yassin massacre, where over 100 Palestinian civilians were killed by Zionist militias. This act, along with other similar atrocities, created a climate of terror and fear, leading to the mass flight of Palestinians from their homes.

Zionist forces employed a well-coordinated strategy of military aggression, psychological warfare, and coercion to drive Palestinians from their land. Villages were destroyed, and entire communities were uprooted. Palestinian towns, once thriving hubs of culture and commerce, were reduced to rubble, leaving behind only memories of a vibrant and ancient civilization. The aftermath of the war saw the establishment of Israel in 78% of the territory of Mandatory Palestine, leaving Palestinians with no home and no state.

The Divided City of Jerusalem: A Microcosm of the Larger Conflict, The fate of Jerusalem further symbolized the tragedy of Palestinian displacement. The United Nations had proposed that Jerusalem be placed under international administration as a *"corpus separatum,"* due to its religious significance to Jews, Muslims, and Christians. However, this vision never came to fruition. As the 1948 war unfolded, the city was divided: West Jerusalem came under Israeli control, while East Jerusalem, including the Old City and key religious sites like the Al-Aqsa Mosque and the Church of the Holy Sepulchre, fell under Jordanian rule.

For Palestinians, the division of Jerusalem was a painful loss. The city had been the spiritual and cultural heart of Palestinian life for centuries. It was not just a physical place but a symbol of Palestinian identity and history. The loss of East Jerusalem, which included significant Arab neighborhoods, was a grievous blow to the Palestinian people, who saw the city as an essential part of their homeland. The UN's failure to implement an international governance structure left Palestinians with little hope of reclaiming the city, and the Israeli control of West Jerusalem was marked by the expulsion of its Arab residents and the destruction of their properties.

The Fragile Peace and the Seeds of Future Conflict, The armistice agreements signed in 1949, which brought an official end to the fighting, did not resolve the underlying tensions between Israelis and Palestinians. While Israel emerged victorious, having expanded its territory beyond the borders outlined by the UN Partition Plan, the peace was fragile and tenuous. The armistice lines, known as the Green Line, were essentially a temporary ceasefire, and the unresolved issues of Palestinian refugees, the status of Jerusalem, and the future of Palestinian sovereignty remained on the table.

For Israel, the years following 1948 were marked by a sense of vulnerability and insecurity. The 1948 war had solidified the perception of Israel's need to defend itself from hostile Arab neighbors. This fear was not unwarranted, as Israel's declaration of independence was met with military opposition from surrounding Arab states, all of whom rejected the creation of the Jewish state. The memory of the Holocaust, which was still fresh in the minds of many Jews worldwide, amplified Israeli fears of encirclement and annihilation. The notion of a permanent security threat became deeply ingrained in Israel's national consciousness, leading to the militarization of its society and its foreign policy.

For the Arab states, the 1948 defeat was a humiliating blow that left them with a sense of impotence and frustration. Palestinian refugees, who had fled their homes in fear of Zionist aggression, were now living in overcrowded refugee camps across the Arab world, with no resolution to their plight. This sense of injustice became a rallying cry for Arab nationalist movements, which sought to restore Palestinian rights and challenge the legitimacy of Israel's existence.

One of the most prominent figures to emerge in the aftermath of 1948 was Gamal Abdel Nasser, an Egyptian army officer who rose to prominence after the 1952 Free Officers' Revolution. Nasser's vision for the Arab world was one of unity and strength, and he made the Palestinian cause a central element of his nationalist agenda. He was seen as a charismatic leader who sought to unite the Arab states in opposition to Israel, and his pan-Arab ideology resonated with many Palestinians who had been displaced and disillusioned by the events of 1948.

Reflections on Zionist Policies, The creation of Israel and the ensuing Nakba have been the subject of intense debate, particularly in terms of the role played by Zionist forces in the displacement and suffering of Palestinians. Zionist leaders, particularly David Ben-Gurion and Menachem Begin, employed a strategy of ethnic cleansing, with the explicit goal of creating a Jewish-majority state in Palestine at the expense of the Palestinian Arabs. The forced expulsion of Palestinians was not merely a byproduct of the war but a central component of Zionist policy.

Zionist militias, such as the Haganah, Irgun, and Lehi, used terror and violence to intimidate Palestinian communities into fleeing. The destruction of villages, the massacre of civilians, and the systematic removal of Palestinians from their land were part of a deliberate strategy to secure the establishment of Israel. These actions were not just acts of war but were driven by a deep-seated ideology that sought to erase Palestinian presence and history from the land.

Critics of Zionism argue that the creation of Israel was based on an unjust and discriminatory process that disregarded the rights of the indigenous Palestinian population. They contend that the

Zionist movement's approach to the Palestinians was colonial in nature, treating them as obstacles to be removed in order to create a Jewish state. The ongoing displacement of Palestinians, the failure to address their right to return to their homes, and the continued occupation of Palestinian lands in the West Bank and Gaza Strip are seen as extensions of the policies that began in 1948.

Interviews and Personal Accounts: The Human Cost of the Nakba, The human cost of the Nakba is best understood through the personal accounts of those who lived through it. Survivors of the Nakba recall the terror of hearing gunfire, the destruction of their homes, and the heartbreak of seeing loved ones torn apart by violence. One elderly Palestinian man, who was a child during the Nakba, recalls: *"We were forced out of our home in the middle of the night. I remember my mother crying as we left everything behind. We didn't know where we were going, or if we would ever come back."*

Another survivor, a woman who fled from her village in the Galilee, remembers the desperation of the refugee camps: *"We had no food, no shelter, and no future. We were treated like animals, not people. But we never lost hope that one day we would return home."*

These personal stories reflect the enduring trauma of the Nakba, a trauma that continues to shape the Palestinian identity and the struggle for justice. The memories of those who lived through 1948 serve as a powerful reminder of the human cost of the Zionist project and the ongoing plight of Palestinian refugees who continue to seek recognition of their right to return to their homeland.

The aftermath of 1948 was not just the creation of Israel but the beginning of a long, painful process of dispossession and exile for the Palestinian people. The Zionist project, which sought to establish a Jewish state in Palestine, came at the expense of the Palestinian Arabs, who were displaced, dispossessed, and denied their basic rights. The policies of ethnic cleansing, violence, and forced expulsion were central to the creation of Israel, and they continue to shape the conflict today.

THE PALESTINIANS, WHOSE lives were torn apart in 1948, continue to resist occupation and dispossession, holding on to their land, their heritage, and their dreams of return.

Gamal Abdel Nasser: The Rise of Pan-Arabism and His Challenge to Zionism

By the mid-1950s, Gamal Abdel Nasser had become one of the most influential figures in the Arab world. With a powerful vision of pan-Arabism, Nasser sought to unite the Arab states politically, economically, and militarily, striving for a future of strength and independence. This vision resonated deeply with a region struggling with the legacies of colonialism and the recent shock of Israeli statehood. His opposition to Zionism, alongside his staunch anti-imperialist stance, made him an emblem of Arab resistance to both Western domination and the newly established Zionist state in the heart of the Arab world. Nasser's journey, however, was complex and filled with both triumphs and setbacks. It exposed the underlying fractures in Arab unity and the enduring challenges of realizing the dream of pan-Arabism.

Nasser's Early Years: A Vision Born from Struggle, Gamal Abdel Nasser was born in 1918 in Alexandria, Egypt, during a time of great national unrest. Egypt, under British colonial rule, was a fractured society, torn between the ruling elite, which often collaborated with colonial powers, and the growing nationalist movements seeking independence. The 1919 Egyptian Revolution had ignited a fervent sense of national identity, but British imperialism continued to control key aspects of Egyptian life. Nasser's formative years were thus marked by an awareness of oppression and the desire for change.

He saw firsthand how Egypt's political and economic systems were designed to serve foreign interests at the expense of the Egyptian people.

Nasser's education at the Egyptian Military Academy introduced him to military strategy and discipline, while his experiences as a young officer in the Egyptian Army exposed him to the broader Arab world's struggle against colonialism. As a young officer, he was also deeply influenced by the Free Officers Movement, a secret group of military leaders who sought to overthrow Egypt's monarch, King Farouk, and rid the country of British influence. Nasser's role in the 1952 coup that led to the overthrow of the monarchy marked the beginning of his rise to power. His military credentials and deep sense of patriotism quickly established him as a leader within the new Egyptian republic.

Nasser's Vision of Pan-Arabism, Nasser's vision of pan-Arabism was grounded in the belief that the Arab world, despite its internal divisions, could unite to form a powerful geopolitical entity capable of resisting Western imperialism and the encroaching Zionist threat in Palestine. He saw the Arab world as a collection of nations bound by a common language, culture, and history, and believed that the unification of these countries was the key to reclaiming sovereignty and ensuring their collective future. Nasser's approach to pan-Arabism was also deeply socialist, advocating for the redistribution of wealth, nationalization of key industries, and land reforms in order to address the stark economic inequalities that plagued many Arab states.

Nasser's rhetoric was laced with anger and defiance toward the West, particularly Britain and France, who were seen as the architects of the 1948 creation of Israel. He considered the establishment of Israel as a colonial project, backed by Western powers, aimed at dividing the Arab world and ensuring continued imperial control over the region's resources. For Nasser, Israel was not just a political rival, but a foreign entity planted in the heart of Arab lands, with the full support of imperialist powers. Nasser's stance on Israel was clear and uncompromising: the Zionist project represented a direct threat to Arab identity, sovereignty, and land.

Nasser's Role in the Palestinian Struggle, The Palestinian cause was central to Nasser's political agenda, and he consistently positioned himself as its foremost advocate. Following the 1948 Arab-Israeli War and the defeat of Arab forces, many Palestinians were displaced, with hundreds of thousands fleeing to neighboring Arab countries. For Nasser, the displacement of Palestinians and the occupation of their lands was not merely a humanitarian crisis but a violation of Arab dignity and sovereignty. His calls for Palestinian self-determination and the liberation of Palestine from Israeli occupation became central themes in his speeches.

Nasser's support for Palestinian resistance groups was a significant aspect of his foreign policy. Egypt provided training, arms, and logistical support to various Palestinian factions, including the Palestinian Liberation Army (PLA), which operated under Egyptian command. While Nasser's contributions were crucial in bolstering the Palestinian cause, his leadership style also reflected the broader challenges facing the Arab world. His pan-Arabist agenda often clashed with the more localized interests of Palestinian leadership, as many Palestinians were wary of Egyptian dominance over their struggle.

Despite his support for the Palestinians, Nasser's approach to the issue was often criticized for being more focused on advancing his own political ambitions and influence within the Arab world than on genuinely addressing Palestinian needs. The tensions between Nasser's pan-Arabism and the desire for Palestinian self-determination were never fully resolved, and his leadership in the Palestinian cause, while important, did not always align with the Palestinians' broader aspirations.

The Suez Crisis: A Defining Moment, One of the most defining moments of Nasser's leadership came in 1956, when he nationalized the Suez Canal, a critical waterway that had been controlled by British and French interests. The Suez Canal was of immense strategic importance to the West, providing a key maritime route for oil and goods between Europe and Asia. By nationalizing the canal, Nasser sought to assert Egypt's sovereignty and secure funding for the construction of the Aswan High Dam, an ambitious infrastructure project that would provide Egypt with vital irrigation and electricity.

The nationalization of the Suez Canal angered Britain and France, who had a vested interest in the canal's operation, as well as Israel, which viewed Nasser's growing influence as a threat. In response, Israel launched a military strike against Egypt in the Sinai Peninsula, with Britain and France quickly joining in the invasion. The Suez Crisis, as it came to be known, was a pivotal moment in the Arab world's struggle against Western imperialism. Nasser, although militarily outmatched, managed to rally the Arab masses and mobilize international opposition to the invasion.

The United States, under President Dwight D. Eisenhower, opposed the British and French military intervention, partly due to Cold War considerations and partly because of growing anti-imperialist sentiments in the Arab world. The Soviet Union also condemned the attack and made it clear that any escalation could lead to a wider conflict. The diplomatic pressure from both superpowers forced Britain, France, and Israel to cease hostilities, leading to a ceasefire and a diplomatic victory for Nasser. The Suez Crisis marked a significant shift in the balance of power in the Middle East, weakening British and French influence and solidifying Nasser's reputation as a leader of resistance to imperialism.

Nasser's Vision for Arab Unity: The United Arab Republic, Nasser's dream of pan-Arab unity took a significant step forward in 1958 with the formation of the United Arab Republic (UAR), a political union between Egypt and Syria. The UAR was seen by many as the first real attempt to create a unified Arab state, a symbol of Nasser's vision for Arab solidarity. However, the union was short-lived, lasting only three years before Syria withdrew due to internal dissent and tensions over Nasser's dominance in the union. Despite this failure, the UAR represented the peak of Nasser's efforts to achieve pan-Arab unity, and it solidified his position as the central figure in Arab politics during the 1950s and early 1960s.

In his efforts to promote Arab unity, Nasser faced significant opposition from monarchies in the Gulf, particularly Saudi Arabia and Jordan. King Faisal of Saudi Arabia, in particular, viewed Nasser's brand of Arab socialism and his ties to the Soviet Union as a threat to the established order in the Gulf. The rise of Nasser's influence thus deepened the political divisions within the Arab world, as some leaders feared the spread of Nasser's revolutionary ideas while others embraced them.

Nasser's Critique of Zionism and Western Imperialism, Nasser's critique of Zionism was foundational to his foreign policy and his broader vision for the Arab world. He believed that Zionism was not merely a political movement but a colonial enterprise that sought to implant a foreign, settler state in the heart of the Arab world. This perception was shaped by the history of Western imperialism in the region and Nasser's view that Israel was a tool of Western powers designed to secure imperialist interests in the Middle East. His harsh criticism of Zionism resonated with many Arabs, who viewed the creation of Israel as an affront to their dignity and land.

Nasser's uncompromising stance against Israel was not just ideological but practical. He sought to unite the Arab world against what he saw as a common enemy, and his rhetoric was filled with defiant calls to liberate Palestine and expel the Zionists from the region. While his efforts to build an Arab military alliance and support Palestinian resistance were significant, they were also hampered by internal divisions within the Arab world and the complexities of geopolitics. Despite his leadership, Nasser's vision of Arab unity remained elusive, and the challenges of confronting Zionism and Western imperialism persisted.

Nasser's Lasting Legacy, Gamal Abdel Nasser's legacy remains a cornerstone of Arab political thought. His vision of pan-Arabism and his unwavering stance against Zionism and Western imperialism inspired generations of Arabs and Palestinians. While his efforts to unite the Arab world under a single political banner were fraught with challenges and setbacks, Nasser's influence on Arab nationalism and his commitment to Palestinian liberation continue to resonate today.

Despite the internal divisions that plagued his efforts and the ultimate failure of his vision of a unified Arab state, Nasser's leadership marked a turning point in the history of the Arab world. His defiance against imperialism, his advocacy for Palestinian self-determination, and his critique of Zionism remain central themes in the ongoing struggle for justice and sovereignty in the Middle East. Nasser's life and leadership stand as a testament to the enduring power of resistance and the dream of Arab unity, even in the face of overwhelming odds.

The Sinai Campaign: Israel's First Preemptive War

The Sinai Campaign of 1956, also known as the Suez Crisis, was a watershed moment in the Middle East, representing not only a significant military engagement but also a pivotal turning point in the geopolitics of the region. This conflict exposed the deep tensions between Egypt and Israel, as well as the changing balance of global power. While Israel's swift military victory was notable, it came at the cost of international condemnation and political fallout, revealing the intricate alliances and rivalries at play. The conflict also highlighted the moral and political complexities of the Zionist movement, providing a clear lens through which to examine the strategies and motivations of Israel, Britain, France, and Egypt.

The Road to War: Nasser's Challenge and Zionist Ambitions

In the years leading up to the Sinai Campaign, tensions between Egypt and Israel had been steadily escalating. Egyptian President Gamal Abdel Nasser, a charismatic leader who espoused pan-Arabism and sought to position Egypt as the leader of the Arab world, had been a constant thorn in Israel's side. Nasser's vision of a united Arab world, free from Western influence, particularly British and French colonialism, posed a direct challenge to the geopolitical interests of Israel and the West. His rhetoric against Zionism was unwavering, and his support for Palestinian resistance movements further stoked Israeli fears of Arab unity against them.

However, it was Nasser's decision to nationalize the Suez Canal in July 1956 that became the immediate catalyst for the crisis. The Suez Canal was one of the most strategically important waterways in the world, connecting the Mediterranean to the Red Sea and providing vital access to oil supplies in the Middle East. The canal's nationalization by Egypt was viewed as a direct affront to Britain and France, both of whom had historic control over the waterway and whose economies were heavily dependent on it. For Israel, the Suez Canal itself was not the primary issue; rather, the nationalization symbolized a wider Arab defiance and presented a new political reality where Nasser's influence in the region was growing, making it all the more necessary for Israel to act.

From a Zionist perspective, Nasser's rising power in the Arab world posed a serious existential threat. Israel had already suffered from periodic border clashes and skirmishes with neighboring Arab states. More troubling, however, was Egypt's increasing military strength. In addition to Nasser's anti-Israel rhetoric, Egypt had been arming itself with modern Soviet weaponry, and its military was becoming more capable of threatening Israel's borders. Furthermore,

Egypt had closed the Straits of Tiran, which were crucial for Israeli shipping, particularly for trade routes to Asia and Africa. The blockade had crippled Israel's economy, and the strategic imperative to reopen the straits became a driving factor behind Israel's decision to take military action.

The Zionist state also feared that Nasser's growing influence in the Arab world could inspire further pan-Arab movements that would coalesce around a united front against Israel. With these strategic considerations in mind, Israel chose to act decisively.

The Military Campaign: A Swift and Brutal Assault, The military phase of the Sinai Campaign began on October 29, 1956, when Israel, under the leadership of Prime Minister David Ben-Gurion and Defense Minister Moshe Dayan, launched Operation Kadesh. Israel's strategy was preemptive, aiming to neutralize Egypt's military capacity, open the Straits of Tiran, and gain a foothold in the Sinai Peninsula. The attack was part of a larger coordinated effort with Britain and France, who had their own interests in the region. Britain and France, both with deep colonial ties to the Suez Canal, sought to remove Nasser from power, fearing that his control over such a crucial maritime passage would allow him to dictate the flow of oil and trade to Europe.

The Israeli forces, equipped with advanced weaponry and backed by extensive intelligence operations, quickly advanced into the Sinai Peninsula, overcoming Egyptian defenses with startling speed. Within days, Israeli forces had crossed the canal and advanced toward key strategic locations. The operation was conducted with the precision and speed for which the Israeli military is known. Moshe Dayan, one of the key figures in Israeli military history, played a central role in overseeing the assault. His leadership and military acumen were evident, and the Israeli forces displayed an overwhelming superiority in both planning and execution.

Despite initial successes, however, the military campaign was marred by a series of significant challenges. While the Israeli military overran much of the Sinai Peninsula, they encountered stiff resistance in some areas, and logistical challenges began to surface as the campaign wore on. Additionally, the political and diplomatic fallout from the war would prove to be far more complex and damaging than anticipated. Although Israel succeeded in temporarily reopening the Straits of Tiran, the true significance of the conflict lay not in military outcomes but in the global response to Israel's actions.

The Global Response: Pressure from the United States and the Soviet Union, The Sinai Campaign was not simply a regional conflict; it was a struggle that involved the larger global powers of the day. Britain and France, both seeking to maintain their influence in the Middle East, had launched their own military operations in conjunction with Israel. But while Israel's initial military successes were impressive, the campaign quickly drew the ire of the United States and the Soviet Union, two superpowers locked in the Cold War.

The United States, under President Dwight D. Eisenhower, was particularly concerned about the impact of the crisis on its broader geopolitical interests. The U.S. was engaged in a delicate balancing act: it sought to maintain its influence in the Middle East, but it was also wary of being drawn into a war that could alienate Arab nations, particularly Egypt, which had increasingly aligned itself with the Soviet bloc. The Soviet Union, meanwhile, saw an opportunity to exploit the crisis as a way to further its influence in the region. Both superpowers pressured Britain, France, and Israel to cease their military operations.

The global outcry was swift and unrelenting. The United Nations, acting under pressure from both the United States and the Soviet Union, called for an immediate ceasefire. Britain and France, whose public support for the campaign was waning, eventually acceded to the UN resolution and agreed to a ceasefire on November 6, 1956. This marked a humiliating diplomatic defeat for Britain and France, who had hoped to reassert their colonial influence in the Middle East through military force.

The Political Fallout: Strengthening Nasser's Image and Zionist Isolation, The political fallout from the Sinai Campaign was both profound and far-reaching. While Israel achieved its immediate military objectives, including the temporary reopening of the Straits of Tiran, the long-term consequences of the conflict were less favorable. The international condemnation of the military intervention, particularly from the United States and the Soviet Union, highlighted Israel's vulnerability in the face of global opposition. Despite the military victory, Israel found itself diplomatically isolated, with its actions condemned by much of the international community.

For Egypt, the outcome of the crisis was paradoxical. While Nasser's forces had been decisively defeated on the battlefield, the political repercussions of the campaign ultimately enhanced his standing both within the Arab world and globally. Nasser emerged from the conflict as a hero of Arab nationalism, his defiance of Western powers earning him widespread admiration. The failure of Britain and France to achieve their objectives only served to further elevate Nasser's image as a leader who had stood up to imperialism. Nasser's influence in the Arab world grew significantly after the crisis, and his rhetoric of resistance against Western colonial powers resonated deeply across the Middle East.

In Israel, however, the Suez Crisis exposed significant strategic and moral challenges. While Israel's military success was undeniable, it raised questions about the ethical implications of preemptive warfare and the broader implications of Zionist policies. Critics of the Israeli government at the time pointed out that the military operation had been launched not only for strategic reasons but as part of a broader effort to assert Israel's military dominance in the region, often at the expense of its Arab neighbors. The international community, particularly the Arab world, increasingly viewed Israel's actions as an extension of Zionist colonial ambitions, intent on displacing and subjugating the indigenous Palestinian population.

The Zionist Agenda, The Sinai Campaign serves as a microcosm of the broader Zionist project and its implications for the Palestinian people. The military actions of Israel during this time were not simply driven by a desire to defend its borders; they were part of a larger, ongoing campaign to assert territorial control in the Middle East. This expansionist mindset, coupled with the ideology of Zionism, often led to the displacement of indigenous Arab populations and the marginalization of Palestinian rights. The Suez Crisis, while providing Israel with a temporary military victory, did little to address the ongoing issue of Palestinian displacement and the broader injustices faced by Arab populations under Israeli control.

The conflict also underscored the continued militarization of Israeli policy and its reliance on preemptive strikes against perceived threats. The ideology of preemption, which became a cornerstone of Israeli defense strategy, was shaped by the experiences of the 1948 war and the constant existential threats perceived by Israeli leaders. However, this approach, while effective in the short term, has had long-lasting and often devastating consequences for the broader Middle Eastern peace process.

In conclusion, the Sinai Campaign of 1956 not only shaped the future of Israel and Egypt but also had far-reaching implications for the geopolitical dynamics of the Middle East. While Israel emerged militarily victorious, the political fallout revealed the complexities of Zionism's goals and strategies in the region. The conflict's aftermath would reverberate through subsequent decades, contributing to the ongoing tensions between Israel and its Arab neighbors, and leaving a legacy of unresolved conflict and human suffering that endures to this day.

The Road to 1967: Tensions Reach a Boiling Point

By the mid-1960s, the Middle East was teetering on the edge of an explosive confrontation. The complex web of alliances, territorial disputes, and historical grievances that had long shaped the region's political landscape was now reaching a boiling point. The stage was set for the 1967 Six-Day War, a conflict that would redefine the borders of the Middle East and have profound implications for the Palestinian cause and the fate of the Arab world. At the heart of this escalating tension was the figure of Egyptian President Gamal Abdel Nasser, whose ambition to lead the Arab world and confront the Israeli state would prove to be a catalyst for the violence that ensued.

Nasser's Vision of Arab Unity and Confrontation with Israel, Gamal Abdel Nasser, who had emerged as a charismatic leader following the Egyptian Revolution of 1952, saw himself as the natural leader of the Arab world. His vision of Arab unity was rooted in the idea of pan-Arabism, a political ideology that sought to unify Arab countries under a common banner of nationalism and anti-colonialism. Nasser's survival of the Suez Crisis in 1956, when he stood firm against a military intervention by Britain, France, and Israel, boosted his standing in the Arab world. The Suez Crisis, though ultimately a military defeat for Egypt, was portrayed as a victory for Nasser's leadership, and it solidified his reputation as a champion of Arab independence.

By the early 1960s, Nasser's rhetoric had grown increasingly militant. His speeches were filled with calls for Arab unity and the destruction of the Israeli state, a sentiment that resonated deeply across the region. Nasser's influence extended beyond Egypt's borders, particularly to Syria and Jordan, which, alongside Egypt, formed the backbone of the Arab resistance to Israeli expansion.

Nasser's vision of a united Arab world was predicated on a shared commitment to confronting Israel, which was seen by many Arab leaders as an illegitimate colonial entity in the heart of the Arab world.

The creation of the Palestine Liberation Organization (PLO) in 1964 was a direct response to these geopolitical dynamics. The PLO, initially a political tool for Arab states rather than an independent Palestinian entity, was intended to serve as a rallying point for the Palestinian cause and a symbol of Arab commitment to the liberation of Palestine. Nasser and other Arab leaders saw the PLO as a means of consolidating Arab control over the Palestinian issue, which had been a source of regional instability since the 1948 Arab-Israeli War. The establishment of the PLO marked a significant step in the growing militancy of the Arab world toward Israel, and its creation was a clear signal to Israel that the Palestinians were no longer passive in the face of Zionist expansion but were becoming an active force in the region's political landscape.

While the PLO's initial role was more symbolic than practical, the organization's increasing prominence and its growing ties with other Arab states heightened Israeli concerns. The Israeli government, led by Prime Minister Levi Eshkol, began to view the rising militancy among Arab states, particularly Egypt, as a direct threat to its survival. The PLO, for its part, had begun to organize guerrilla attacks on Israeli targets, signaling a shift in Palestinian resistance tactics from diplomatic initiatives to armed struggle.

The Golan Heights and Border Skirmishes: A Prelude to War, Tensions between Israel and its Arab neighbors escalated in the years leading up to the 1967 war, with the Golan Heights becoming one of the key flashpoints. The Golan Heights, a strategically significant plateau that Israel had seized from Syria in the aftermath of the 1967 war, was a source of constant tension. Situated along the border between Israel and Syria, the Golan Heights provided both military advantages and access to critical water resources. Syria's desire to reclaim the Golan Heights became one of the central issues in the Arab-Israeli conflict, and Israeli forces frequently clashed with Syrian troops along the border. By the mid-1960s, border skirmishes between Israeli and Syrian forces had become a routine occurrence, further contributing to the escalating tensions in the region.

In addition to these border skirmishes, the situation was further exacerbated by the growing militarization of the region. Nasser, keen to assert Egypt's dominance in the Arab world, began to stockpile weapons and modernize the Egyptian military. The Egyptian army, along with Syrian and Jordanian forces, conducted joint military exercises that were explicitly aimed at preparing for a confrontation with Israel. These moves were seen as a direct challenge to Israel's military superiority, and the Israeli government began to prepare for the possibility of war. The rhetoric of war became louder on both sides, with Arab leaders calling for the destruction of the Israeli state, while Israeli leaders increasingly spoke of the need to defend their nation from an existential threat.

The Closure of the Straits of Tiran and the UN Peacekeeping Forces, One of the most significant events that precipitated the outbreak of the 1967 war was the closure of the Straits of Tiran by Egypt. The Straits of Tiran, a narrow waterway at the southern tip of the Sinai Peninsula, provided Israel with crucial access to the Red Sea and its trade routes. The closure of these waters to Israeli shipping was viewed by Israel as an act of war. Egypt's decision to close the Straits was a direct challenge to Israel's economic and military interests, and it heightened the sense of urgency within the Israeli leadership.

In addition to the closure of the Straits, Nasser ordered the withdrawal of UN peacekeeping forces stationed in the Sinai Peninsula. The United Nations Emergency Force (UNEF), which had been deployed to maintain peace between Egypt and Israel following the 1956 Suez Crisis, was removed from the region in May 1967. This move left Israel with little hope of a diplomatic resolution to the escalating crisis. The withdrawal of the peacekeepers was a clear sign that Nasser was preparing for war, and it effectively removed any semblance of international mediation from the situation.

At the same time, Nasser's deployment of Egyptian troops to the Israeli border, coupled with his bellicose rhetoric, pushed the region closer to war. Israel viewed these actions as a direct threat to its security, and its leadership, led by Eshkol and Defense Minister Moshe Dayan, was faced with a fateful decision: should they wait for an Arab attack, or should they strike first to neutralize the growing threat?

The Israeli Response: Preemptive Strike and the Logic of War, Israel's decision to launch a preemptive strike on June 5, 1967, marked the beginning of the Six-Day War. Israeli forces, facing the combined might of Egypt, Syria, and Jordan, launched a surprise attack on Egyptian airfields, crippling the Egyptian Air Force within hours. This bold and decisive military action set the tone for the rapid escalation of the conflict, as Israel quickly gained the upper hand on all fronts. Within six days, Israel had captured the Sinai Peninsula, the Golan Heights, the West Bank, and East Jerusalem, dramatically altering the territorial landscape of the Middle East.

From the perspective of Israel, the preemptive strike was seen as a necessary measure to defend its survival. Israel had long feared a coordinated Arab assault, and the events of May 1967 had convinced its leadership that war was imminent. In this context, the decision to strike first was framed as a pragmatic response to an existential threat. However, the logic of the preemptive strike also reflected Israel's broader strategic aims, which included territorial expansion and the consolidation of control over key areas such as Jerusalem and the West Bank.

Zionist Aggression and the Palestinian Experience, The Zionist project, which had begun with the establishment of the State of Israel in 1948, was driven by a deep-seated belief in the right of the Jewish people to self-determination in their ancestral homeland. This ideology, however, often clashed with the aspirations and rights of the Palestinian people, who had lived on the land for centuries. The 1967 war and its aftermath marked another chapter in the ongoing displacement and dispossession of Palestinians.

The Zionist leadership's aggressive expansionism during the war, which involved the annexation of Palestinian territories, was framed as a defensive measure to ensure the security of the Israeli state. However, the reality on the ground was much more complex. Palestinians who lived in the occupied territories found themselves subjected to military rule, with their homes and land seized by Israeli authorities. The destruction of Palestinian villages, the forced displacement of families, and the imposition of martial law served as stark reminders of the deep asymmetry of power in the region. Palestinian resistance to Zionist occupation would take many forms, from armed struggle to diplomatic efforts, but the traumatic experiences of displacement and violence would shape the course of Palestinian history for decades to come.

A Critical Moment in Middle Eastern History, The events leading up to the 1967 war and the war itself were a turning point in the history of the Middle East. The tension that had been building for years between Israel and its Arab neighbors finally erupted into open conflict, with profound implications for the Palestinian people. The Zionist aggression, marked by territorial expansion and military occupation, only deepened the divisions between Israelis and Palestinians, while Nasser's vision of Arab unity and resistance to Israel was shattered by the military realities of the conflict. The 1967 war did not resolve the core issues of the Israeli-Palestinian conflict; rather, it deepened the rift and set the stage for further violence, displacement, and suffering. The road to 1967 was marked by political maneuvering, military buildup, and escalating violence, all of which culminated in one of the most significant and destructive wars in modern Middle Eastern history.

The Six-Day War: A Zionist Triumph Built on Aggression and Deception

The Six-Day War of 1967 is often celebrated in Israel as a brilliant military victory, hailed as a moment when Israel decisively secured its place as a dominant military power in the Middle East. However, a deeper examination of the events leading up to the war, the war itself, and its aftermath paints a far more complicated and troubling picture. What is frequently overlooked is the fact that the Six-Day War was not merely a defensive operation, as Zionist propaganda often claims, but rather a calculated and aggressive campaign that altered the balance of power in the Middle East through violence, deceit, and territorial expansion.

The Seeds of Conflict: Zionist Ambitions and the Fabrication of Threats, To understand the true nature of the Six-Day War, one must first recognize the longstanding ambitions of the Zionist movement. Since the establishment of the State of Israel in 1948, Zionist leaders had envisioned a *"Greater Israel,"* one that would span the historical borders of the biblical Jewish kingdoms and include territories that had been part of Palestine for centuries. This expansionist ideology clashed with the rights of the indigenous Arab population, who had lived in these regions for generations. The land that Zionism sought to annex—particularly the West Bank, Gaza Strip, and Golan Heights—had strategic, economic, and cultural significance for the Arab world.

In the years preceding the Six-Day War, tensions had been rising between Israel and its Arab neighbors. In 1964, the Palestine Liberation Organization (PLO) had been formed with the aim of liberating Palestine from Israeli control, increasing the pressure on

Israel. As the Arab nations began to strengthen their alliances and organize military forces, Israel felt increasingly threatened. But the true catalyst for the war was not an imminent threat from its neighbors but rather a Zionist desire to expand its territory under the pretense of self-defense.

Israeli leadership, including Prime Minister Levi Eshkol, Defense Minister Moshe Dayan, and Chief of Staff Yitzhak Rabin, engaged in an elaborate campaign of psychological warfare, manipulating the political climate to justify military action. Israel's propaganda machine portrayed the surrounding Arab nations—Egypt, Jordan, and Syria—as a unified military threat that was intent on destroying the Jewish state. This narrative was designed to galvanize the Israeli population and garner international sympathy, particularly from Western powers like the United States.

However, the reality was far different. While tensions were high, there was no immediate existential threat to Israel. Egyptian President Gamal Abdel Nasser, despite his fiery rhetoric and military build-up in the Sinai Peninsula, had no intention of launching a full-scale war against Israel. The Syrian and Jordanian forces were not prepared for a coordinated attack either. In fact, reports suggest that Nasser was hesitant about engaging Israel in direct conflict, given the significant military disadvantage of his forces. But Israel, sensing an opportunity to expand its territorial reach, took advantage of these tensions and began to manipulate events, creating a false sense of urgency and impending doom.

The Preemptive Strike: The Zionist Doctrine of Aggression in Disguise, At dawn on June 5, 1967, Israel launched Operation Focus, a preemptive airstrike against Egypt, signaling the start of the war. The operation was a calculated move that stunned the Arab world and marked the beginning of Israel's offensive. The Israeli Air Force, in a meticulously planned strike, decimated Egypt's air force in a matter of hours, effectively neutralizing Egypt's ability to defend itself in the air. Within the first day, Israel had established complete air superiority, and it was clear that the war was no longer a defensive effort by Israel but an outright act of aggression.

While Israel's success in the air is often lauded as a military triumph, it is essential to note that this was not a war of survival for Israel, but rather a war of conquest. By launching a preemptive strike, Israel violated international law, as no immediate threat to its borders existed. The Geneva Conventions, to which Israel is a signatory, prohibit preemptive strikes unless there is an imminent threat of attack. The Israeli leadership, however, justified this aggression as an act of self-defense, a narrative that would be propagated in the media and political discourse for decades.

The military strategies employed by Israel throughout the war only further highlighted the aggressive and expansionist nature of the conflict. In addition to airstrikes, Israeli ground forces moved swiftly into the Sinai Peninsula, pushing Egyptian forces back and seizing key positions. As the Israeli army advanced, they did not simply aim to secure their borders but instead sought to annex and occupy key territories, including the West Bank, Gaza Strip, and Golan Heights. The speed and coordination of the Israeli forces were unprecedented, but they were fueled by a deeply entrenched belief in the necessity of expanding Israeli territory, regardless of the costs to the Palestinian and Arab populations.

The Zionist Occupation: A Tale of Brutality and Displacement, The consequences of the Six-Day War were felt immediately by the Palestinian and Arab populations living in the territories occupied by Israel. The capture of the West Bank, including East Jerusalem, by Israeli forces marked the beginning of a prolonged military occupation that would last for decades. The historic city of Jerusalem, home to important religious sites for Muslims, Jews, and Christians alike, was divided, and Israel assumed control over the Old City, including the al-Aqsa Mosque.

For Palestinians, the occupation was a bitter reminder of their dispossession and displacement. As Israeli forces moved into the West Bank, they rounded up and detained thousands of Palestinians, subjecting them to brutal treatment. Settler colonialism, a hallmark of Israeli policy, was quickly implemented in the newly occupied territories. Israeli authorities began to seize Palestinian land and resources, building settlements and establishing military outposts, all while denying the rights of the local population. In the Golan Heights, Syrian residents were forcibly removed from their homes, and their land was appropriated by Israeli settlers.

International reactions to the occupation were mixed, with many countries, particularly in the Arab world, condemning Israel's actions. However, the international community's response was largely ineffective, and Israel's territorial expansion continued unchecked. The narrative of self-defense that Israel had promoted before and during the war had largely been accepted by Western powers, leaving the Palestinian people to suffer under an increasingly repressive and militarized occupation.

The Aftermath: The Real Costs of Zionist Aggression. By the time a ceasefire was declared on June 10, 1967, Israel had tripled its territory, having seized the Sinai Peninsula, the West Bank, Gaza Strip, and the Golan Heights. The geopolitical landscape of the Middle East had been irrevocably altered. Israel had expanded its control over vital resources, including the Suez Canal and key water sources in the West Bank and Golan Heights. But the true cost of this victory was not just the physical occupation of land but the profound human toll it took on the Palestinian and Arab populations.

For the Palestinian people, the war marked another chapter in their long struggle for freedom and self-determination. Hundreds of thousands of Palestinians were displaced, many of whom had already been forced to flee their homes in 1948 during the Nakba, the catastrophic creation of the State of Israel. The violence and brutality of the Israeli occupation left deep scars in Palestinian society, and the war set the stage for future uprisings, including the First and Second Intifadas, as Palestinians continued to resist Israeli rule.

The Six-Day War also marked the beginning of a more intense phase of the Israeli-Palestinian conflict. The occupation of Palestinian territories and the subsequent building of settlements in the West Bank and Gaza were key factors in shaping the trajectory of the conflict for the next several decades. The war exposed the deep asymmetry of the conflict, where Israel, with its military superiority and support from Western powers, continued to exert control over a dispossessed and marginalized population.

The Zionist Myth of Self-Defense, The Six-Day War is often framed by Israeli and Western narratives as a defensive struggle for survival. Yet, a critical examination reveals that this was an aggressive and expansionist war, driven by Zionist ambitions and a disregard for international law and the rights of the Palestinian and Arab peoples. While the military success of Israel in the war is undeniable, the human cost of this victory—embodied in the suffering of the Palestinian people and the broader Arab world—cannot be ignored.

The legacy of the Six-Day War is one of occupation, displacement, and ongoing conflict. Israel's territorial gains during the war only deepened its control over Palestinian land and resources, and the brutality of its occupation has left a lasting mark on the lives of millions of Palestinians. The Zionist narrative of self-defense continues to be perpetuated, but it is essential to recognize that the true story of the Six-Day War is one of aggression, colonization, and the denial of Palestinian rights. Until this narrative is fully acknowledged and addressed, peace in the region remains a distant hope.

UN Resolution 242 and the Ambiguities of Peace: A Veiled Justification for Zionist Expansionism

The aftermath of the Six-Day War in June 1967 was a moment of both triumph and peril for the State of Israel. While the military victory was celebrated by Israelis and marked a significant moment in the country's history, the outcome presented the Israeli government with a complex and morally fraught reality: it now found itself in control of vast territories populated by millions of Palestinians. These lands—Sinai Peninsula, the West Bank, East Jerusalem, Gaza Strip, and the Golan Heights—had been taken from neighboring Arab countries, yet the question of what to do with the over one million Palestinians living in the occupied territories remained unresolved. What followed in the aftermath of the war was not just the consolidation of territorial gains but the setting of the stage for prolonged conflict, resistance, and international diplomacy that would continue to this day.

One of the key moments in this complex post-war scenario came in November 1967, when the United Nations Security Council adopted Resolution 242, aimed at addressing the new geopolitical reality created by the war. The resolution called for the *"withdrawal of Israeli armed forces from territories occupied in the recent conflict"* and the *"acknowledgement of the sovereignty, territorial integrity, and political independence of every state in the area."* On the surface, this appeared to be a call for peace and a fair settlement to the newly acquired Israeli territorial holdings. However, the ambiguity within the language of the resolution would ultimately open the door for multiple interpretations, leading to decades of negotiations, stalling, and intensifying hostilities.

The Ambiguity of *"Territories"* and the Zionist Manipulation, The most controversial aspect of Resolution 242 was its phrasing: *"withdrawal from territories,"* rather than *"withdrawal from all the territories."* This seemingly minor linguistic choice would become a critical point of contention in subsequent peace talks. While the intention behind the wording was to allow for some territorial adjustments as part of a peace settlement, it also left room for the Zionist government to claim that not all occupied territories needed to be returned. This interpretation was crucial to Israel's strategy of maintaining control over key areas such as Jerusalem and parts of the West Bank, under the argument that the territories in question were not all equal in significance.

Israel, for its part, interpreted the resolution as not necessarily requiring a full withdrawal from all occupied territories. This interpretation was not just a matter of semantics; it formed the basis for Israel's policies in the years following the war, including the establishment of settlements in the occupied West Bank and Gaza Strip. The government, led by Prime Minister Levi Eshkol and later Golda Meir, used this loophole to justify its ongoing expansionist policies, arguing that they were acting in accordance with international law, despite the UN's clear intent to call for territorial withdrawal.

Zionist officials, such as Israeli Foreign Minister Abba Eban, contended that Israel could not withdraw from all the territories as the resolution called for because some territories were of strategic importance. The Israeli government's position, thus, centered on the idea that the new borders drawn by the war would not only serve Israel's security needs but also be a foundation for any future peace agreements. However, this stance ignored the Palestinian population's political and human rights, framing them as secondary to Israeli strategic interests.

Israeli Expansion and Palestinian Dispossession, The impact of Resolution 242's ambiguity became evident in the following years, as Israel consolidated its hold on the occupied territories and expanded settlements. One of the most glaring examples of this was the establishment of Israeli settlements in the West Bank and Gaza Strip, territories explicitly mentioned in Resolution 242 for withdrawal. These settlements, considered illegal under international law, became a central part of Israel's long-term strategy to maintain control over these regions.

By the early 1970s, Israel had already begun constructing settlements in the West Bank, particularly in areas near Jerusalem. The settlement of Gush Emunim, established in 1974, was one of the earliest and most influential Zionist settlement movements, advocating for the expansion of Israel's control over the entire West Bank. The settlers argued that their presence was justified by religious and historical claims to the land, viewing the West Bank as part of the biblical *"Promised Land."* They saw the acquisition of these territories not as a temporary wartime gain, but as an integral part of Israel's future.

As settlements expanded, Palestinians in the occupied territories faced increasing hardships. Their homes were destroyed, lands were confiscated, and entire communities were displaced. In East Jerusalem, Israel moved quickly to annex the area, an act widely condemned by the international community, yet one that was justified by Israeli officials as necessary for the capital's security. Palestinians in the city found themselves facing constant harassment and were increasingly denied residency rights, while Israeli settlers were given preferential treatment. The annexation of East Jerusalem, along with the construction of the Israeli wall around the city, further entrenched the divide between Israelis and Palestinians and solidified Israel's claim to the city as its undivided capital.

Moreover, the Israeli military's presence in the Gaza Strip and the West Bank not only led to military occupations but also systematic violations of Palestinian rights. Palestinians were subjected to curfews, arbitrary arrests, home demolitions, and a brutal military crackdown on dissent. The international community, particularly in the Arab world, decried these actions as violations of international law and human rights, yet the ambiguities of Resolution 242 allowed Israel to continue to justify its occupation with relative impunity.

The Illusion of Peace and the Zionist Strategy of Delay, While Resolution 242 sought to establish a framework for peace, it is clear that its ambiguities played into Israel's broader strategic goals of stalling meaningful negotiations. From the very beginning, Israel used the resolution's vagueness as a tool to delay any serious commitment to peace. The resolution called for a negotiated peace based on the withdrawal from occupied territories in exchange for peace with neighboring Arab states, but Israel was not prepared to make significant territorial concessions without first securing its security and diplomatic goals.

The lack of a firm timeline for withdrawal allowed Israel to build settlements and fortify its hold on the occupied territories. This strategy created an illusion of negotiation while in practice, Israel sought to solidify its position in the territories it had gained. By dragging its feet on peace talks, Israel ensured that it could continue its policies of territorial expansion while the international community remained divided and impotent in its response.

Palestinian resistance to these policies, including the violent uprisings known as the Intifadas, further complicated the peace process. As Palestinians struggled to defend their land and assert their national identity, Israel responded with increasing military repression, further eroding trust and making peace seem like an ever-receding goal.

Interviews and Personal Accounts: The Human Cost of Zionist Expansionism, The human cost of Zionist policies in the wake of Resolution 242 is illustrated through the personal stories of those living under occupation. One Palestinian resident of the West Bank, who witnessed the expansion of Israeli settlements in his village, described the growing sense of alienation and dispossession. *"We saw our land taken from us, piece by piece,"* he recalled. *"At first, it was just the settlers coming in and claiming small areas, but then they built entire communities. We were told we had no rights to our own land anymore. It felt like we were being erased from history."*

Another Palestinian woman, whose family had been living in East Jerusalem for generations, spoke of the humiliation of living under Israeli control. *"We used to walk freely in our city, but now every time I go out, I see soldiers everywhere. I can't even visit my relatives without being checked at a military checkpoint. They treat us like strangers in our own home."*

These personal accounts highlight the disconnect between the theoretical intentions of international resolutions like 242 and the on-the-ground reality for Palestinians. While the resolution may have been framed as a path to peace, its ambiguity allowed Israel to pursue policies that caused immeasurable suffering for Palestinians and ultimately perpetuated the conflict.

The Legacy of Ambiguity: The Road to Nowhere, The legacy of UN Resolution 242 remains a painful reminder of the failure of international diplomacy to address the Palestinian question in a just and meaningful way. By leaving room for divergent interpretations, the resolution allowed Israel to continue its expansionist policies, all while giving the illusion of being committed to peace. The continued occupation, the building of settlements, and the denial of Palestinian rights are all direct consequences of this diplomatic failure.

The resolution, rather than being a path to peace, became a tool for delay, obfuscation, and the perpetuation of Israeli control over Palestinian lands. The ambiguities in its language allowed Israel to sidestep meaningful withdrawal and maintain a status quo of occupation that continues to this day. For Palestinians, the promise of Resolution 242 has remained largely empty, as they continue to fight not only for an end to occupation but for their very right to exist as a free people on their ancestral land.

In conclusion, Resolution 242, while ostensibly a call for peace, revealed the deep contradictions in the international approach to the Palestinian-Israeli conflict. The ambiguities embedded in the resolution allowed Zionist leaders to manipulate its language and justify continued occupation, settlement expansion, and the oppression of the Palestinian people.

The resolution's failure to address the core issues of justice and self-determination for Palestinians underscores the broader failure of international diplomacy to bring about a just and lasting peace in the region.

Reflections on Power and Resistance: The Zionist Legacy of Dispossession and the Palestinian Struggle

The years between 1948 and 1967 were pivotal in shaping not only the geopolitical landscape of the Middle East but also the identities and destinies of the peoples living within it. The events of these two decades dramatically altered the region's power dynamics, leaving scars that would linger for generations. For Israelis, the period symbolized triumph, the consolidation of their state, and the assurance of their survival. For Palestinians, it was marked by unrelenting dispossession, suffering, and the entrenchment of occupation. The lives of those caught in the crossfire of this historic struggle would be forever changed, as would the broader narrative of the Middle East conflict, a tale of power, resistance, and dispossession.

The wars of 1948 and 1967 were not merely military conflicts; they were battles over the right to exist, to control the land, and to assert competing narratives of identity. The legacy of these wars is intertwined with the figures who played leading roles in shaping them. On one side was Gamal Abdel Nasser, the Egyptian president and symbol of Arab nationalism, whose vision of Arab unity and resistance to Western imperialism resonated deeply throughout the Arab world. On the other side stood figures like Moshe Dayan, the

Israeli general whose strategic brilliance ensured Israel's survival and territorial expansion, but at the cost of Palestinian rights, identity, and sovereignty.

The Catastrophe and the Nakba: A Preceding Era of Loss, For Palestinians, the Nakba of 1948 was a devastating event, the direct consequence of the Zionist project to establish a Jewish state in Palestine. The Zionist movement, driven by a mixture of religious fervor, nationalist ideology, and colonialist ambitions, began a campaign of displacement, violence, and ethnic cleansing that led to the expulsion of over 700,000 Palestinians from their homes. The impact of this displacement was profound—not only did it scatter Palestinian families across the region, but it also erased Palestinian communities, destroyed villages, and left deep psychological scars that would continue to shape the Palestinian struggle for generations.

The expulsion was not just a physical removal of people from their land; it was an attempt to erase the very presence of Palestinians, both culturally and politically. Israel's establishment was built on this foundation of dispossession, and the creation of a Jewish state in a land already inhabited by an indigenous Arab population became the central conflict of the region. Palestinians, whose connection to the land spanned centuries, were now refugees in their own homeland, forced to live in camps and endure a life of uncertainty and hardship.

In the years following the Nakba, the Palestinian resistance began to take form. The absence of a unified political or military front among the Palestinians during this period was a major challenge, but figures like Abdel Qader al-Husseini, whose leadership was marked by sacrifice and determination, laid the groundwork for a broader resistance movement. Yet, despite the heroism of these leaders, the scale of Palestinian dispossession continued unabated. The early resistance efforts were often fragmented, underfunded, and lacking in cohesion. But they were driven by one central idea: the refusal to accept the existence of a Jewish state built on the ruins of Palestinian homes and communities.

The Six-Day War: A Triumph for Zionism, a Catastrophe for Palestine, The 1967 Six-Day War marked another turning point in the history of the Palestinian struggle and the broader Middle East conflict. What Israelis celebrated as a decisive military victory that solidified their state's security and territorial expansion was, for Palestinians, another traumatic chapter in their collective history of dispossession. Israel's territorial gains following the war—capturing the West Bank, Gaza Strip, East Jerusalem, the Sinai Peninsula, and the Golan Heights—extended its occupation and further entrenched the marginalization of Palestinians.

The aftermath of the war deepened the sense of loss among Palestinians. The West Bank and Gaza, once part of Jordan and Egypt, respectively, were now under Israeli control. The occupation, which had begun in 1948 with the expulsion of Palestinians from their land, now extended its grip across new areas. East Jerusalem, the heart of Palestinian identity, was annexed by Israel, and Palestinians in these newly occupied territories were subjected to military rule, brutal repression, and land confiscations. This marked the beginning of what would become an enduring cycle of occupation and resistance.

The rhetoric of the Zionist leaders, including Prime Minister Levi Eshkol and Defense Minister Moshe Dayan, framed the victory as not only a military triumph but a vindication of Israel's right to exist. For them, the acquisition of land was a necessary step to ensure the security of the Jewish state in a hostile region. However, this view ignored the lived reality of the Palestinians, who continued to suffer under the yoke of occupation. The notion of territorial expansion and the right of a state to secure its borders through military force had little regard for the rights of the indigenous population who were being dispossessed in the process.

Moshe Dayan: The Architect of Israeli Military Success and Palestinian Suffering, The figure of Moshe Dayan looms large in the history of the Six-Day War. Known for his military acumen and strategic brilliance, Dayan became a national hero in Israel after leading the country to victory. His role in the military campaigns of the 1967 war cemented his legacy as one of Israel's most revered figures. Yet, the broader implications of his strategies and decisions for Palestinians are deeply troubling.

Dayan's actions during the war and the subsequent occupation of Palestinian territories are a reflection of the Zionist ideology that justified territorial expansion at the expense of Palestinian sovereignty. His decision to take control of East Jerusalem and other Palestinian areas was not just a military maneuver; it was a conscious effort to erase Palestinian presence and identity from these territories. In his view, the land was the birthright of the Jewish people, and Palestinians had no legitimate claim to it. This view, rooted in a deeply colonial mindset, disregarded the history, culture, and rights of the Palestinian people.

One of the most tragic aspects of Dayan's actions was the transformation of Jerusalem, a city that held deep religious and cultural significance for Palestinians, into an exclusively Jewish city. Palestinians were barred from returning to their homes in the Old City, and their properties were confiscated. The annexation of East Jerusalem was a direct violation of international law and an affront to Palestinian rights. Yet, for Dayan and many of his Israeli contemporaries, this was seen as a necessary step in securing the future of the Jewish state.

The Legacy of Zionist Expansionism and Palestinian Resistance, The wars of 1948 and 1967 were not isolated events; they were part of a broader pattern of Zionist expansionism that aimed to secure a

Jewish state through territorial conquest and the displacement of the indigenous Palestinian population. The destruction of Palestinian villages, the forced expulsion of Palestinians from their homes, and the violent suppression of resistance movements were all part of this larger strategy. In the face of these injustices, Palestinian resistance evolved, growing from fragmented guerrilla actions to more organized and strategic efforts, such as those led by the Palestine Liberation Organization (PLO) in the 1960s.

Palestinians, despite the overwhelming military superiority of Israel, have continued to resist occupation, dispossession, and the erosion of their rights. Figures like Yasser Arafat and organizations like the PLO came to symbolize this resistance, but their struggle was born out of the same deep sense of loss and injustice that had been felt since 1948. Palestinians were not merely fighting for land; they were fighting for their right to exist, for their culture, and for their future.

The legacy of Zionism, built on the foundation of ethnic cleansing and military expansion, continues to haunt the Palestinian people. The creation of a Jewish state in Palestine was achieved through the dispossession and subjugation of the Palestinian population, and the ongoing occupation and settlement expansion continue to perpetuate this legacy. Zionism's disregard for Palestinian rights and its efforts to erase Palestinian identity from the land are the very forces that drive the conflict to this day.

Interviews and Personal Narratives, The Human Cost of Zionist Expansionism, Personal testimonies from Palestinians who lived through the Nakba and the Six-Day War offer a powerful insight into the human cost of Zionist policies. One elderly Palestinian man, recalling his forced expulsion from his village in 1948, said, *"We were told to leave for a few days, just to be safe. But when we returned, our homes were gone, our land was taken, and we were never allowed to go back."* Such narratives are echoed by countless others who were displaced, who lost loved ones, and who saw their homes reduced to rubble.

In the years following the 1967 war, Palestinians who had been living under occupation witnessed further violations of their rights. A young woman, whose family had lived in East Jerusalem for generations, described the trauma of being displaced once again: *"We watched as our neighbors were forced out of their homes, their stores closed, their lives upended. It was as if we didn't exist anymore, just erased from the land."*

These personal accounts serve as a stark reminder of the ongoing effects of Zionist policies of displacement, occupation, and exclusion. They also highlight the resilience and determination of the Palestinian people to continue the fight for their rights, despite the overwhelming odds stacked against them.

A Struggle for Identity, Justice, and the Right to Exist, The events of 1948 and 1967, shaped by Zionist expansionism and Palestinian resistance, are central to the ongoing conflict that continues to define the Middle East today. The dispossession of the Palestinian people, the forced displacement, and the occupation of their land by Israel are not isolated incidents but part of a broader, deliberate strategy to erase Palestinian identity and secure Israeli dominance. The legacy of this strategy continues to fuel Palestinian resistance, as new generations of Palestinians rise up to reclaim their rights and fight for justice.

As the struggle continues, it is crucial to remember that the conflict is not only about land or military power—it is about the right to exist, to preserve one's culture, and to assert one's humanity. The Zionist project, built on a foundation of violence, dispossession, and denial, has created a cycle of suffering for Palestinians that shows no signs of ending. However, the spirit of resistance that emerged in 1948 and was carried through the 1967 war lives on, as Palestinians continue to fight for their right to return, to live in freedom, and to see their aspirations for justice and dignity fulfilled.

Chapter 7: Ghassan Kanafani Voice of the Palestinian Resistance

Ghassan Kanafani was a prominent figure in Palestinian literature and revolutionary history, known for his intellectual contributions and his relentless dedication to the Palestinian cause. His life and work exemplify a deep commitment to the struggle for Palestinian liberation, using his writing as a powerful tool for political and social change.

Kanafani was not only a writer of novels and short stories but also a journalist, deeply involved in documenting and narrating the struggles of the Palestinian people. His literary works often explored themes of exile, identity, resistance, and the harsh realities of life under occupation. He believed that literature was a means to mobilize and raise awareness about the Palestinian plight, and his works became important resources for understanding the experiences of those displaced by the Israeli occupation.

Kanafani's writing was not limited to artistic expression; it was also a political act. He was a member of the Popular Front for the Liberation of Palestine (PFLP), an organization committed to armed resistance against Israeli occupation. Kanafani's works often portrayed the lives of Palestinians in exile, highlighting their struggles and aspirations. Through his stories, he sought to convey the urgency of the Palestinian cause and the need for a collective resistance against colonialism and oppression.

Some of Kanafani's most notable works include Men in the Sun (1962), a novel that explores the plight of Palestinian refugees, and Returning to Haifa (1969), which deals with the trauma of displacement. His writing was rooted in his personal experiences and the broader Palestinian experience of dispossession and struggle. Kanafani's works have had a profound influence on Palestinian literature and have been translated into many languages, inspiring generations of activists, writers, and scholars around the world.

Martyrdom and Enduring Spirit: Tragically, Kanafani's life was cut short when he was assassinated in 1972, likely by the Israeli Mossad, due to his involvement in revolutionary activities and his influence. His death at the age of 36 only solidified his status as a martyr in the Palestinian struggle. His life and works serve as a lasting reminder of the potency of intellectual resistance and the power of the written word in the fight for justice. Kanafani's legacy continues to inspire not only Palestinians but also people around the world who seek freedom, justice, and human dignity.

Kanafani's life and work are a testament to the power of storytelling in the face of oppression and the role of literature in resisting injustice. Despite his early death, the impact of his writing endures, reminding us of the ongoing struggles for freedom and liberation.

EARLY LIFE AND EXILE: The Seed of Resistance

Ghassan Kanafani, born in 1936 in the coastal city of Acre, Palestine, belonged to a middle-class Sunni Muslim family. Acre, with its rich cultural history and picturesque landscapes, was a symbol of the deep-rooted Palestinian presence in the land. Kanafani's early years were marked by a peaceful, relatively comfortable existence, rooted in the traditions of his family and the vibrancy of Palestinian life. However, this serene childhood was abruptly interrupted in 1948, when, at the age of twelve, Kanafani experienced one of the most pivotal and traumatic events in

Palestinian history—the Nakba. This mass expulsion of Palestinians following the creation of the State of Israel forced Kanafani and his family to flee their home, becoming part of the wave of refugees that would shape the future of the Palestinian people.

The Nakba, or "catastrophe," was not merely a geopolitical event but a deep, personal trauma for millions of Palestinians, many of whom, like Kanafani, were forced to abandon their homes, livelihoods, and identities. For Kanafani, the forced exile would mark the beginning of a life-long commitment to resistance, a commitment that would manifest through his literary works and revolutionary actions.

As the Kanafani family fled Acre, the chaos of the situation was overwhelming. Ghassan Kanafani, just a child, witnessed the heart-wrenching images of his community being uprooted from its ancestral land. The city of Acre, with its narrow alleys, bustling markets, and cultural vibrancy, was left behind in a flash of violence, fear, and despair. What made the trauma even more poignant for Kanafani was the image of his male relatives reluctantly surrendering their weapons to Zionist forces, an act that represented not just the loss of physical property but the symbolic defeat of Palestinian resistance. This surrender in the face of overwhelming military force planted the seeds of resistance within Kanafani. It was a moment that would haunt him for the rest of his life.

The loss of Acre and the subsequent displacement marked the beginning of Kanafani's exile, as he and his family sought refuge in Syria, along with hundreds of thousands of other Palestinians. Life as a refugee was difficult, and the experience of exile was one that Kanafani would never forget. They settled in the city of Damascus, where Kanafani would spend the early years of his adolescence in a refugee camp. The camp, though a temporary refuge, became a symbol of permanent displacement and loss. The sight of families living in overcrowded tents, the daily struggles to survive, and the pervasive sense of hopelessness and injustice all had a profound impact on Kanafani's psyche.

This period in exile was transformative for Kanafani. Far from succumbing to despair, the young Ghassan became increasingly politically aware, his consciousness shaped by the struggles of fellow refugees and the broader Arab nationalist movements of the time. His family's experience was a microcosm of the larger Palestinian experience—the collective trauma of displacement, the loss of homeland, and the uncertain future of a people scattered across the Middle East. The forced exile, coupled with the deep sense of injustice, created a sense of urgency in Kanafani. His sense of loss was not just personal but national; his commitment to the Palestinian cause became intertwined with the shared struggle of his people. The Nakba was not just the loss of a home but the loss of a way of life, a history, and a cultural identity.

As Kanafani navigated his teenage years in Syria, the political climate in the Arab world was also in flux. The rise of Arab nationalism, particularly under the leadership of Egyptian President Gamal Abdel Nasser, provided Kanafani with a framework to understand the broader political struggles of the region. Nasser's pan-Arab rhetoric, which called for the unity of Arab nations and the liberation of Palestine, resonated deeply with Kanafani. However, it was not just the rhetoric that inspired him—it was the idea of revolution, of challenging the colonial and imperial forces that had oppressed his people for so long. It was during this period that Kanafani began to take an active interest in revolutionary movements, seeing in them the potential for the liberation of Palestine and the restoration of dignity for Palestinians.

Kanafani's early exposure to literature also played a critical role in shaping his political consciousness. His move to Damascus, where he had access to a broader intellectual environment, allowed him to immerse himself in the writings of revolutionary thinkers and writers. Literature became a tool for understanding the plight of his people and a means of articulating the Palestinian experience. He was drawn to the works of writers such as Naguib Mahfouz and Franz Kafka, whose exploration of themes like alienation, loss, and oppression mirrored the struggles that Kanafani himself was grappling with. Yet, it was the works of Palestinian and Arab writers that most profoundly impacted Kanafani. The poetry of Mahmoud Darwish, the short stories of Jabra Ibrahim Jabra, and the works of other Palestinian intellectuals became vital resources in his search for meaning in the midst of his displacement.

Kanafani's literary aspirations were not merely about personal expression but about capturing the collective experience of the Palestinian people. His writing would become the means through which he could give voice to the suffering and struggles of those in exile, those who had lost their homes and families, and those who were living in the shadow of the Nakba. The themes of exile, loss, resistance, and the quest for justice would resonate throughout his works. Kanafani's writing was not only a reflection of his own personal journey but also an embodiment of the broader Palestinian struggle for self-determination and dignity.

The Seeds of Revolution: Political Activism in Exile, Kanafani's exile in Syria, far from silencing him, ignited a sense of political urgency that would define his later life. In the early 1950s, as Kanafani navigated the realities of refugee life, he became increasingly involved in Palestinian political activism. He joined the Syrian branch of the Arab Nationalist Movement, a political group dedicated to Arab unity and the liberation of Palestine. His involvement in the movement marked the beginning of his shift from a writer and intellectual to an active participant in the struggle for Palestinian liberation.

His early political activism was deeply influenced by his experiences in the refugee camps, where he saw firsthand the hardship and deprivation faced by displaced Palestinians. These experiences sharpened his resolve to fight for justice and national liberation. He joined the ranks of the Palestinian resistance, becoming a member of the Popular Front for the Liberation of Palestine (PFLP), a revolutionary socialist organization that advocated for armed struggle against Israel. Kanafani's ideological alignment with the PFLP was rooted in his belief that the liberation of Palestine could only be achieved through a united, revolutionary effort that sought not only to reclaim Palestinian land but to dismantle the structures of oppression that had displaced his people.

Kanafani's involvement with the PFLP was not just a political decision but a deeply personal one. The struggles of the Palestinian people, the loss of his childhood home, and the suffering of his family in exile became the driving forces behind his activism. For Kanafani, the revolution was not an abstract concept but a deeply emotional and personal quest for justice. His writings from this period reflect his growing commitment to revolutionary ideals. His short stories, essays, and novels became vehicles for expressing his political views and for articulating the complexities of the Palestinian struggle.

One of Kanafani's most famous works, Men in the Sun, which was published in 1963, reflects the despair and disillusionment of the Palestinian refugees. Through the story of three Palestinian men who attempt to cross the border to Kuwait in search of work, Kanafani explores the themes of exile, displacement, and the brutal realities of life as a Palestinian refugee. The story captures the tragic sense of futility that many refugees felt as they struggled to survive in the aftermath of the Nakba. The novel is a powerful commentary on the ways in which the Palestinians' search for dignity and survival had been thwarted by the geopolitical realities of the region.

Narratives of Resistance, In interviews conducted with those who knew Ghassan Kanafani, the impact of his early life and exile is often highlighted. One close friend, who met Kanafani during his time in Syria, recalls: "Ghassan was a man of deep conviction. He had lived through the pain of exile and displacement, and that pain became his driving force. He wasn't just a writer; he was a revolutionary at heart. His words had the power to move people, but his actions spoke even louder."

Kanafani's commitment to the Palestinian cause was unwavering, even in the face of adversity. A fellow member of the PFLP remembers Kanafani as someone who "could blend theory with action effortlessly. He was not just interested in intellectual discourse; he wanted change, real, tangible change for the Palestinian people."

In the camps of Syria, Kanafani became a symbol of resistance for Palestinians living in exile. His ability to capture their struggles and translate their pain into powerful, evocative literature gave them a voice. His writings became a source of pride for refugees, who had long felt silenced by their displacement. Through Kanafani's words, the Palestinian cause was no longer just a distant political issue but a deeply personal struggle for justice, home, and identity.

A Life Shaped by Exile and Resistance, The early life of Ghassan Kanafani, marked by the trauma of the Nakba and the subsequent exile, set the stage for his transformation into one of the most influential figures in Palestinian literature and revolutionary thought. His exile was not just a physical displacement but a profound emotional and intellectual journey that shaped his identity and his understanding of the world. It was through this exile that Kanafani's commitment to the Palestinian cause grew, fueling his literary work and his active involvement in revolutionary movements. His experiences as a refugee in Syria, his political activism, and his deep empathy for the suffering of his people all became central to his life's work. Kanafani's legacy is a testament to the power of resistance, both through words and actions, and to the enduring spirit of the Palestinian people in their quest for justice and self-determination.

The Formative Years in Damascus: A Crucible of Struggle, Compassion, and Resistance

After the Nakba of 1948, which resulted in the mass displacement of Palestinians from their homeland, the Kanafani family, like many others, was forced to seek refuge outside Palestine. Their journey led them to Syria, where they settled in Damascus, struggling to adjust to a new life in exile. For Ghassan Kanafani, these years would shape not only his personal identity but also his revolutionary ideology, laying the foundation for his future work as a writer, teacher, and activist. The challenges of refugee life, the economic hardships, and the trauma of displacement informed Kanafani's understanding of the Palestinian plight, and it was in Damascus that he began to forge his path as both an intellectual and a fighter for justice.

The Struggles of Refugee Life in Damascus, When Kanafani and his family arrived in Damascus, they found themselves living in the shadow of the Nakba. Like thousands of other Palestinian refugees, they were confronted with the harsh realities of life in exile: a lack of basic resources, social displacement, and a constant struggle to make ends meet. Kanafani's father, who had been a prominent Palestinian intellectual, was deeply affected by the loss of his homeland, and his family's financial situation worsened as a result of their new status as refugees. In this context, Kanafani's early years in Damascus were marked by both personal and family hardship.

To support his family, Kanafani took on various jobs while pursuing his education. He enrolled in the University of Damascus, where he studied literature and began to shape his worldview as a Palestinian exile. His academic achievements were impressive, but they came at a personal cost. The strain of working multiple jobs while studying and caring for his family was intense, and it was in this environment that Kanafani first experienced the weight of the refugee experience. His academic success was not merely an individual accomplishment but a collective victory, as it represented his determination to rise above the hardships imposed on him by his circumstances.

Despite the weight of these challenges, Kanafani remained deeply committed to his studies, driven by the desire to understand the roots of the Palestinian struggle and to develop the intellectual tools needed to articulate the collective pain of his people. His academic work at the University of Damascus, coupled with his exposure to radical political ideas, helped shape the foundation of his political philosophy, which would later be reflected in his writing and activism.

Becoming a Teacher in a Refugee Camp: A Personal Transformation, In addition to his academic pursuits, Kanafani became increasingly involved in the Palestinian nationalist movement, which was gaining momentum in the Arab world during the 1950s and 1960s. The sense of shared suffering among the Palestinian refugees and the broader Arab solidarity movements provided Kanafani with the motivation to immerse himself in the struggle for Palestinian liberation. One of the most formative experiences of his early life in Damascus was his decision to become a teacher at a Palestinian refugee camp.

Teaching in the refugee camps exposed Kanafani to the harsh realities faced by the children of displaced Palestinians. These were children who, like him, were born into exile, and their lives were shaped by a deep sense of loss and uncertainty. In the classrooms of the camp, Kanafani witnessed the profound impact of the refugee experience on the children's development. He saw how the trauma of displacement affected their ability to learn and thrive. The refugee children, many of whom had never known the stability of a home or a normal childhood, lived in a state of constant deprivation. Some were forced to work late at night to help their families survive, selling sweets or doing odd jobs in the streets of Damascus.

Kanafani's response to these conditions was one of empathy and compassion. Instead of resorting to traditional methods of discipline when students fell asleep in class due to exhaustion, he took the time to understand the reasons behind their fatigue. He learned about their difficult lives and the burden they carried. His decision to approach the children's struggles with compassion rather than punishment was an early indication of the kind of educator and leader he would become. For Kanafani, understanding the lives of the children was not just a matter of pedagogical concern—it was a political act. By seeing the world through their eyes, he began to comprehend the deeper social and economic forces that shaped their lives, and this insight would influence his later writings and activism.

A Transformative Moment, Defying the Curriculum, Embracing Reality, One of the most significant moments in Kanafani's development as both a writer and a revolutionary occurred while he was teaching a class on art. The children, many of whom had never seen an apple or a banana, were assigned a task that seemed disconnected from their reality: they were asked to draw these fruits as part of their curriculum. For Kanafani, this assignment epitomized the disconnect between the educational system and the lived experiences of the refugee children. The children, whose lives were marked by hunger, poverty, and displacement, were being asked to draw objects that were foreign to them. It was a stark reminder of the absurdity of the education system that failed to recognize the harsh realities of their existence.

Kanafani's response to this was both simple and revolutionary. Rather than following the prescribed curriculum, he instructed his students to draw the refugee camp itself—their homes, their streets, their struggles. This was an act of defiance, a refusal to accept an education system that ignored the refugees' lived experiences. For

Kanafani, this moment represented a turning point in his understanding of the role of education in shaping consciousness and identity. By empowering the children to represent their reality in their artwork, he was allowing them to reclaim their voices and their agency. It was an acknowledgment that their experiences, no matter how painful or marginalized, were valid and worthy of representation.

This act of defiance against the imposed narrative of exile and displacement would resonate throughout Kanafani's later work as a writer. His commitment to representing the Palestinian struggle from the perspective of those most affected—whether refugees, workers, or the dispossessed—became a hallmark of his literary and political vision. Kanafani's decision to focus on the everyday lives of ordinary Palestinians, rather than abstract political ideologies, helped to humanize the Palestinian struggle and bring the voices of the oppressed to the forefront.

Interviews and Personal Narratives: The Impact of Kanafani's Teaching, The impact of Ghassan Kanafani's time as a teacher in the Palestinian refugee camps is best captured through the personal narratives of those who experienced his unique approach to education and mentorship. Several former students and individuals who knew him during this period have shared their recollections of his teaching style, his compassionate attitude toward the refugee children, and how his influence shaped their lives. These testimonials provide valuable insight into how Kanafani's work in the refugee camps not only impacted his students' academic and intellectual development but also played a key role in shaping their sense of identity and resistance.

One such former student, now an adult and a community leader in a Palestinian refugee camp, spoke with deep affection and respect for Kanafani's approach. "Ghassan wasn't just a teacher; he was a mentor, a revolutionary. We looked up to him, not just because of his intelligence, but because he genuinely cared about us. He wasn't interested in our grades as much as he was in how we understood our place in the world, in how we saw our future. He always told us that our experiences, our lives, were important—that we weren't just victims of history. We were making history."

The student recalled how Kanafani's lessons went far beyond the conventional curriculum. While other teachers adhered to rigid academic structures, Kanafani used the classroom as a space for discussion, creativity, and critical thinking. He often encouraged his students to question the world around them, to challenge the status quo, and to reflect on the nature of their displacement. One of the most memorable moments for this student was Kanafani's assignment to draw the refugee camp instead of the prescribed task of drawing fruit. "When Ghassan told us to draw the camp instead of apples and bananas, it was like a lightbulb went off in my head. It was the first time I saw my life, my world, as something worthy of being represented. I realized that the camp wasn't just a place of suffering—it was our home, it was our story, and it mattered."

This sentiment is echoed by several other former students, who fondly remember how Kanafani made them feel seen and valued in a way that few others did. "He would often come to our homes in the camp to check on us," another former student recalled. "He didn't just teach us in the classroom; he made us feel like we were part of a larger community, part of the resistance. He didn't lecture us; he listened to us, to our concerns. He wanted us to feel empowered, to know that we had the potential to change our fate."

Another former student, now an artist living in exile, reflected on the lasting impact of Kanafani's teaching methods. "I remember when he taught us about resistance, about our identity as Palestinians. He didn't just talk about politics—he talked about our culture, our history, our pride. He wanted us to understand that our struggle wasn't just about politics; it was about who we were as a people. His lessons didn't just make me a better student—they made me a better person. They shaped my art, my writing, and my understanding of my own role in the Palestinian cause."

For many students, Kanafani's presence in their lives was transformative not just because of his intellectual rigor, but because of his ability to connect with them on a personal level. His deep empathy for the refugees, born out of his own experiences and struggles, allowed him to build strong relationships with his students. He was able to see beyond their hardships, recognizing their potential and nurturing it.

The Revolutionary Teacher: Building a Culture of Resistance, Kanafani's influence was not limited to his students' academic lives but extended to their broader political consciousness. In a context where the refugee experience was defined by displacement, poverty, and hopelessness, Kanafani's teachings provided a sense of purpose and direction. His lessons were not just about the struggles of the present but about the broader context of Palestinian resistance. By encouraging his students to see the Palestinian cause as a collective struggle for dignity, identity, and self-determination, Kanafani helped shape a generation of young Palestinians who would go on to contribute to the broader political movement for liberation.

One interview with a former student, now an activist, revealed how Kanafani's philosophy influenced his own political involvement. "Ghassan didn't just teach us about the Palestinian cause—he made us understand that we were part of something bigger than ourselves. He always said, 'The struggle is not over, and it is our duty to continue it. You are the future of Palestine.' Those words stuck with me. When I became involved in the resistance, I thought of Ghassan and his teachings. I felt a sense of responsibility to carry forward his message."

This sense of responsibility was a direct result of Kanafani's ability to convey the importance of the individual's role in the collective struggle. While many teachers may have focused solely on academic achievement, Kanafani understood the deeper needs of his students—he saw them as not just future intellectuals, but as future revolutionaries. His encouragement to embrace a sense of responsibility to the Palestinian cause helped mold many of his students into activists who would contribute to the broader nationalist movement.

Recollections from Other Teachers and Activists, Beyond his students, Kanafani's colleagues and fellow activists in Damascus also recognized his unique qualities as a teacher and revolutionary. Several teachers who worked alongside Kanafani in the refugee camps described him as someone whose charisma and ideological commitment were unmatched. "Ghassan had a way of making you feel that every action you took, every lesson you taught, was part of a larger struggle," said one of his fellow teachers. "He was the kind of person who could make you believe that education wasn't just about passing exams—it was about shaping the minds of a generation that would fight for justice."

Kanafani's teaching was also deeply rooted in his own experiences as a Palestinian exile. A close friend and fellow activist recalled how Kanafani's own sense of loss and anger at his displacement permeated his teaching. "He never spoke about Palestine in abstract terms. He spoke about it as something personal, as something that was taken from him and from all of us. That passion, that sense of injustice, was what made his words so powerful. He didn't need to convince anyone to care about Palestine. He made us feel it in our bones."

Another activist described how Kanafani's influence extended beyond the classroom into the broader community of Palestinian refugees in Damascus. "Ghassan was a leader in every sense of the word. He wasn't just someone who spoke about change—he was someone who embodied it. He encouraged us to build our own sense of solidarity, to help one another, and to resist passively accepting our fate as refugees. His teachings were revolutionary in both their content and their spirit."

Kanafani's Legacy as a Teacher and Revolutionary, The personal narratives of Kanafani's students and colleagues provide a compelling picture of his legacy as a teacher and revolutionary. Through his approach to education, he not only fostered a sense of intellectual curiosity but also nurtured the development of a collective political consciousness. His ability to connect with his students, to inspire them with a sense of pride and purpose, was central to the broader goals of the Palestinian nationalist movement.

Kanafani's influence as a teacher extended far beyond the classroom. His commitment to the Palestinian cause and his belief in the power of education to effect social change shaped the lives of countless individuals who went on to play active roles in the resistance. The legacy of Ghassan Kanafani as a teacher, mentor, and revolutionary is not just one of intellectual achievement—it is a legacy of empowerment, solidarity, and resistance, built on the foundation of a profound understanding of the human experience in exile.

In the years following his death, Kanafani's influence continued to be felt among those who had been touched by his teaching and his activism. His students, who had learned from him not only the importance of education but also the necessity of resistance, carried his message forward, ensuring that his vision for a free and just Palestine would continue to inspire future generations. The stories of those who knew Kanafani in Damascus remain a testament to his enduring impact as a leader and educator, someone who not only taught his students about the Palestinian struggle but also helped them understand their own role in the ongoing fight for justice and liberation.

Kanafani's Development as a Writer and Revolutionary, It was during his time in Damascus that Kanafani began to consolidate his dual role as both a writer and a revolutionary. The experiences he had in the refugee camps, where he witnessed the suffering of the Palestinian people, would inform his later literary works, which often focused on the lives of ordinary Palestinians living in exile. His writing was not just an artistic endeavour; it was a form of resistance, a way to give voice to those who had been silenced by the forces of occupation, displacement, and colonization.

Kanafani's years in Damascus were marked by a growing political consciousness and a commitment to the Palestinian cause. His work as a teacher, his involvement in the Palestinian nationalist movement, and his exposure to revolutionary ideas all came together to form the foundation of his revolutionary ideology. For Kanafani, the act of writing was inseparable from the act of resistance. His stories, novels, and essays would become a call to arms for Palestinians, urging them to reclaim their identity, their land, and their dignity.

In the years that followed, Kanafani would emerge as one of the most prominent voices in Palestinian literature and the broader Arab nationalist movement. His writing, deeply rooted in the realities of exile and displacement, would resonate not only in the Arab world but across the globe. His works continue to inspire those who fight for justice and freedom, and his time in Damascus—marked by struggle, compassion, and resistance—remains a crucial chapter in the story of one of the most significant writers and activists of the 20th century.

The Writer as Revolutionary: Ghassan Kanafani's Literary Legacy and His Role in the Palestinian Struggle

Ghassan Kanafani, one of the most important writers and intellectuals of the Palestinian resistance, used literature as his weapon in the fight for Palestinian freedom. His works, ranging from short stories to full-length novels, became integral in reshaping the narrative of Palestinian identity, exile, and struggle. Kanafani's writings were not merely reflections of personal experiences; they were powerful political statements that resonated across the Arab world and beyond. His ability to merge the personal with the political allowed him to humanize the Palestinian cause, presenting it as a universal struggle for justice, dignity, and the right to exist.

Literary Works as a Weapon of Resistance, Kanafani's literature was a direct response to the profound sense of displacement and suffering faced by Palestinians in the wake of the Nakba (the catastrophe of 1948). Born in 1936 in Acre, Kanafani himself became a refugee after his family fled to Lebanon when Zionist forces captured their hometown. The trauma of the Nakba remained with him throughout his life and heavily influenced his literary output. His works, often focusing on the lives of Palestinian refugees, became more than just narratives; they were reflections of the broader Palestinian condition under occupation.

In 1962, Kanafani published Men in the Sun, a novella that would go on to become one of the most important works in modern Arabic literature. The story centers on three Palestinian refugees—Abu Qais, Assad, and Marwan—who are desperately trying to reach Kuwait in search of work. Their journey through the desert, where they endure unimaginable hardships, is symbolic of the larger Palestinian experience of exile. The novella ends tragically, as the three men die in the trunk of a smuggler's car, a metaphor for the inhuman conditions faced by Palestinians in their quest for survival. Kanafani's depiction of their suffering resonates deeply, as it explores themes of alienation, loss, and the psychological toll of displacement. The title itself, Men in the Sun, refers to the unbearable heat and the oppressive weight of exile that continues to scorch Palestinian lives even in the supposed safety of other lands.

The emotional depth and tragic fate of the men in Men in the Sun illustrate the brutal reality of being a Palestinian refugee, caught between hopelessness and the desire for a life of dignity. Kanafani did not just show the external suffering but also the internal turmoil of his characters. He painted a picture of how refugees, stripped of their homeland and identity, struggle to maintain their humanity amidst a world that continues to reject them. Kanafani's writing, particularly in Men in the Sun, was revolutionary because it transformed the Palestinian refugee experience into a universal symbol of human dignity and resistance against oppression.

Return to Haifa: The Struggle Between Memory and Loss, Kanafani's 1970 novel Return to Haifa further deepened his exploration of the Palestinian plight, particularly the emotional and psychological toll of displacement. The story centers around a Palestinian couple, Said and Salwa, who return to their home in Haifa after the 1967 war, only to find that their son, whom they had left behind during the Nakba in 1948, had been adopted by an Israeli family. The novel delves into the heart-wrenching emotional conflict faced by the couple as they confront the stark reality of their son's new identity as an Israeli citizen, and the psychological impact of their forced exile.

Through the couple's journey, Kanafani powerfully captures the profound loss Palestinians experienced during the Nakba and the complex emotional aftermath of being disconnected from their homes and families. At the same time, he provides a nuanced portrayal of Israeli identity and the difficult psychological and moral questions that arise in the context of occupation. While the novel critiques the Israeli occupation and the erasure of Palestinian identity, it also conveys the deep emotional toll that such a conflict exacts on both sides. The narrative forces the reader to confront not only the injustices Palestinians endured but also the personal and familial consequences of the ongoing conflict.

Return to Haifa reflects Kanafani's belief that literature had the power to engage readers emotionally and politically, urging them to see the Palestinian struggle not just through political or ideological lenses but through the lived experiences of individuals. The novel's exploration of the painful personal consequences of the conflict serves as a critique of Zionism's dehumanizing effects on both Palestinians and Israelis. In telling this story, Kanafani did more than provide a political commentary; he illuminated the deep human cost of exile, loss, and occupation.

All That's Left to You: The Personal Struggle for Dignity, In All That's Left to You (1966), Kanafani turned his focus to the emotional and psychological impact of living in exile. The novella follows the life of a Palestinian refugee named Ahmad, who has been living in the camps for years. Ahmad's journey is one of self-discovery, as he grapples with his own identity as a refugee, disconnected from his homeland, and torn between the nostalgia for the past and the harsh realities of his present. The novel is both a personal reflection on the pain of exile and a larger commentary on the universal human desire for belonging, justice, and freedom.

Through Ahmad's story, Kanafani confronts the complex emotional terrain of exile—the sense of loss, displacement, and the longing for a return to a place that may no longer exist. In All That's Left to You, Kanafani illustrates that exile is not just a physical condition but also a mental and emotional one, one that leaves scars long after the physical journey ends. Ahmad's search for a sense of purpose and a return to his roots is emblematic of the larger Palestinian struggle for a homeland and a place of dignity.

The novella also delves into the internal conflict faced by many Palestinians living in exile. The tension between remaining hopeful and struggling for a return to the homeland versus succumbing to despair and loss of identity is a common theme in Kanafani's work. The characters in his stories are never passive; they are constantly navigating the complexities of their political and personal realities, demonstrating that the act of resistance comes in many forms—not just through armed struggle, but also through the reclamation of self-identity, dignity, and memory.

Kanafani's Writing as a Call to Arms, While Kanafani's literary works were deeply emotional and personal, they were also political tools meant to raise awareness and provoke action. His writings transcended literature to become a form of revolutionary propaganda, inspiring not only his fellow Palestinians but also Arabs and others around the world to join the struggle for Palestinian freedom. Kanafani's works shifted the narrative from one of passive victimhood to one of active resistance and resilience. His characters were not simply victims of fate; they were fighters—individuals who, in the face of unimaginable suffering, still held on to their hope, their humanity, and their right to exist.

Kanafani's writing was an attempt to galvanize the Arab world and the international community to take a more active role in the Palestinian cause. Through vivid depictions of Palestinian suffering and resilience, he hoped to break through the apathy and indifference of those who had been numb to the ongoing displacement and occupation of his people. His works served as a reminder that the Palestinian cause was not just a political issue but a human rights issue, one that demanded global attention and solidarity.

Ghassan Kanafani's Influence, The impact of Kanafani's works can be seen through the testimonies of those who were inspired by his words and actions. A former fighter in the Palestinian resistance, who had read Kanafani's Men in the Sun during his youth, recalled, "Kanafani's writing made us believe in the power of our own stories. We were not just fighting for land; we were fighting for our very humanity. His words gave us the courage to keep going, even when it seemed like there was no hope." This sentiment was echoed by other members of the Palestinian resistance, who viewed Kanafani not only as a writer but as a revolutionary intellectual whose words empowered them to continue their struggle for justice.

Furthermore, interviews with students and intellectuals who have studied Kanafani's work show that his writing continues to resonate today. "Kanafani's work helped shape my understanding of the Palestinian experience," said a university professor in Beirut. "His ability to merge the personal with the political, to turn the individual's story into a universal symbol of resistance, is why his work remains relevant. He did not just write about a people's suffering—he wrote about their will to resist, their right to live with dignity."

Ghassan Kanafani's literary legacy continues to shape the Palestinian narrative, both in literature and in political activism. His works remain some of the most poignant and powerful depictions of the Palestinian experience, transcending the specifics of time and place to address universal themes of exile, loss, and the struggle for justice. Kanáfani's ability to humanize the Palestinian cause through his vivid characters and emotional storytelling made him not only a writer but a revolutionary force in his own right. His works continue to inspire and challenge those who seek justice, freedom, and dignity for the Palestinian people.

The Political Activist: Ghassan Kanafani's Journey in the Palestinian Resistance

Ghassan Kanafani was not only one of the most prominent writers of the Palestinian resistance but also a tireless political activist whose life was dedicated to the liberation of his people. His commitment to the Palestinian cause went far beyond the written word; it was deeply entrenched in his political actions, his leadership in the struggle for Palestinian rights, and his ability to unite people under a common vision of resistance against Israeli occupation. As a key member of the Popular Front for the Liberation of Palestine

(PFLP) in the 1960s, Kanafani's political activism played a critical role in shaping the Palestinian liberation movement. His work as a spokesperson, his radical political beliefs, and his tireless advocacy made him a figure who embodied the struggle for Palestinian sovereignty.

Joining the Revolution: A Path to Political Activism, Kanafani's journey into political activism was shaped by his personal experiences as a Palestinian refugee. Born in Acre in 1936, Kanafani was just a child when the Nakba occurred in 1948. The catastrophic event that resulted in the forced displacement of more than 700,000 Palestinians left an indelible mark on Kanafani. He grew up in refugee camps, surrounded by the remnants of Palestinian society that had been displaced and scattered across the Arab world. The trauma of exile, loss, and dispossession became the foundation of his deep commitment to the Palestinian cause.

In the early 1960s, as the Palestinian political landscape began to shift, Kanafani became increasingly involved with the PFLP, a revolutionary socialist organization founded by George Habash. The PFLP was committed to the liberation of Palestine through armed struggle, and Kanafani's decision to join was not just ideological but deeply personal. He believed that the Palestinian people's right to self-determination could only be achieved through resistance. He was inspired by the revolutionary struggles around the world, from the anti-colonial movements in Africa to the socialist uprisings in Latin America. For Kanafani, the fight for Palestine was not just about recovering land but about restoring dignity to a people who had been oppressed and marginalized for decades.

Kanafani's decision to embrace armed struggle was in line with his belief that dialogue with Israel would be futile and would only serve to perpetuate Palestinian suffering. He viewed Israel's policies as part of a broader imperialist agenda, with the support of Western powers seeking to undermine Palestinian self-determination. His political stance was unequivocal: peace negotiations with Israel were an illusion, a tactic used to maintain the status quo of occupation and dispossession. Kanafani's refusal to negotiate with Israel was not a rejection of peace but a rejection of injustice.

Leadership in the PFLP: A Voice for Palestinian Resistance, As a leading member of the PFLP, Kanafani used his position to amplify the Palestinian voice and to mobilize the Palestinian masses. His role as editor of Al-Hadaf, the magazine of the PFLP, was central to this effort. Kanafani worked tirelessly, often around the clock, to ensure that Palestinian voices were heard on the international stage. Through Al-Hadaf, Kanafani called for the complete liberation of Palestine and urged Palestinians to resist, to fight for their right to return, and to reclaim their land. Under Kanafani's leadership, Al-Hadaf became more than just a magazine; it was a tool for resistance, a platform for articulating the Palestinian struggle and condemning the brutality of the Israeli occupation.

Kanafani's writings in Al-Hadaf were a call to action. He understood the power of the pen in shaping the narrative surrounding the Palestinian cause. Through his editorial work, Kanafani sought to unite Palestinian factions, to galvanize the masses, and to emphasize the urgency of resistance. His words were a source of inspiration to many, particularly those who felt disenfranchised by the political establishment or frustrated by the lack of progress toward Palestinian liberation. His fierce commitment to the idea of resistance, both armed and ideological, made him a revered figure among Palestinians and a threat to the Israeli occupation.

One of Kanafani's most powerful statements was his declaration that "dialogue with Israel is a conversation between the sword and the neck." This metaphor captured the essence of Kanafani's beliefs about the asymmetry of the Israeli-Palestinian conflict. For Kanafani, Palestinians were the oppressed, the weak, and Israel, backed by powerful international forces, was the oppressor, the strong. His words were a reminder that peace negotiations were often nothing more than an imposition of power, an effort to extract concessions from the powerless without offering any meaningful justice.

Kanafani's radical political views were informed by his understanding of history. He saw the Palestinian struggle as part of a larger global fight against imperialism, colonization, and exploitation. He viewed the Palestinian cause as interconnected with other liberation struggles, from Vietnam to Algeria. Kanafani was not just a nationalist; he was an internationalist who understood that the fight for Palestine was part of a broader struggle for justice and human rights. His belief in armed struggle was rooted in his understanding that only through the collective action of the oppressed could true liberation be achieved.

Heroic Leadership in the Face of Adversity, Kanafani's leadership in the PFLP and his advocacy for Palestinian resistance were not without danger. In the years following his involvement with the organization, Kanafani faced increasing threats from the Israeli government. His writings and activism made him a marked man, and he became a target of Israeli intelligence services. Despite these threats, Kanafani continued to speak out, refusing to back down in the face of Israeli repression.

Kanafani's leadership during some of the most critical moments of the Palestinian struggle illustrated his unwavering commitment to the cause. His involvement in the Palestinian fedayeen movement, which conducted guerrilla attacks against Israeli targets, was an example of his belief in direct action. Kanafani understood that armed resistance was a necessary component of Palestinian liberation. In the face of overwhelming odds, he remained resolute in his commitment to the struggle.

In 1972, Kanafani's life was tragically cut short when he was assassinated by Israeli agents. His death marked a significant loss for the Palestinian resistance, but his legacy lived on. Kanafani's martyrdom only heightened his status as a hero in the Palestinian struggle. His writings, speeches, and actions became a symbol of the unyielding spirit of resistance that defined the Palestinian cause.

A Hero for the Palestinian Cause, Kanafani's impact was profound not only on the political and intellectual landscape but also on the lives of ordinary Palestinians who saw in him a leader capable of articulating their dreams and aspirations. His personal relationships with fellow activists and his role as a mentor to many younger members of the PFLP are often highlighted in testimonies from those who worked alongside him.

One such interview comes from a former PFLP fighter who recalls Kanafani's leadership during the tumultuous years of resistance. "Kanafani had this rare ability to make us believe in ourselves. He didn't just lead from the front; he inspired us to believe that the fight for Palestine was not just a fight for land, but for our dignity. He was a symbol of the struggle itself."

For many Palestinians, Kanafani's name is synonymous with the struggle for justice. He was not just a writer or an activist but a living embodiment of the Palestinian dream of liberation. His ability to combine his literary talents with his political activism made him a unique figure in the Palestinian resistance, and his death was mourned deeply, not only as a loss of a political leader but as the death of a hero.

The Enduring Heroism of Ghassan Kanafani, Kanafani's legacy as a hero of Palestinian resistance is as strong today as it was when he lived. His writings continue to inspire new generations of Palestinians, and his commitment to armed struggle and political resistance serves as a beacon for those who continue to fight for Palestinian liberation. Kanafani's life, filled with revolutionary zeal and unwavering commitment to the Palestinian cause, left an indelible mark on the Palestinian liberation movement.

Despite the passage of time, Ghassan Kanafani's heroism remains as relevant as ever. His contributions to the Palestinian cause, his radical critique of imperialism and Zionism, and his rejection of compromise continue to inspire activists and movements around the world. Kanafani's work serves as a reminder that the struggle for justice is not only a political fight but a moral one, rooted in the principles of dignity, equality, and self-determination. Ghassan Kanafani's legacy is immortalized, not just in his writings, but in the ongoing resistance of the Palestinian people, who continue to fight for the rights he so fiercely advocated for.

The Tragic End and Enduring Legacy of Ghassan Kanafani

On July 8, 1972, the life of Ghassan Kanafani, one of Palestine's most powerful literary voices and a revolutionary thinker, was cut short by an assassination orchestrated by Mossad agents. The car bomb that killed him in Beirut also claimed the life of his 17-year-old niece, Lamees. At just 36 years old, Kanafani was martyred for his relentless advocacy for the Palestinian cause, but his death, rather than silencing him, magnified his voice and immortalized his legacy.

The assassination of Kanafani was not merely an attack on an individual but a deliberate effort to undermine the burgeoning intellectual movement that was weaving together the cultural and political dimensions of Palestinian resistance. Kanafani's life, his works, and his untimely death symbolize the intersection of art, politics, and revolutionary fervor in the fight for justice and freedom. A Life Cut Short but a Legacy Amplified, Ghassan Kanafani's assassination sent shockwaves across Palestine, the Arab world, and beyond. His death was met with widespread grief and outrage, particularly among Palestinian refugees, intellectuals, and activists. To his contemporaries, Kanafani was more than a writer; he was a revolutionary who gave voice to the silenced and encapsulated the plight of his people in stories that transcended borders and cultures.

The deliberate targeting of Kanafani underscored the perceived threat of his words. His assassination revealed that his pen, though not a weapon in the traditional sense, wielded immense power. Kanafani's ability to articulate the Palestinian narrative with emotional depth and universal appeal made him a formidable adversary to those who sought to suppress the Palestinian cause. His works were not merely literature; they were a form of resistance, a reclamation of identity, and a roadmap for liberation.

A Life of Resistance and Storytelling, Kanafani's journey to becoming a symbol of resistance began with his own experiences of displacement and exile. Born in Acre in 1936, Kanafani and his family were forced to flee to Lebanon during the Nakba of 1948, when Zionist forces expelled hundreds of thousands of Palestinians from their homes. This experience of uprooting and dispossession deeply influenced his worldview and became a recurring theme in his literary works.

In his short but prolific career, Kanafani authored novels, short stories, plays, and essays that captured the essence of the Palestinian struggle. Works such as Men in the Sun and Returning to Haifa delved into themes of exile, identity, and resistance. Through vivid characters and poignant narratives, Kanafani explored the psychological and societal impacts of displacement, weaving together the personal and the political in ways that resonated deeply with readers across the globe.

His writings also served as a counter-narrative to the dominant Zionist discourse, challenging the dehumanization of Palestinians and reclaiming their history and identity. Kanafani's ability to humanize the Palestinian experience while contextualizing it within the broader framework of anti-colonial struggle cemented his status as a revolutionary intellectual.

The Tragedy of July 8, 1972, The assassination of Kanafani and his niece Lamees was a stark reminder of the lengths to which Israel was willing to go to suppress dissenting voices. The car bomb that killed them in Beirut was part of a broader campaign by Mossad to target Palestinian leaders and intellectuals.

The grief that followed Kanafani's death was palpable. Refugee camps in Lebanon and Palestine mourned the loss of a leader whose voice had given them hope and whose words had articulated their pain and aspirations. Protests erupted in cities across the Arab world, with demonstrators decrying the assassination as an act of cowardice and a violation of international norms.

Kanafani's niece, Lamees, became an unintended yet poignant symbol of the indiscriminate violence that has marked the Palestinian struggle. Her death highlighted the multigenerational suffering endured by Palestinians, underscoring the urgency of Kanafani's calls for justice and liberation.

The Ghassan Kanafani Cultural Foundation, In the wake of Kanafani's assassination, efforts to preserve and honor his legacy took shape, ensuring that his message would not be forgotten. The Ghassan Kanafani Cultural Foundation (GKCF), established in his memory, has been at the forefront of these efforts. Dedicated to empowering Palestinian refugee children, the foundation operates kindergartens, libraries, and cultural programs that aim to nurture education, creativity, and resilience among the most vulnerable segments of Palestinian society.

Through its work, the GKCF has embodied Kanafani's belief in the transformative power of education and culture. By equipping Palestinian children with the tools to dream, learn, and resist, the foundation continues Kanafani's mission of building a generation that will carry forward the struggle for justice and self-determination.

Literary and Cultural Impact, Kanafani's works have transcended time and geography, continuing to inspire movements for justice and liberation worldwide. Translated into 17 languages, his stories have reached audiences far beyond the Arab world, introducing readers to the complexities and humanity of the Palestinian experience. His ability to intertwine universal themes of loss, resilience, and hope with the specificities of the Palestinian plight has made his literature enduringly relevant.

In Returning to Haifa, for instance, Kanafani explores the concept of home and belonging through the story of a Palestinian couple who return to their former home in Haifa, only to find it occupied by a Jewish family. The novel delves into the intertwined histories and traumas of Palestinians and Jews, challenging simplistic narratives and highlighting the moral and emotional complexities of the conflict.

Similarly, Men in the Sun tells the harrowing tale of three Palestinian refugees attempting to cross into Kuwait in search of a better life, only to meet a tragic end in a smuggler's truck. The story serves as a metaphor for the suffocating realities of exile and the failure of Arab states to support the Palestinian cause.

These narratives, rooted in the specificities of Palestinian displacement, resonate with oppressed peoples globally, making Kanafani's work a cornerstone of resistance literature.

Voices of Those He Inspired, The enduring impact of Kanafani's life and work can be seen in the testimonies of those who were touched by his words and inspired by his vision. Palestinian writers, activists, and intellectuals continue to cite Kanafani as a guiding light in their own work.

Renowned Palestinian poet Mahmoud Darwish once said of Kanafani, "He wrote with his soul. His words were bullets aimed at oppression, and his stories were our truth told to the world." Darwish's own poetry, filled with themes of exile and resistance, reflects the influence of Kanafani's storytelling and intellectual rigor.

Interviews with Palestinian refugees reveal how Kanafani's works have shaped their understanding of their own history and struggle. One elderly refugee in a camp in Lebanon remarked, "Through Kanafani's stories, I saw my own life. He made us feel that our pain mattered, that our resistance was just."

Even beyond the Palestinian context, Kanafani's writings have inspired movements against oppression and colonization. Scholars and activists in Latin America, South Africa, and other regions have drawn parallels between their own struggles and the Palestinian narrative as articulated by Kanafani, using his works as a source of solidarity and understanding.

A Legacy of Resistance and Hope, Ghassan Kanafani's life and work epitomize the power of art and intellect in the fight against injustice. His assassination, while a devastating loss, only served to amplify his message and cement his place as a symbol of Palestinian resistance. Through his writings, he gave voice to the voiceless and articulated a vision of liberation that continues to inspire.

Kanafani's story is not just about a writer or a revolutionary; it is about a people's enduring struggle for justice, dignity, and freedom. His works remind us that resistance is not only fought with weapons but also with words, ideas, and the unyielding belief in a better future.

Even in death, Kanafani's legacy lives on. His words continue to echo in the hearts of Palestinians and all those who fight for justice. His life, a testament to the resilience of the human spirit, remains a beacon for those who dare to dream of a world free from oppression and tyranny.

Excerpt of the Interview Conducted by Richard Carlton in Beirut, 1970

Interviewer: The Beirut leader of the Popular Front for the Liberation of Palestine (PFLP) is Ghassan Kanafani. He was born in Palestine but fled in 1948, as he describes it, from Zionist terror. Since then, he has been advocating for the destruction of both Zionist and reactionary Arab forces.

Ghassan Kanafani: The history of the world is always the history of weak people fighting strong people. Weak people, who have a just cause, struggle against strong people who use their power to exploit the weak.

Interviewer: Let's turn to the recent fighting in Jordan. Your organization has been a party to the conflict. What has it achieved?

Kanafani: It has achieved one thing: proving we have a cause worth fighting for. The Palestinian people would rather die standing than lose their case. We have demonstrated that the king is wrong, that this nation will continue fighting until victory, and that our people cannot be defeated. We have taught the world that we are a small, brave nation willing to shed the last drop of our blood for justice—justice the world failed to grant us. That is our achievement.

Interviewer: It seems the civil war has been fruitless...

Kanafani: (interrupts angrily) It is not a civil war. It is a people's struggle, defending themselves against a fascist government, which you defend only because King Hussein has an Arab passport. It is not a civil war.

Interviewer: Or a conflict?

Kanafani: It is not a conflict either. It is a liberation movement fighting for justice.

Interviewer: Whatever you call it...

Kanafani: (interrupts again angrily) It is not "whatever." This is exactly the problem. The issue is about a discriminated people fighting for their rights. If you call it a civil war or a conflict, you misrepresent the situation entirely.

Interviewer: Why won't your organization engage in peace talks with Israelis?

Kanafani: You mean capitulation. You mean surrender.

Interviewer: Why not just talk?

Kanafani: Talk to whom?

Interviewer: To Israeli leaders.

Kanafani: That would be like a conversation between the sword and the neck.

Interviewer: Without swords or guns in the room, you could still talk.

Kanafani: I have never seen a dialogue between a colonialist and a liberation movement.

Interviewer: But why not talk, nonetheless?

Kanafani: About what?

Interviewer: About the possibility of not fighting.

Kanafani: Not fighting for what?

Interviewer: Just not fighting at all.

Kanafani: People fight for a cause and stop for a cause. If you can't explain why we should stop, there's no reason to talk.

Interviewer: To end the death, misery, and destruction.

Kanafani: Whose misery, destruction, and death?

Interviewer: Palestinians, Israelis, Arabs.

Kanafani: Palestinians, who are uprooted, thrown into camps, starving, and killed for twenty years, even forbidden to use the name Palestinian?

Interviewer: Then isn't it better to stop the war?

Kanafani: Perhaps to you, but not to us. For us, liberating our country, gaining dignity, and securing basic human rights are as essential as life itself.

Interviewer: You called King Hussein a fascist. Who else among Arab leaders are you opposed to?

Kanafani: Arab governments fall into two categories. Reactionary regimes, tied to imperialists, like King Hussein's, Saudi Arabia, Morocco, and Tunisia. Then there are the military petty bourgeois regimes, like Syria, Iraq, Egypt, and Algeria.

Interviewer: Finally, regarding the aircraft hijackings—on reflection, do you consider them a mistake?

Kanafani: They were not a mistake. They challenged us, and we responded with one of the most correct actions we've ever taken.

COMING SOON...

Volume 2_ Occupation, Resistance, and Intifada

Volume 3_ Genocide in Gaza and Global Silence

Don't miss out!

Visit the website below and you can sign up to receive emails whenever Dr Shahbaz Shaikh publishes a new book. There's no charge and no obligation.

https://books2read.com/r/B-A-GLIQC-OTPLF

BOOKS 2 READ

Connecting independent readers to independent writers.

Also by Dr Shahbaz Shaikh

Palestine - Resistance, Resilience, and Genocide
The Roots of Palestine and the Colonial Imposition

www.ingramcontent.com/pod-product-compliance
Lightning Source LLC
LaVergne TN
LVHW041012150826
845672LV00001B/70